Teaching About Religion
in Public Schools

TEACHING
ABOUT
RELIGION
IN
PUBLIC
SCHOOLS

Edited by
Nicholas Piediscalzi
and
William E. Collie

87
Argus Communications • Niles, Illinois

ARGUS COMMUNICATIONS
7440 Natchez Avenue
Niles, Illinois 60648

International Standard Book Number 0-913592-79-X
Library of Congress Number 77-80623

1   2   3   4   5   6   7   8   9   0

Dedicated

to

JAMES VINCENT PANOCH

Pioneering Leader in Public-Education Religion Studies

Acknowledgments

The editors express appreciation to Diane C. Johnson and Mary Beth Horn for their assistance in preparing and typing the final manuscript. Also they, on behalf of Wright State University and the Public Education Religion Studies Center (PERSC), express gratitude to the contributors to this volume who assigned and contributed their rights and royalties to PERSC's operating budget.

Contents

Contributors

Catherine L. Albanese, Ph. D., is Associate Professor of Religion at Wright State University, Dayton, Ohio, and during 1976–77, Visiting Associate Professor of Religious Studies at the Pennsylvania State University. She is author of two forthcoming books on American religion and a number of articles.

Rodney F. Allen, Sr., is Associate Professor, Department of Social Studies Education, and Principal Investigator, Religion Social Studies Curriculum Project, Florida State University, Tallahassee. He is the coauthor of numerous books in the field of religion studies, including instructional materials for secondary school social studies students (*Religious Issues Series,* Addison-Wesley) and for elementary school children (*Learning About Religions/Social Studies* program, Argus).

David L. Barr, Ph.D., is Assistant Professor of Religion at Wright State University, Dayton, Ohio. He is coauthor of the book *Religion Goes to School* (Harper) and has written a number of articles on teaching about religion in public schools.

Jon T. Barton has been a member of the English department at Santa Monica High School for the past ten years, where he teaches The Bible as Literature, Philosophy, and Introduction to Religion Studies. He has a Master of Theological Studies degree from Harvard Divinity School, where he served as Codirector for the Program on Religion and Education during the 1974–75 academic year while on study sabbatical. He is a contributing author to the textbook *Religion and Public Education* (Harper & Row, 1975) and has conducted numerous workshops and seminars on the academic study of religion in the public schools.

Wesley J. Bodin, B.A., Project Codirector of the World Religions Curriculum Development Center, has completed over seventy hours of graduate work in anthropology and social studies education at the

University of Minnesota. He has conducted several workshops and made numerous presentations at professional meetings, colleges, and universities on public education religion studies.

William E. Collie, Ed.D., is a member of the faculty of the Division of Teacher Education, Director of Student Services of the College of Education, and Codirector of the Public Education Religion Studies Center at Wright State University, Dayton, Ohio. His publication, workshop, and professional presentations have been in the fields of social studies, teacher education, and religion studies.

Joan G. Dye, M.Ed., was Project Coordinator for the Religion in Elementary Social Studies Project at Florida State University. She was formerly an instructional television teacher for the Georgia Educational Television Network.

John L. Esposito, Ph.D., is Associate Professor and Chairman, Department of Religious Studies, College of the Holy Cross, Worcester, Massachusetts. He is the author of several articles on Islamic law and the role of women in Muslim society.

William C. Fenton, Ed.D., is Professor of Music and Chairman, Department of Music, Wright State University, Dayton, Ohio. He is Director of the University Chamber Singers and has conducted concert tours in both the United States and Europe. In addition, his experience as a church musician spans twenty-nine years.

Joseph Forcinelli, Ph.D., is Director of the Program on Religion and Education and Lecturer in Religion and Education at The Divinity School, Harvard University. He established the pilot program in Religion Studies for Secondary Schools at Claremont High School, Claremont, California. He prepared the proposal for the certification of teachers in Academic Studies of Religion for the State of California. He has contributed to the publication of anthologies and is the author of numerous articles on religion and moral education.

Ruth D. Hallman is a teacher and Chairperson, Department of English, as well as Humanities Coordinator at Walter E. Stebbins High School, Dayton, Ohio. She has contributed chapters to two books and is the author of several articles.

Ann M. Hildebrand is a member of the Department of English and teaches Children's Literature at Kent State University. She is a former public school teacher, the author of several articles, and the initiator of the Religion Studies Program at Kent State University, Kent, Ohio.

Mark R. Lester, A.B., is a graduate student in the Department of Philosophy, San Diego State University.

Nicholas Piediscalzi, Ph.D., is a professor and Chairman, Department of Religion, and Codirector of the Public Education Religion Studies Center at Wright State University, Dayton, Ohio. He is coeditor of two books, *Contemporary Religion and Social Responsibility* (Alba House) and *From Hope to Liberation: Towards a New Marxist-Christian Dialogue* (Fortress Press), and has published a number of articles on related topics.

Geraldine H. Rosenthal, Ed.D., is Associate Supervisor for Social Studies and coordinator for Law Studies, Tulsa Public Schools, and Adjunct Professor, Department of Education, University of Oklahoma. She is the author of several articles and an active member of the National Council for the Social Studies.

Lee H. Smith, Ph.D., Project Codirector of the World Religions Curriculum Development Center, has conducted numerous workshops and presentations at professional meetings, colleges, and universities on public education religion studies. Dr. Smith is also a former director of the National Council for the Social Studies.

Barbara Ann Swyhart, Ph.D., is Associate Professor and Coordinator of Religion and Public Education at San Diego State University in the Department of Religious Studies. During 1975–76, she was a Visiting Lecturer and Director of the Program in Religion and Education at The Divinity School, Harvard University. She is the author of *Bioethical Decision Making: Releasing Religion from the Spiritual* and various articles on ethics and on religion and public education.

Thayer S. Warshaw is a teacher of English and Coordinator of Student Teaching at Newton (Massachusetts) North High School and Associate Director of the Indiana University Institute on Teaching the Bible in Literature Courses. He is coauthor of a student textbook, general coeditor of a series of books on The Bible in Literature courses, and has published several articles.

Paul J. Will developed a high school World Religions course in the early 1960s. Since 1969 he has taught a variety of religion courses, including several workshops for teachers at Eastern Michigan University, Western Michigan University, the University of Detroit, and the University of Michigan. Among his scholarly contributions are specialized studies on Asian religions as well as curricular materials for public education religion studies.

Rika Zimmerman, B.S. (Education), is certified as both a secondary social studies teacher in Ohio and as a religious school teacher by the Union of American Hebrew Congregations. She is currently a Hebrew School and religious school teacher.

Introduction

Nicholas Piediscalzi
and
William E. Collie

Teaching About Religion in Public Schools is an attempt to provide a response to the numerous requests of interested school officials, teachers, and members of the public who have become aware of the fact that religion studies legally can take place in a public school setting and who favor its inclusion in the curriculum but who ask the practical question: How can it be done?

This book is a product of its time: it reflects both the degree of sophistication in curriculum development which has been achieved by those committed to the academic study of religion in the public schools and the still unsure search for appropriate form and for definitive status of the more traditional curricular subjects. The establishment of a place for religion studies in the public school curriculum is in one sense easier than might have been possible in earlier times, since the elementary and secondary curriculum now is more fluid, more flexible, and more open to new and varied interdisciplinary approaches. Paradoxically, however, the very fact that curricular offerings are in a state of flux means that religion studies as a possible area for inclusion in the curriculum appears in competition for time and resources with many other recently identified school concerns such as values education, environmental studies, and ethnic studies. To some, religion studies may be viewed only as another "in" topic destined to find its way into and quickly out of an already crowded curriculum. Furthermore, the very interdisciplinary emphasis of current curricular developments makes it difficult for religion studies to find an academic place in the curriculum as a distinct discipline legitimate in its own right. In practice, as we shall see, religion studies usually appears in the curriculum under the rubric of another, already established, curricular area—most frequently language arts or social studies.

1

This book is an outgrowth of the development of religion studies as a curricular concern at the elementary and secondary levels in the last dozen years. While the academic study of religion at these levels has been identified as "public education religion studies" to clearly distinguish it from religious study or religious education (which are not constitutionally appropriate for a public school setting), the name is, in a sense, a misnomer, since many advocates of the development of the academic study of religion have been individuals and groups involved in private or parochial school education who also support a religion studies approach. Thus, while the suggestions provided in this book for religion studies in the elementary and secondary schools are designed specifically for a public school setting, they are adaptable for any school at the same levels committed to including an academic study of religion as a part of the curriculum.

The articles which follow both detail current practice and hold portent for future religion studies curriculum development in elementary and secondary schools. The contributors are themselves a representative sample of those involved in religion studies curriculum development—classroom teachers, school-district curriculum specialists, curriculum project directors, university-level teacher educators, and subject-matter and religion studies scholars. The religion studies programs they describe vary from portions of overall curricular conceptualizations for grades K–12 to more limited, discrete units of study within particular subject areas. Some of the studies outlined are the product of years of testing, experimentation, and revision— programs that have survived over long periods of time. Other studies described are being newly implemented and doubtlessly will be revised on the basis of trial runs. Still other studies are mere suggestions of possible approaches which might be utilized but which at this point have not been developed beyond the conceptual stage. Some of the studies are the products of large, funded curriculum projects; others are the results of individual teacher initiative and endeavor.

The articles describing different approaches to religion studies in the elementary and secondary schools attempt to place religion studies within the disciplinary structures most commonly found, hence the emphasis on language arts in the humanities and fine arts and on social studies. Even the division of the curriculum into humanities and the fine arts and social studies is an uneasy categorization, since what subjects fit under these labels is unclear. For example, does a study of the history of religion most appropriately belong under humanities or social studies? Likewise, a study of the cultural impact of religion might logically be identified as an artistic study, a social study, a humanistic study, or a religion study! Pragmatically, we have encouraged schools to incorporate religion studies wherever appropriate and under whatever designation is necessary. We have supported the natural inclusion of religion studies, believing that the curricular presence of a consideration of the role of religion in the development and functioning of individuals and societies is far more significant than arguing endlessly about where to pigeonhole it in the curriculum.

The authors have included exemplary units and courses of study to provide specific instances of what may be done in religion studies within their area of subject-matter concern. The units and courses are as detailed as possible so as to provide information for those who wish to examine concrete examples of religion studies programs. The studies, while quite thorough, are not intended to be seen as the final, finished version of what should be taught on each of the topics discussed. Rather, the studies should be viewed as working models of curriculum development at differing levels of refinement. The studies are intended to be suggestive in nature rather than complete programs of study ready to be directly implemented without alteration by the classroom teacher. It is hoped that these guidelines for religion studies will encourage teachers to see the many possibilities for the inclusion of religion studies in their curricular planning. It is further hoped that teachers will build on the recommendations provided and develop religion studies consistent with their own particular needs, interests, resources, and abilities.

In the first article, the authors succinctly review the background of curriculum development in religion studies in elementary and secondary education. They trace the significant growth of the inclusion of religion studies in the curriculum in recent years. They clarify the legal position of religion studies in the public schools as defined by Supreme Court rulings. They address several practical questions: Why is religion studies needed? What are the objectives of religion studies in the public schools? How is religion defined for public school study? In what ways can religion be studied in public schools?

Much of the ferment in religion studies in the schools has come in courses which fall under the general rubric of humanities and the fine arts. Joseph Forcinelli's article describing a program of studies he calls

"Relational Humanities" details the development of a humanities program at Claremont (California) High School, as an outgrowth of courses first offered as a part of the social science department. He provides a general overview of the teaching strategies and objectives for one of the course offerings, a year-long History of World Religions. Forcinelli includes a thorough description of two units in the course, "What Is Religion?" and "Three Religions That Aid Student Understanding of Religious Experience: Jainism, Zoroastrianism, and Taoism." The course follows a somewhat formal structure, combining lectures, in-class tutorials based on outside readings, weekly discussion seminars, student research, concluding symposium, and examination.

Jon Barton utilizes California's proposed humanities curriculum model for grades K–12 as a format to suggest ways for the inclusion of religion studies in literature, drama, dance, and film. Barton feels that the teacher potential for religion studies can be brought into congruence with course potential by concurrent development in three areas: the identification of goals which the various subject areas share in common with religion studies, development and utilization of instructional materials for religion studies, and professional encouragement for teachers to explore ways to incorporate religion studies into the curriculum. His chapter contains a wealth of suggestions for interdisciplinary implementation of religion studies at different grade levels.

William Fenton furthers the position for the natural inclusion of religion studies in the fine arts as he traces aspects of religious influence on architecture, painting, and music in a historical survey of Western culture. He outlines an exemplary resource unit entitled "Religious Aspects of Gothic and Renaissance Art" appropriate for use in an art course at the secondary level.

Ann Hildebrand develops an approach mentioned by Jon Barton in her recommendation for a study designed for upper elementary language arts entitled "Beginnings, Mythic and Scientific." Hildebrand suggests the primary objective of presenting mythic as well as scientific versions of Creation is "to give children a reassuring multiplicity of views on the origin of the cosmos while keeping alive the imaginative faculty which is natural and primary to childhood." She encourages concurrent studies in science and social studies to parallel the language arts emphasis. The annotated bibliography identifying reading levels should prove particularly useful for teachers.

Ruth Hallman's chapter on the inclusion of religion studies in secondary language arts presents a telling argument for the study of the Bible as a part of secondary literary studies. Among other reasons, she posits that one cannot adequately understand the literature of Western civilization without some familiarity with the Bible. Hallman's unit outline for a study of Exodus could fit into various course structures—a minicourse, semester, or year-long format. The unit's emphasis on the study of different literary forms and the extension of Bible stories and themes in opera, hymn, folk song, painting, sculpture, novel, and drama supports her contention that the Bible is an integral part of Western culture. Her emphasis on the Bible in literature is consistent with national trends in secondary language arts. The increasing tendency among language arts teachers to include examination of religious themes in their analysis of literature may well lead to broader grounds for the inclusion of religion studies which has yet to be fully explored.

Thayer Warshaw's distinctions of how the Bible may be studied *as* literature and *in* literature complement Hallman's article. His article is rich with suggestions for how both approaches may be used as well as another emphasis, the Bible *and* literature. Warshaw describes a semester elective Bible Literature course offered at Newton (Massachusetts) North High School utilizing the book *The Bible as/in Literature* he edited with James Ackerman. The book is based on the course and on the efforts of the authors in the Indiana Institute on Teaching the Bible. His examples are drawn from a survey of the Creation accounts in Genesis which approaches the study of the Bible *as* literature.

Because social studies has become such an all-inclusive curricular area, it should not be surprising that many of the religion studies emphases which have been instigated have appeared in the public school curriculum under the social studies label. This is particularly appropriate since many social studies educators stress that social studies is a practical integration of information drawn from the social sciences rather than merely an umbrella title to encompass discrete disciplines such as history, political science, economics, sociology, anthropology, and geography. Indeed, many social studies educators would argue for the inclusion of the academic study of religion as a necessary component of an integrated social studies program.

Joan G. Dye reviews the variety of ways students learn about religions through elementary social studies programs and argues convincingly for a curriculum infusion method in keeping with current efforts to encourage interdisciplinary social studies programs. She argues that religion studies ought to be part of a clearly articulated scope-and-sequence of social studies objectives identified for the elementary program. She outlines the major concepts, main ideas, and sensitivities included in the six-level Learning About Religions/Social Studies program developed for the elementary grades by the Religion in Elementary Social Studies Project at Florida State University. Dye details a second-level unit on Java to exemplify how the program is implemented. The program itself is the first inclusive curriculum project in religion studies at the elementary level to be commercially published. The Learning about Religions/Social Studies program published by Argus Communications may well be the forerunner of increasing involvement by commercial publishers in the development and dissemination of religion studies instructional materials.

Along with a survey of possible ways religion studies may be included in secondary social studies, Geraldine Rosenthal raises practical concerns about the context for religion studies. She deftly deals with those who would use religion studies for *religious* study by arguing for the academic study of religion within the constitutional limitations defining separation of church and state. Her chapter raises multiple possibilities for religion studies by listing numerous societal issues with religious implications. She provides specific proposals for religion studies approaches for use in American Government and World History courses. Rosenthal completes the general overview with the outline of an introductory unit for a two-semester senior high school course entitled: World History with Emphasis on Religion. Her annotated bibliography would be a worthwhile starting point for a teacher interested in implementing a similar course.

Rika Zimmerman's recommendations for the inclusion of Jewish studies in the social studies present a telling argument for an examination of some of the Jewish roots of Western culture which historically have been overlooked and often misrepresented. Zimmerman's study negates the natural fears of those who suggest that such study may only lead to further misunderstanding, and suggests that if we err, we must do so on the side of enlightenment, making every possible effort to treat new ideas appropriately rather than avoid them. Her exemplary unit on "The Misunderstood Pharisees: Their View of Life and Humanity" is actually a seedbed of multiple ways to study the sayings of the Pharisaic philosophers of the period from 200 B.C.E. to 300 C.E.* Such studies would be particularly enlightening for students who have a Christian conception of Pharisaic Judaism. Since such a study would be totally new for most social studies teachers, the bibliography provided is especially significant.

The concluding article on religion studies in the social studies outlines a number of exemplary courses and units of study. Lee Smith's and Wesley Bodin's description of "Religion in Human Culture," an elective social studies course about world religions for the senior high school level, is an outgrowth of the World Religions Curriculum Development Center funded by a grant received under Title III–IV C of the Elementary-Secondary Education Act. *Religion in Human Culture* is to be published by Argus Communications and will include multimedia instructional materials.

John Esposito's presentation of "An Introduction to Islam" would fit well into an upper-level social studies course on Western religions. Esposito's outline of the course content integrating reading references with the subject matter should be particularly beneficial to teachers delving into the study of a religious tradition with which they have had limited contact.

Paul Will describes a one-semester course entitled "Hinduism and Buddhism" offered at Kimball High School, Royal Oak, Michigan, open to high school juniors and seniors. (The course parallels a similar one which covers major Western religions.) Will outlines the salient characteristics and basic religious components of the two complex Asian traditions in a generalized chronological treatment.

Catherine Albanese and David Barr entitle their article "Toward a Public Education Course on Christianity." These university-level religion studies scholars present a lucid analysis of many of the pitfalls of trying to teach about Christianity in a public school setting in ways consistent with constitutional guidelines. They suggest a history-of-religions approach for a course with a central focus on religious experience and interpretation, particularly emphasizing the distinctive forms of religious experience in each major Christian tradition. The study attempts to help the student discover what is religious about this religion, thus bringing about some comprehensive interpretation of the nature of Christianity. The contributors qualify their article as

*Parallels the Gregorian calendar.

being the outline of a course in the process of development which may need subsequent revision. Though perhaps too comprehensive for the secondary school level as presented, the outline should contribute useful insights to the secondary teacher. The clear outline of the course of study, with sound, scholarly references understandable to the teacher, should prove invaluable for those committed to presenting a balanced academic study of Christianity in the public schools.

Continuing a theme earlier recommended for elementary and secondary language arts, "The Meeting of Science and Religion: Narratives About Origins" by Barbara Ann Swyhart and Mark Lester describes the development of a curriculum unit on cosmic and human origins for use in senior high school anthropology courses in the San Diego, California schools. The resulting syllabus, entitled "Narratives About Cosmic and Human Origins," includes philosophical, religious, and scientific interpretations. Though the materials could be used for a semester course or a unit within an anthropology course, in this article Swyhart and Lester present an approximate two-week segment centered on Western scientific interpretations. The course encourages students to recognize that on basic questions of life, thoughtful people have produced a variety of explanations which reflect differing perspectives but which need not be mutually exclusive. The course Swyhart and Lester describe is an example of new curricular considerations rich with potential for religion studies which are being, or could be, developed if we are willing to break out of the traditional mind sets that have defined our public school curriculum.

In the last article, Rodney Allen discusses the implications for religion studies in programs which incorporate values clarification and moral education. In his argument for the necessity of including consideration of values and moral issues in the public school curriculum, Allen himself articulates a value position on the role of education in American society. He suggests that the schools must help develop democratic persons by confronting conflicts in student and societal values in the classroom. Regardless of whether one accepts Allen's view of the role of education, it is important to recognize that the social education he describes, including analysis of public issues and moral dilemmas plus values clarification, raises definite concerns related to religion studies. Allen points out that in considering these issues, students will confront religious philosophical commitments. Too often the bases for decision making in these vital areas of human life are treated as though they were secular in nature only, while for many individuals their ultimate concerns are religious in nature. Allen asserts that social education should sensitize its analysis of the commitments of individuals to recognize that these commitments stem from diverse religious-philosophical traditions. Finally, Allen provides a number of specific examples drawn from curriculum materials for both elementary and secondary levels developed by the Religion-Social Studies Curriculum Project at Florida State University which incorporate the principles he suggests.

Part 1

Public Education and Religion Studies

Legal, Theoretical, and Practical Issues

Nicholas Piediscalzi
and
William E. Collie

Religion studies courses and units on religion are being introduced at a rapid rate in our nation's public schools. Between 1967 and 1974 the number of Pennsylvania public schools offering the course Religious Literature of the West grew from 31 to 100, and the number of students involved in this course increased from 700 to 4,000. Another 8,000 students, reports Dr. John Whitney, formerly of Pennsylvania State University, were enrolled in other religion-studies programs in Pennsylvania public schools in 1974. Professor Thomas Love of California State University, Northridge, identifies at least 80 new religion-studies courses appearing within a 60-mile radius of his campus between 1968 and 1972. In addition, innumerable units on religion were included in regular courses. Dr. Lambert Ponstein's survey of Michigan's secondary schools reveals that 50 out of the 96 respondents inaugurated religion-studies courses between 1970 and 1973. In a 1974 follow-up study, Professor Henry Hoeks discovered 19 additional high schools offering religion-studies courses and a substantial number of religion courses in junior high schools in addition to units in regular courses. A study by the National Council of Teachers of English reports that The Bible as Literature ranks high among the top 25 mini-courses most requested by students. This is just a sampling of the reports received by the Public Education Religion Studies Center (PERSC) on the introduction of religion studies in public education.[1]

Since this change is taking place quietly, it goes unnoticed by most citizens and educators. Hence, whenever the topic of religion studies in public education arises, a series of recurring questions are asked: Are public education religion studies illegal? Why should religion studies be included in the public schools? What are the objectives of religion studies? How should religion be defined for public school study? How do you study religion in public education? Where is the best place to include religion studies in the curriculum? How do you find and select materials for public education religion studies? This chapter seeks to answer these questions and to prepare the way for the articles, units, and selected courses presented in the remainder of the book.

THE BIG BAD SUPREME COURT

Gross misunderstanding prevails in our nation regarding the Supreme Court decisions on prayer and religion studies in the public schools. The Court did not ban all prayer from the schools. Neither did the Court prohibit the academic study of religion. The Court ruled against public schools and their teachers requiring students to pray and/or recite passages from the Bible for devotional purposes. This is in keeping with the First Amendment of the United States Constitution, which prohibits the government and its agents—in this case the public schools—from establishing a religion.

At the same time, the Court made it clear that the academic study of religion is not prohibited by the Constitution: "Nothing we have said here indicates that such a study of the Bible or of religion, when presented objectively as part of a secular program in education, may not be effected consistent with the First Amendment" *(Abington* v. *Schempp).*

The Court also stated that "one's education is not complete without a study of comparative religion and its relationship to the advancement of civilization. . . .[Moreover] the Bible is worthy of study for its literary and historic qualities" *(Abington* v. *Schempp).*

Even though these statements of the Supreme Court establish beyond a doubt that it is legal to study religion academically in the public schools, citizens and educators continue to confuse the propagation of a religious faith with the study of religion. This is due in large part to the long period in our national history when the public schools were used first to inculcate Calvinistic Protestantism and, later, a nonsectarian religious patriotism.[2] Against this Protestant hegemony, minority religious communities founded parochial schools to preserve their own religious integrity and heritages. However, these schools pursued religious indoctrination rather than the academic study of religion. Due to this history, it is difficult to alter our consciousness, which automatically and erroneously identifies religious indoctrination with religion studies. Therefore we Americans often find it difficult to understand how the Supreme Court could rule in favor of the academic study of religion while prohibiting indoctrination in public schools and how the schools can be objective in their teaching about religion.

James V. Panoch developed a set of what he calls "pair-words," which may be used to determine what constitutes legal and illegal religion studies in the public schools and to distinguish the difference between the propagation of a religious faith and the study of religion.

> The school may sponsor the *study* of religion, but may not sponsor the *practice* of religion.
>
> The school may *expose* students to all religious views, but may not *impose* any particular view.
>
> The school's approach to religion is one of *instruction,* not one of *indoctrination.*
>
> The function of the school is to *educate* about all, not to *convert* to any one, religion.
>
> The school's approach to religion is *academic,* not *devotional.*
>
> The school should *study* what all people believe, but should not *teach* a pupil what he should believe.
>
> The school should strive for student *awareness* of all religions, but should not press for student *acceptance* of any one religion.
>
> The school should seek to *inform* the student about various beliefs, but should not seek to *conform* him to any one belief.[3]

In summary, the study of religion in public education is legal, according to the Supreme Court, when it is an integral part of the school's academic program, when it neither gives preferential nor derogatory treatment to any single religion or religion in general, and when it is not introduced or utilized for devotional purposes.

BUT WHY ADD RELIGION STUDIES TO AN ALREADY CROWDED CURRICULUM?

The religious factor in human history is a significant one. It is deeply embedded in most of the world's history, in its literary documents, and in its social institutions. Consequently a curriculum which does not include study about religion is incomplete. Raymond English, Director of the Educational Research Council of America's Social Science Program, maintains:

> To study human behavior and societies without paying attention to religious motivations is like studying chemistry without recognizing the presence of oxygen in the atmosphere. Men behave as they do for a variety of reasons, and one powerful causal factor is their value system—their beliefs about life's meaning and purpose. These beliefs are their religion—their ultimate concept of reality.[4]

Furthermore, to omit religion studies from the school is, as the American Association of School Administrators suggested in 1964, to present a truncated and distorted view of human history:

> A curriculum which ignored religion would itself have serious religious implications. It would seem to proclaim that religion has not been as real in men's lives as health or politics or economics. By omission it would appear to deny that religion has been and is important in man's history—a denial of the obvious. In day-by-day practice, the topic cannot be avoided. As an integral part of man's culture, it must be included.[5]

Thus, since one of the public schools' tasks is to provide students with a complete education, study about religion must be made a part of the curriculum.

Also, in a time like ours, when societal values are changing and world cultural values come into conflict, it is important to study about the sources of values. Religion is a source of values for many societies and peoples. Therefore it is important for the public schools to help students understand the role of religion in value information and value conservation or transformation.

In summary, commitment to comprehensive education requires the inclusion of religion studies in the curriculum.

WHAT ARE THE GOALS OF PUBLIC EDUCATION RELIGION STUDIES?

According to the authors, religion studies in public education should pursue five general goals. They are to develop a broad and discerning understanding of:

1. the religious dimension of human existence and the many and diverse ways in which it is embodied and expressed in historical groups and individual lives;
2. the way in which religions function in history and culture, with special emphasis on how religions influence institutions and in turn are influenced by them;
3. the meaning and significance of making a religious commitment and living by it;
4. the numerous different ways in which religion may be studied;
5. the difference between practicing and studying about religion.

The remainder of this book delineates specific ways these goals may be achieved.

HOW IS RELIGION DEFINED FOR PUBLIC SCHOOL STUDY?

Like most contemporary teachers about religion, the authors of this article find it necessary to utilize two definitions of religion, one narrow and the other broad.

The narrow definition comes to mind immediately when the word "religion" is used: an institutionalized set of beliefs, dogmas, ethical prescriptions, and cultic practices which center around devotion to and service of a particular deity or set of deities. Hinduism, Judaism, Christianity, Islam, and Baha'i, for example, are religions of this type.

The broad definition envisions religion as any faith or set of values to which an individual or group gives ultimate loyalty. Theravada Buddhism, Taoism, Ethical Culture, secularism, humanism, scientism, nationalism, and the attainment of money and/or power illustrate this concept of religion.

There are at least three important factors which make it necessary for those who teach about religion to use both of these definitions in their work. First, the United States Supreme Court in recent years has broadened the legal definition of religion. For example, in the 1961 *Torcaso* case, the Court, hearing the suit of a Maryland notary public who had been barred from office because he would not profess belief in the existence of God, stated that "neither a State nor the Federal Government can constitutionally . . . aid those religions based on a belief in the existence of God as against those religions founded on different beliefs."

17

To make certain that no one misunderstood this position, the Court added: "Among religions in this country which do not teach what would generally be considered a belief in the existence of God are Buddhism, Taoism, Ethical Culture, Secular Humanism, and others." At the same time, the court related its opinion in the *Torcaso* case to *Everson* v. *Board of Education* (1947) and *McCollum* v. *Board of Education* (1948), pointing out that the legal definitions and principles used in the *Torcaso* case had been applied previously in the *Everson* and *McCollum* decisions. By relating the *Torcaso* decision to these educational cases, the Court made clear that the broad definition of religion applies to the field of education.[6]

Second, religions, in the narrow sense of the term, are no longer institutions of primary influence and power in most Western and many Eastern societies. They have been replaced by what Paul Tillich calls "quasi-religions," for example, secularism, scientism, nationalism, and humanism.[7] These faiths by which individuals live function as religions. Also it is possible for people to use traditional religious symbols to justify an ultimate commitment which is contrary to the meaning those symbols originally conveyed. Will Herberg, for example, suggests that most Americans live by a civil religion which he calls "The American Way of Life," although they use the symbols and institutions of the Jewish and Christian traditions to justify and uphold this primarily secular-nationalistic commitment.[8]

Third, contemporary life is filled with intense religious quests and attempts at religious reform. Many of these activities take place outside the boundaries of traditional religions. They are found in the works of artists and scholars and protest and counterculture groups. For example, the novels of Albert Camus and John Updike, the works of Picasso and Chagall, the compositions of Leonard Bernstein and Gian-Carlo Menotti, and the writings of Erick H. Erikson and Paul Goodman are replete with serious religious questions and quests. There are significant parallels and similarities between the pronouncements and judgments of the Hebrew prophets and some contemporary protest and counterculture movements. Many of the recent experiments at communal living and new life-styles share the same religious intensity and attempts at religious reform found in the monastic movements of the West and in the utopian sect groups which have had an ongoing history of experimentation since the founding of our country.

18

Confronted with such complex and sensitive issues as these, teachers clearly need not only a broadened definition of religion but also a special approach to study about religion.

HOW DO YOU STUDY ABOUT RELIGION IN PUBLIC SCHOOLS?

Academic study of religion is a nondoctrinal, open, critical, and empathetic examination of all religions, narrowly and broadly defined, both past and present. This approach seeks to avoid condemnation and defamation and to produce understanding and appreciation. Through such a study of religion, the student is able eventually to understand the role religion plays in forming, conserving, reforming, or stultifying societies and cultures.

Robert A. Spivey and Rodney F. Allen recently wrote that the aim of the academic study of religion is to develop religious literacy. The role of teachers in this process, they suggest, is to help students raise and consider three questions: (1) What is religion? (2) What are some of the significant religious traditions? (3) What is the relationship of religion to culture?[9]

Since religions, both broadly and narrowly defined, are highly complex systems, religious literacy cannot be achieved if the study of them is confined solely to a review of their scriptures, written documents, and major beliefs. Their rituals, forms of worship, traditions, polity, organizational structures, and systems of ethics must also be considered. Failure to examine these elements as integral and interrelated parts of a complex whole leads to a distorted and inadequate understanding of religion.[10]

Teachers who engage in religion studies must strive to prevent personal religious faith and values from distorting the learning process. This does not mean that they must become cold and detached in their presentations. On the contrary, teachers about religion, like other effective teachers, must engage in what Philip H. Phenix calls "disciplined intersubjectivity." According to Phenix, to be academic and objective about religion "is to enter into the subjectivity of persons other than oneself in a disciplined way. . . . This is the fundamental mark of human intelligence. We are humanly intelligent to the degree that we are capable of getting inside points of view other than our own, in a way that is genuinely appreciative."[11] Margherite LaPota adds that objectivity also entails presenting "a plurality . . . of interpretations, attitudes, and materials; . . . [encouraging] free pursuit of related information; and [maintaining] reciprocal respect for contrary positions."[12]

Admittedly, human beings cannot be totally objective about the subjects they teach. However, teachers of religion—like other teachers—can make their own and students' biases a teaching tool by pointing out their lack of objectivity. They can help students identify the preconceived notions they bring to their study about religion and other subjects which prevent them from being objective. Ideally, such awareness is a major goal of education. For this reason it must be stated once again that there is a difference between the study about religion and the practice and propagation of religion. The public school is not a church or a religious institution. It is a place for academic pursuits, a community where students and instructors can join in an objective study of events, beliefs, practices, and issues, including secular commitments. Such study should lead to a deeper understanding and appreciation of these aspects of their lives and the lives of others.

Before concluding, it is also necessary to note that the study of ethics and values is included in religion studies. Religions, both narrowly and broadly defined, present their adherents with an explicit or implicit ideal of the "good" life and the consequences of that ideal for human conduct. In addition, as Ninian Smart points out, some value problems contain or ask religious questions which evoke religious answers. For example:

> Since much of life seems to get its value from ongoing projects and institutions, death represents a question mark over that value. Hence the grim horror and hopelessness of *On the Beach*. If death claims us, then does it not thereby claim the long-term purposes in which we cooperate with our fellow men?[13]

When ethical and value questions are treated in religion studies, the major focus is on understanding the relationship of religious commitments to ethics and of ethics to values. Hence it is important not to confuse religion studies with contemporary popular forms of moral education and values clarification. In the former, the focus is upon religion as an integrative view of human life which provides the foundation for the community's and the believer's ethics and values. Moral education and values clarification, on the other hand, usually focus on the principles and skills of making moral decisions, identifying and clarifying the values by which groups and individuals live, and discovering the different consequences produced by different moral and values commitments. While these approaches serve useful educational purposes and raise religious questions implicitly or explicitly, they do not constitute religion studies. Furthermore, they are methods derived from ideologies which function as religions, according to the broad definition of the term. Therefore they, too, must be studied critically and comparatively within religion studies as the foundations of different moral and value positions. These points are made neither to denigrate nor reject outright moral education or values clarification. They are noted in order to clarify the goals and objectives unique to moral education, values clarification, and religion studies and the relationships among them.[14]

NOTES

1. Parts of this chapter are revisions and expansions of sections from Peter Bracher et al., *PERSC Guidebook, Public Education Religion-Studies: Questions and Answers* (Dayton, Ohio: Public Education Religion Studies Center, 1974) and are used here by permission of the publisher.

2. For a penetrating and succinct description of the developmental changes in the religio-moral character of American public education, see: William B. Lauderdale, "Moral Intentions in the History of American Education," *Theory into Practice,* 14 (October 1975): 264–70.

3. Bracher, *PERSC Guidebook,* p. 2.

4. Raymond English, "Focus on Religious Ideas," *Scholastic Teacher,* 22 (December 1968): 12.

5. *Religion in the Public Schools: A Report by the Commission on Religion* (Washington, D.C.: American Association of School Administrators, 1964), p.55.

6. For a more detailed discussion of this case and a justification for broadening the definition of religion, see: Donald Oppewal, "Religion and Public Education: An Emerging Quandary," *Educational Forum,* 31 (March 1967): 323–31. Cf. John J. Paris, S.J., "Toward an Understanding of the Supreme Court's Approach to Religion in Conscientious Objector Cases," *Suffolk University Law Review,* (Spring 1973): 449–517.

7. D. Mackenzie Brown, *Ultimate Concern: Tillich in Dialogue* (New York: Harper & Row, 1965), pp. 25–26.

8. Will Herberg, *Protestant, Catholic, Jew: An Essay in American Religious Sociology,* rev. ed., Anchor Books (Garden City, N.Y.: Doubleday, 1960), pp. 72–90.

9. Robert A. Spivey and Rodney F. Allen, *The Supreme Court Speaks: Learning About Religion in the Public Schools* (Tallahassee, Fla.: Religion-Studies Curriculum Project, Florida State University, 1972), 26–27.

10. Cf. Ninian Smart, "What Is Religion?" in Ninian Smart and Donald Horder, eds., *New Movements in Religious Education* (London: Temple Smith, 1975) pp. 14–17; and Jean L. Holm, *Teaching Religion in School* (London: Oxford Univ. Press, 1975), pp. 7–11.

11. Philip H. Phenix, "Religion in Public Education: Principles and Issues," *Religion and Public School Curriculum: Proceedings of the National Council on Religion and Public Education,* Richard U. Smith, ed., *Religious Education,* 67 (July–August 1972, Pt. 2), p. 19.

12. Margherite LaPota, "Religion: Not 'Teaching' but 'Teaching About,' " *Educational Leadership: Journal for the Association for Supervision and Curriculum Development,* 31 (October 1973), p. 32.

13. Smart, *New Movements,* p. 18.

14. For a complete discussion of this topic, see: Nicholas Piediscalzi and Barbara A. Swyhart, eds., *Distinguishing Moral Education, Values Clarification and Religion-Studies: Proceedings of the 1976 American Academy of Religion Group on Religion-Studies in Public Education* (Missoula, Mont.: Scholars Press, 1976).

Part 2

Religion Studies in the Humanities and the Fine Arts

Relational Humanities
and Religion Studies

Joseph Forcinelli

To write and, presumably, to read about humanities topics in educational materials evokes almost instant interest. As people, we rarely stop examining our humanity or cease wondering what it means to be human. This is historically true, and it suggests that humanities education appropriately reflects the values of tradition as well as change. But more importantly, such education allows the student to examine the meaning of his or her own individual humanity.

Writing an essay in 1975, I suggested three ways to include religion studies in the high school humanities program:[1] (1) *Global Humanities,* as an interdisciplinary and thematic concept; (2) *Humanities Electives,* such as Philosophy and The History of World Religions; and (3) *Coordinate Humanities,* which focus more on the interrelation of certain area studies and humanities such as English Humanities and Social Science Humanities.

For the purposes of this article, I am suggesting what may be a more cogent designation for Global Humanities and Humanities electives when they include religion, namely, "Relational Humanities and Religion Studies." This approach emphasizes both the integrative and independent appeal of religion studies to students. Also, it characterizes independent courses such as I have been teaching— Humanities I, in which the theme "Man, the Religious Animal" is explored; The History of World Religions, a study of individual religions and cultures of the world; and Philosophy, which is an inquiry into philosophical issues, including the relationship between religion and ethics.

When I began teaching about religion at Claremont High School in 1963, I was struck by the obvious truth that historical, scholarly, academic, and independent elective study in world religions was the most acceptable way to include religion studies in the school program. I extended this truth to include a philosophy course that same year and, three years later, an interdisciplinary humanities course. Because these courses were unique in the history of the school district, they had to be approved by the school faculty, members of the social science department, the administration, and the school board. In 1970, I established a separate humanities department, having committed my thinking to a philosophy of education that was based on a relational-humanities approach to learning. New courses added to the program included: Oriental Studies, The Bible as Literature, Western Philosophy, Eastern Philosophy, Religion in America, and African Studies.

In 1973, two self-directed courses were added, using television and the news media as basic materials: "The Humanities Film Forum" and "America and the Future of Man." The most recent courses to be included in the department program were: Philosophies and Religions of the Middle East and Religion: Past, Present, and Future.

All of these courses were offered as electives and have remained that way to the present. This model for relational humanities and religion studies illustrates that teachers prepared with adequate foundations in humanities, history, religion, and philosophy can implement a respectable humanities program that explores the interrelationships of religion and culture. At the same time, an underlying philosophy persists: when religion is presented as a separate and substantive entity, it must not lose the distinctive characteristics and integrity of its cultural origins. Likewise, when religion is studied in a relational sense, such considerations also must preserve the personal integrity of the individual students.

The following illustrative model demonstrates only partially the varieties of independent courses in the humanities program described above. I am extracting a five-week segment from what would normally be a full-year course in The History of World Religions. I have deliberately chosen those sections of the course which demonstrate the nature of religion, how we study it, and what it means when a Jain, a Parsee, and a Taoist relate the sincerity of their faith. Prior to dealing with these sections of the course, I would like to present an overview of the teaching strategies and objectives of the course generally.

TEACHING STRATEGIES

I believe it is important to introduce the course with the question, "What is religion?" A study of the nature of religion, or what is commonly called the phenomenology of religion, provides students with a basic starting point for the study. The students are motivated to define religion for themselves, and then they examine the definition used by Paul Tillich, namely, religion is that which is one's "ultimate concern." Invariably, this approach to the nature of religion leads to a brief study of theories as to how religion found expression in such phenomena as animism, mana, totemism, and magic.

I begin with the religions of Jainism, Zoroastrianism, and Taoism. After studying these religions, the students become aware of what a serious adherent feels when he or she worships. Students also become interested in and fascinated with little-known religions—those whose unique characteristics of belief and ritual inform us of basic patterns of religious experience. Examples would be the emphasis the Jain adherent places on self-denial, nonviolence, the nature of evil, and the ways of being saved from evil. Later on in the course, the students are able to link Jainism with the study of Hinduism and Buddhism, clearly unfolding for them the whole subject of Indian culture.

The Middle East becomes the cultural environment for students as they study the religion of Zoroaster. Again, the unique monotheism of the Parsee later opens the way for noticing corollaries with the monotheism of Judaism, Christianity, and Islam.

Taoism not only introduces the student to the culture of China, but the Taoist philosophy of quiescent nature mysticism perceived by the student is seen against the backdrop of the more formal Confucian philosophy which is studied later.

A brief outline of these units follows:

Unit I. What Is Religion?
  A. The Nature of Religion Defined
  B. The Religious Quality of Experience
  C. Religion in Its Infancy
  D. Questions That Concern Students
  E. On Being Students of Religion

Unit II. Three Religions That Aid Student Understanding
         of Religious Experience

27

A. Jainism, A Religion of Self-Power
B. Zoroastrianism, A Religion of Other-Power
C. Taoism, A Religion of Inaction and Passivity

GOALS AND OBJECTIVES

Performance objectives,[2] sometimes called behavioral objectives, consist of experiences verifiable in the classroom and later accounted for by learning indicators, usually in the form of tests, written papers, oral reports, etc. The following objectives are prescribed for the student: objective research, tutorial-type reading assignments, maintaining a lecture notebook, providing student data services, participating in symposia, and open-note examinations.

More specifically, the performance objectives are stated this way:

1. The student will follow an objective historical study of the world's religions.
2. The student will become a "student of religion."
3. The student will develop a sense of appreciation of religions of the world.
4. The student will perform objective research.
5. The student will engage in directed readings.
6. The student will visit and participate in dialogues with adherents of particular religions.
7. The student will participate in a symposium on religions.
8. The student will write religion papers relevant and meaningful to his or her knowledge and understanding of the religions.

All of these activities will occur in the classroom (except for excursions), which will also become a student resource center.

TEACHER'S GUIDANCE OF LEARNING ACTIVITIES

1. Lectures containing the data and phenomena of the learning unit will be presented on Mondays. Students will keep notes on lecture data. Comprehensive and carefully delineated reading lists will be given the students in printed form every Monday.
2. In-class tutorials based on reading lists are planned for Wednesdays. The instructor will clarify and supplement material

questions raised. Students will keep reading logs containing data. These discussion-type tutorials will be extended when interest is generated. Discussion-type seminars are projected for Fridays.

3. Student data services are integral to the research performance papers and symposium. For each learning unit, seven to ten primary segments of the substantive material will be assigned to students on the basis of three to five students per segment. In researching these segments in depth, these students will also be responsible for providing the class with their data findings, which are then filed for student use in an open-book format during the writing of performance papers and the conduct of the symposium.

4. The symposium will be held toward the conclusion of each five-week learning unit. The intent here is to allow the students to perform as "experts" in an interaction of knowledge fields.

5. The functional examination affords the student an opportunity to employ all the knowledge gained in the five-week unit. This examination will be conducted in open-book format as a "research performance" lasting two class periods.

PERFORMANCE INDICATORS

It is my intention in this section to outline a variety of teacher-directed activities which will integrate and monitor the various levels of student performance. This will be done for each of the two units described in earlier pages of the article.

Unit I. What Is Religion?

VOCABULARY

animism	sacrament	prophet
nature religion	magic	dance
ritual	breath	chant
symbolic forms	spirit	mantra
water	religious garb	psalm
mountains	prayer	festival
rivers	meditation	celebration
blood	enlightenment	libation

fire	saint	funeral
sacrifice	holy man	cult
baptism	priest	worship
exorcism	shaman	

SEMINAR QUESTIONS

Toward a definition of religion

1. A modern theologian has defined religion as "ultimate concern." What is the difference between an immediate concern and an ultimate concern? If we accept this definition of religion, in what sense are all human beings religious?
2. What is the difference between a "religious question" and a "question about religion"? Give examples of each type of question.
3. Is religion best described as a human invention or as a human response? To what extent are both definitions useful?
4. What is the difference between faith and belief? Is one more crucial to religion than the other? What generates faith? What causes belief? Is there such a thing as blind faith, or unfounded faith?
5. How do myth, symbol, and ritual interrelate?

Unit II. Jainism, Zoroastrianism, Taoism

VOCABULARY

Jainism

asceticism	ajivas	monastic life
karma	jina	angas
caste system	Kaivalya	samsara
Mahavira	Digambaras	fordfinder
Shvetambaras	Sthanakvasis	tirthankara
Tapas	rebirth	Nataputta
ahimsa	atheism	Vardhamana
jivas	the three jewels	Nirvana
		Parsva

Zoroastrianism

Avesta	Mithra	haoma
Yasna	Rita	Agni
Gathas	Asha	Ishtar
Visperad	yima	Zoroaster
Yasht	yama	Zarathustra
Kordah Avesta	fravashi	Vohu Manah
daivas	Pitras	Aphrodite
Mitra	soma	Dakhmas

Taoist Sayings

The Tao that can be expressed is not the eternal Tao.

The name that can be defined is not the unchanging name.

Nonexistence is the mother of all things.

Nonexistence is the antecedent of heaven and earth.

From eternal nonexistence, therefore, we serenely observe the mysterious beginning of the universe.

From eternal existence we clearly see the apparent distinctions.

SEMINAR QUESTIONS

1. Survival is basic to human nature. When do people feel dependent and when do they feel independent—when it means survival?
2. Why is asceticism based primarily on independent self-effort?
   Why do people go in training for athletics, for diet, for health, or fast for religious purposes?
3. What is the connection between respecting all living things and nonviolence?
4. Is there a struggle between good and evil?
5. What does "natural order" suggest to you?

CONCLUSION

There is clearly a place in education for developing an awareness of the interdisciplinary quality of religion studies and the opportunities for its application within the substantive areas of the liberal arts and sciences. In the American school, we are now approaching a subject which is, as in no other time in American history, open to the scholarly mind and academic discipline in the same way that all school subjects must measure up to academic standards. Because we are operating in a new area of educational responsibility, the implementation of present activities and the planning of future frameworks should be guided by intellectual honesty and a respect for the intellectual integrity of all subjects fields. This responsibility, no less for religion studies, should be supportive of quality education that upholds academic soundness, competency of teachers, and a method which assures professional accountability.

The public schools are enjoined to plan for and conduct programs in religion studies which view religion as an integrated aspect of life. Such studies allow for due recognition of religious expression in the culture and beliefs of humankind while at the same time, insuring a faithful, accurate, and cogent understanding of those beliefs. It is my conviction that the professional educator can accomplish this most effectively through a relational-humanities program.

NOTES

1. Joseph Forcinelli, "The Humanities and Religion Studies," PERSC *Newsletter*, (Spring 1975), 1–2.
2. See Forcinelli, "The Humanities and Individualized Instruction" in Lloyd K. Bishop, *Individualizing Educational Systems* (New York: Harper & Row, 1971).

INSTRUCTIONAL RESOURCES

Basic Text

Hutchinson, John A. *Paths of Faith*. Rev. ed. New York: McGraw-Hill, 1968.

Bibliography Used for Assigned Readings and Special Reports

Ballou, Robert O., ed. *The Portable World Bible*. New York: Viking, 1944.

de Bary, William Theodore, ed. *Sources of Indian Tradition*. New York: Columbia Univ. Press, 1960.

———. *Sources of Chinese Tradition*. New York: Columbia Univ. Press, 1960.

———. *Sources of Japanese Tradition*. New York: Columbia Univ. Press, 1958.

Fung Yu-Lan. *A Short History of Chinese Philosophy*. Paperback. New York: Macmillan, 1948.

Gaer, Joseph. *How the Great Religions Began*. Paperback. New York: Doubleday, 1966.

Gaustad, Edwin Scott. *A Religious History of America*. Paperback. New York: Harper & Row, 1966.

Lessa, William A., and Vogt, Evon Z. *Reader in Comparative Religion*. Paperback. New York: Harper & Row, 1967.

Noss, John B. *Man's Religions*. New York: Macmillan, 1963.

Ross, Floyd H., and Hills, Tynette. *The Great Religions by Which Men Live*. Greenwich, Conn.: Fawcett, 1956.

Schoeps, Hans-Joachim. *The Religions of Mankind*. Paperback. New York: Doubleday-Anchor, 1966.

Smart, Ninian. *Religious Experience of Mankind*. Paperback. New York: Scribner, 1969.

Smith, Huston, *The Religions of Man*. Paperback. New York: Harper & Row, 1958.

Zaehner, R. C., ed. *The Concise Encyclopedia of Living Faiths*. Paperback. Boston: Beacon Press, 1967.

Sights, Sounds, and Narrative Media

Publisher: The Center for Humanities, Inc.
Titles: *Man and His Gods: An Inquiry into the Nature of Religion*
Myths and Legends: Mirrors of Mankind
Man's Search for the Meaning of Life
The Bible as Literature: In the Beginning Was the Word
Man and His Values: An Inquiry into Good and Evil
East Meets West: A Contrast in Values and Cultures
Publisher: Time-Life, Inc.
Title: *The Religions of Mankind*
Publisher: Science and Mankind, Inc. (A division of the Center for Humanities)
Title: *An Inquiry into the Origin of Man: Science and Religion*
Publisher: Scholastic, Inc.
Title: *Art and Man Series*

Religion in Literature, Drama, Dance, and Film

Jon T. Barton

Literature, drama, dance, and film are excellent disciplines through which to pursue religion studies in public education because they are replete with religious themes, symbols, and allusions. However, there is no single model for this pursuit. At best we may suggest only representative models. Hence, for purposes of illustration, I shall offer as a model curricular structure for grades K–12 the one proposed by the Humanities Framework Committee for the California Public Schools.[1] It should be noted that the humanities construct proposed for California schools is, at this time, nothing more than a proposal (albeit, an excellent one). As such, its contents remain subject to change before they are implemented. But given the facts (1) that California specifically allows the academic study of religion in the public schools, (2) that some sort of positive action regarding the implementation of a humanities program throughout California is, at the very least, probable in the foreseeable future, and (3) that my twelve years' teaching experience have all been spent in California, I feel using the California humanities model is especially in concert with the intent of this article.

In the chart on page 48,[2] we see the curricular progression for grades K–12 as proposed in the California model. In addition, we see that five components (visual and tactile arts, body education, music, drama and language arts, and social sciences) form a core which does not change throughout the period of public schooling. During the early elementary years, foreign languages are added; during the later elementary years, math and science are added. Then, in junior high school, industrial and household arts are added, leaving only the addition of philosophy and religion in senior high.

Presumably there are a number of educational considerations responsible for this kind of curricular progression. I would suggest the following as being the considerations: (1) increase in cognitive skills, (2) increase in attention span, (3) increase in self-awareness, (4) increase in intragroup awareness, and (5) increase in intergroup awareness. Again, I believe it is imperative that religion studies, at least initially, assume a supportive role in such curricular progression. That religion studies may eventually emerge as a discipline standing on its own academic merit remains an Elysian hope; but if it is ever to achieve such merit, it will first have to demonstrate the productivity of its supportive character.

One further consideration I would wish to raise before proceeding with an examination of how to implement religion studies in existing curricular structures involves arriving at a workable division of grade levels. Apart from the placement of kindergarten as the starting point in public education, there is no consensus regarding where transitions should be made between elementary and secondary levels. The California model calls for a subdivision during the elementary years. Where more traditional structures prevail, this probably presumes a grouping of grades 1–3 and 4–6. On the other hand, where intermediate schools separate elementary and secondary levels, there would doubtless be a K–5, 6–8, and 9–12 grouping. Needless to say, a 7–8 (or 9) and 10 (or 9)–12 secondary grouping seems to be the dominant structure. To simplify matters, I will direct my discussion regarding implementation of religion studies in existing curricular structures along three educational planes: primary, intermediate, and advanced.

INTERDISCIPLINARY IMPLEMENTATION OF RELIGION STUDIES

The first point to be emphasized regarding this consideration is that the fundamental components in our curricular model are intrinsically related to the fine arts and can all be supported significantly by the subject matter of religion studies. Visual and tactile arts provide opportunities both to imitate and to create; body education is frequently synonymous with dance (again, both imitatively and creatively so); music, drama, and language arts (especially literature) are, by definition, fine arts; and social sciences (insofar as they are concerned with exploration of cultural development) never wander far from the arts. While comparable arguments can successfully be offered for extra-foundational courses such as foreign languages, philosophy, and—by all means—religion, less persuasive ones attend math, science, industrial arts, and household arts. However, the most difficult task in establishing an academic base of operations for religion studies within existing course structures is not merely to demonstrate how such courses can be enhanced by such implementation, but to convince the teachers of these courses that they can indeed implement them. Too often, for example, literature teachers feel the major prerequisite for teaching the Bible as literature is a "Sunday School" background; in doing so, they fail to see that their background in literature itself is, by far, the most essential qualification. Similar illustrations could be drawn regarding teachers in other subject areas where a religion studies content is possible.

How can teacher potential be brought into alignment with course potential? There are, I believe, three factors that make such alignment possible: (1) identification of *goals* which the various subject areas share with religion studies (books such as this one do much to help in this direction); (2) development and utilization of *materials* which demonstrate both the supportive and autonomous character of religion studies (clearly, this is the least fulfilled need concerning religion studies at this time); and (3) *professional encouragement* for teachers who wish to explore the many ways in which religion studies can augment the public school curriculum. Tangible encouragements may range from understanding department chairpersons to innovative administrators. A teacher might even be granted a study sabbatical for the express purpose of developing religion studies curricula (as a colleague and I from Santa Monica High School were granted during the 1974–75 school year).

It is with the hope of demonstrating how course potential and teacher potential can be brought into common focus that I now turn from the theoretical to the practical aspect of this chapter. Using "primary," "intermediate," and "advanced" as the agreed-upon levels of learning differentiation, I will survey (not exhaustively, but representatively) the subject areas which are the concern of this chapter and suggest ways in which religion studies can both strengthen and make more pleasurable its educational potentials.

LITERATURE AND RELIGION STUDIES

Primary Level

Literature moves more rapidly as a learning tool at the primary level than at any other. At one end of the spectrum, the preliterate child is entirely dependent upon teacher selection, presentation, and evaluation of materials; at the other end, cognitive and critical skills are just beginning to come into their own, leaving the child at the very threshold of unlimited discovery. Interestingly, there is one religion studies component capable of helping children successfully negotiate such wide-ranging progress: mythology.

It is Northrop Frye's contention that "literature follows after a mythology."[3] If he is correct, the primary level is the ideal starting point for reading myths. To be sure, Western culture is, at its core, a fusion of classical and biblical traditions; and few traditions are as rich with myths as are these two. Of course, I am using "myth" here in a generic sense, whereby I intend it to mean *an attempt to explain the otherwise unexplainable in profound—if not poetic—language.* Hence I am in total agreement with Professor Frye's assessment that "the Bible forms the lowest stratum in the teaching of literature" as well as with his agenda for teaching it "so early and so thoroughly that it sinks straight to the bottom of the mind, where everything that comes along later can settle on it."[4] Again, the classroom teacher without special training or a "Sunday School" background may balk at this as a starting point for integrating religion studies with the regular reading program; but we have strong, critical evidence that the Bible should—as well as clear constitutional evidence that it can—be that starting point.

Since the Bible stories will first only be heard, it is essential that language not serve as a barrier. Whereas the King James Version is generally the translation suggested for a literary study of the Bible, I would suggest instead the *Living Bible.* Its narratives read like stories, and its language is in the contemporary idiom. That the *Living Bible* has been, by far, the best-selling version of the Bible in recent years should serve as added argument for its use. However, if direct reading from the Bible is not the preference of the teacher, then a text such as Pearl Buck's *The Story Bible* can be used without any significant loss of literary integrity.

Greek and Roman myths should also be read in story fashion, which means that they can be utilized early in the primary stage. Here, choice of text does not pose the same kinds of problems as does selecting a source for reading Bible stories. Certainly, Edith Hamilton's *The Greek Way* and *The Roman Way* could serve as sources although the teacher will want to simplify them for the student.

How many additional levels of myth can be built on top of these two is dependent upon teacher initiative and student receptivity. The California humanities model goes so far as to suggest that children at this level also learn about "vegetation and animal myths from American Indian, Asian, African, and other cultures" in order for them to "see other relationships than those presented solely from human adult male points of view."[5] As pointed out earlier, materials presently available have not necessarily kept pace with need, so venturing beyond the biblical and classical traditions may require some do-it-yourself preparation; but the rewards of such efforts should prove inestimable.

Intermediate Level

By the time the intermediate level is reached, students are no longer dependent entirely upon teacher presentation of materials; nor are they restricted to the narrative as the principal form of literary exposure. Poetry, drama, and fiction all come alive for intermediate readers, especially as creative expressions of the myths they have been learning about. The biblical account of the creation becomes an anthropomorphic odyssey in James Weldon Johnson's "The Creation," a "with it" happening in Harry Scarborough's "The Hippie Creation," and an ecological prophecy in Kenneth Ross's "Genesis: Last Chapter." Given a wide range of poems such as these for examples, students can easily be encouraged to try writing a "myth poem" of their own. The same may be said for short fiction: a story such as Jesse Stuart's "As Ye Sow So Shall Ye Reap" can enable a student to correlate a personal experience with an archetypal motif and express that correlation in the form of a short story.[6]

Advanced Level

It is at the advanced level that the entire range of literary possibilities is encountered. Poetry now becomes as important for its critical potential as it does for its pleasure content. Whether the piece is short, such as D. H. Lawrence's "Only Man," or an epic, such as Milton's *Paradise Lost,* students can begin to explore not only what is related in a myth but also why and how well it is being related (in this case, the Fall of Man). Moreover, given the addition of philosophy and religion as subject areas consonant with the advanced level, a wider sampling of poetry from non-Western traditions can be explored. Consider this short Sanskrit poem from the early eighteenth century:

> When a special nectar, made up of the workings
> of word and meaning, with its delightful current bathes
> the minds of men of taste, we have true poetry;
> but the finest subtlety therein
> is that which bursts upon our inner sense
> although not designated by the words.[7]

Or this nineteenth-century Zen poem:

> It's as if our heads were on fire, the way
> We apply ourselves to perfection of That.
> The future but a twinkle, beat yourself,
> Persist: the greatest effort's not enough.[8]

Or this classic from the *Tao Te Ching:*

> The best captain does not plunge headlong
> Nor is the best soldier a fellow hot to fight.
> The greatest victor wins without a battle:
> He who overcomes men understands them.
> There is a quality of quietness
> Which quickens people by no stress:
> "Fellowship with heaven," as of old,
> Is fellowship with man and keeps its hold.[9]

Indeed, a wider sampling of fiction, especially novels, can also be explored. Old Testament figures treated in fiction can be studied in such works as: Thomas Mann's *Joseph,* Sholem Asch's *Moses,* Frank Slaughter's *David: Warrior and King,* and Richard Hubler's *Love and Wisdom* (Solomon). New Testament figures can be found in Taylor Caldwell's *Dear and Glorious Physician* (Luke) and *Great Lion of God*

(Paul), and Lloyd C. Douglas's *The Big Fisherman* (Peter). A critical comparison of Christ-image treatments can be gleaned from Fulton Oursler's *Greatest Story Ever Told,* Sholem Asch's *The Nazarene,* and Nikos Kazantzakis's *The Last Temptation of Christ.* A smaller-scale comparison using peripheral subject matter can be made between Par Lagerkvist's *Barabbas* and Marie Corelli's *Barabbas.* Of course, Hermann Hesse's *Siddhartha* is in a class by itself and needs little introduction to students of Eastern thought or teachers of modern literature.

DRAMA AND RELIGION STUDIES

Primary Level

Since by definition drama involves both reading and acting out parts in a play, the kind of drama we have in mind at the primary level will usually have its emphasis on the latter element. We are reminded in the California model that "drama and language merge naturally in early education"[10] and that "wordless or spoken dance-dramas can grow out of listening to stories" inasmuch as "vivid, dramatic reading by teachers will stimulate the children to act out a sequence, imitate a character, or create . . . gesturally and verbally."[11]

Again, the initial layer of myth can serve as a boundless resource for such imitation and creativity:

> Examples of the tales that can be represented by . . . children who have heard religious and mythological stories are those of a child found by a pharaoh's daughter, brought gifts by wise men, promised a blessing under certain conditions, sent out on a quest, put in charge of other children, given power to heal, selected in her cradle to become chief priestess, or revealed after having been hidden in infancy.[12]

Intermediate Level

After the primary stage, an appreciation for drama as a disciplinary form can be established. Upon discovering the rudimentary elements which constitute drama (e.g., character, dialogue, and plot), students can begin to make up their own plays based on existing story lines with the notion that they can be reenacted—either by themselves or by someone else—with time, space, distance, and even cultural differences being transcended in the process.

To explore this approach, I would suggest having the students listen to a recording of Bill Cosby's "Noah." Then have the students choose a figure of their own from mythology and try a similar treatment, either humorously or seriously. Of course, spontaneity and brevity should be encouraged. Any efforts drawing favorable response from the rest of the class should be recorded for subsequent use (audio, video, or—with teacher assistance—written).

Advanced Level

As usual, it is the advanced level which offers the widest range of religion studies materials for integration with existing curricula. Here a play such as Paddy Chayefsky's *Gideon* can be read in a simple classroom setting with a considerable number of students participating, and the overall effect can be just as invigorating as that achieved by a full-stage production of, say, *Inherit the Wind,* with a limited number of drama students participating. I do not mean by this comparison to denigrate drama programs; I merely wish to point out that the immediacy of drama which has been carefully nurtured during the primary and intermediate stages should not suddenly be disenfranchised in the process of educating all students. It is at the advanced level that the *Iliad* and the *Odyssey* are generally read. If the attention due mythology has indeed been given in the earlier years, readings of these two classics will not be sterile or perfunctory—as has so often been the case.

Moreover, musical theater becomes a viable option at this level. Students will need little prompting to hear and/or see performed *Godspell* and *Jesus Christ, Superstar.* Those who have shown an earlier inclination for dramatic writing can be encouraged to adapt their talents to musical drama; those who have not shown such inclinations but who do have creative interests in music, either lyrically or melodically, can be drawn into the creative, dramatic process. The same might be said for those whose talents are merely supportive: playing instruments, singing, or dancing.

Exploration beyond Western drama also can be encouraged. Introduction to the Japanese form of theater called *No* could be fruitful at this level, especially since the historic *No* theater "in many respects . . . resembled the Greek drama":

First of all, there was the combination of text, music and dance. Secondly, both theaters used a chorus, although in the *No* the chorus never takes any part in the action, confining itself to recitations for the principal dancer when he is in the midst of his dance. Again, the *No* uses masks, as did the Greek drama, but their use is restricted to the principal dancer and his companions, especially when they take the parts of women. Mask-carving has been considered an important art in Japan, and together with the gorgeous costumes, the masks add much to the visual beauty of the *No*. In contrast, the scenery is barely sketched, consisting usually of no more than an impressionistic rendering of the main outlines of the objects portrayed. The music, at least to a Western listener, is not of great distinction, very rarely rising to the level of melody, and most often little more than an accentuation of the declaimed or intoned word. [13]

We are further informed that "behind these plays, as behind the *haiku*, were the teachings of Zen Buddhism, whose greatest influence is probably found in the form of the *No* itself."[14]

DANCE AND RELIGION STUDIES

Primary Level

We have already been reminded that a natural by-product of listening to a vivid reading is the "dance drama." Indeed, it is difficult at this stage of development to draw clear lines of distinction between dance and drama (or drama and language, for that matter). The interwoven nature of dance, drama, and literature is the watershed of creativity for young children, according to the California model:

Bodily and verbal languages should be combined inventively in "dance plays," poetry-mime activities, and interpretive presentations of children's stories. Teachers should interrelate all the forms of human communication in such activities. Children can choose a favorite story and then select some favorite passages from it and begin their individual interpretations in body language. Dance plays can be composed in small groups and performed for the rest of the class. [15]

Such favorite stories can, again, be drawn from the layering of myth: the children of Israel marching around the walls of Jericho; King David dancing before the ark of the convenant as it was being returned to Jerusalem; various native dances of the American Indian—most notably the rain dance. In the former case, additional variations can be explored by having the children dance to the story and then to the music which recounts the story, "Joshua Fought the Battle of Jericho."

Intermediate Level

Whereas the primary level accentuates almost total spontaneity with regard to dance, the intermediate level should provide an opportunity to see the evolution of dance into a particular form. To be sure, the form most important to our study at this point is the "ethnologic dance." By ethnologic dance I mean that form which portrays the traditional characteristics of an ethnic group, past or present, which—at least originally—was designed to teach, entertain, and exhalt. Since the ethnologic dance is not generally executed without special instructions, teachers might at this point invite an appropriate expert to introduce such a dance. Certainly a good beginning point would be the *hora,* a folkdance of Romania and Israel that can be danced (and sung) to the music of *"Hava Nageela"* ("Come Let Us Rejoice and Sing"). In this instance, a member of a local Jewish congregation might be invited to speak to the students about the dance as a form of celebration in his tradition; then either he, or someone he has brought along, can introduce the entire class to the *hora.*

Advanced Level

By the time students reach the advanced stage, dance (more often than not) has been removed from the general classroom setting and placed either in a separate program by itself or in some sector of the physical-education program. The principal aspect of religion studies content stressed at this point is one of cultural enrichment. It might be pointed out, for instance, that Greek drama is greatly indebted to the *dithyramb,* a vigorous, leaping dance associated with spring festivities dedicated to Dionysius; or that in Hinduism, one of the Hindu trinity, Siva, is said to have been born of dance and, as Lord of Dancers (Nataraja), continues to create through dance. Moreover, the distinction between ethnologic and primitive dance can be drawn, pointing out that practically every primitive culture had its corporate dance expressions for harvest, exorcising of evil spirits, rites of passage, and propitiation of the gods.

FILM AND RELIGION STUDIES

Primary Level

Children today have already had years of exposure to television before they begin their formal education. For that reason, the level of sophistication with regard to film will be significantly higher than it will be for other genres. Whereas a ten-year old is not likely to have read *Ben-Hur,* he may indeed have seen the motion-picture version one or more times on television. In fact, the layering of biblical myth for which we argued earlier in this chapter can be greatly augmented by students viewing biblical films such as *The Bible—In the Beginning, The Ten Commandments, King of Kings,* and *The Greatest Story Ever Told.* Other films are less prodigious but still reinforce biblical story lines for the younger student: *Samson and Delilah, David and Bathsheba, Solomon and Sheba,* and *Esther and the King.* Moreover, television has itself produced biblical programs of note in recent years: *Jacob, Joseph and His Brothers, Moses—the Lawgiver,* and *David.* The most important responsibilities for teachers at this stage, then, include keeping abreast of television programming, informing students about scheduled showings of appropriate films, and encouraging students to share their responses to the films.

Intermediate Level

As critical abilities develop, students will be open to a wider range of religious subject matter in films. Instructional films concerned with various mythologies are readily available and should be used. Moreover, critical insights into biblical material can be tested by introducing students to films such as *Moby Dick, Billy Budd,* and *The Red Badge of Courage* and helping them to identify the biblical allusions present in the films. If students have read any of the novels or plays which have been produced for the screen, they may also wish to comment on the degree of authenticity they believe has or has not been achieved in the adaptation.

Advanced Level

At the advanced level, film remains in the domain of the classroom in general, although there will be, in some instances, special film classes offered by the English, art, fine-arts, humanities, or even social studies departments. Attention may still be directed to the source from

45

which the film has been adapted; it may turn to discussion of techniques involved in filmmaking; or it may be centered on how cinematic treatment of a story is similar to or different from treatments in other media. Film can provide an excellent insight into religious history, as does *A Man for All Seasons* in its portrayal of the struggle between Sir Thomas More's spiritual consciousness and Henry VIII's political maneuvering; it can analyze inner religious life in realistic degrees of intensity, as it does in *The Pawnbroker;* or it can explore the realm of symbolic, religious meaning, as do any number of Ingmar Bergman films—though perhaps most notably *The Seventh Seal.*

Since philosophy and religion are added at this level in our suggested model, the use of film becomes particularly fruitful. Certainly it would be impossible to believe the bass undertones chanted by Tibetan Buddhist monks if you did not actually hear them, as you do in Huston Smith's *Requiem for a Faith.* Similarly, depicting the life of Siddhartha in modern terms would be only verbally theoretical were it not for a film such as *Awareness,* which makes it visually so. And of course instructional films, such as those produced by Time-Life, are basic to the study of any major religion.

Finally, do not be surprised by the number of students at this level who have seen *The Exorcist* and *The Omen.* The Gothic form has long been a favorite of filmmakers. What is so notable about these films is (1) their phenomenal box-office success and (2) their use of religious themes to sustain plot (often at the expense of confusing—if not also disturbing—the viewer). Although these are overtly negativistic examples, the question might nonetheless be raised: Does film achieve unusual heights in utilizing the religious, or does the religious achieve unusual heights in the utilization of film?

ACADEMIC POSTSCRIPT

The content of this article, as mentioned earlier, makes no claim to being exhaustive; but it is, I believe, both representative and practical. It is offered with the hope that as *ideas* it will reproduce in kind. Like the medicine taken by Voltaire's philosopher, these ideas may not always be "beautiful" in themselves but if they do indeed "attain their object"—reproduction, either imitatively or creatively, I will have been academically rewarded and personally satisfied.

NOTES

1. *Proposed Humanities Framework for California Public Schools* (Sacramento: 1975). This text is not copyrighted.
2. Implied from table of contents of *Humanities.*
3. Northrop Frye, *The Educated Imagination* (Bloomington: Indiana Univ. Press, 1964), p. 110.
4. Frye, *Educated Imagination,* p. 110.
5. *Humanities,* p. 58.
6. For a comprehensive listing of germane materials, see Thayer Warshaw's article in this publication, "The Bible as/in Literature," as well as his text by the same title published by Abingdon, 1975.
7. Vidyakara, Ed., Daniel H. H. Ingalls, trans., *Sanskrit Poetry from Vidyakara's Treasury* (Cambridge, Mass.: Harvard Univ. Press, 1968), p. 316.
8. Lucien Stryk and Takashi Ikemoto, eds. and trans., *Zen: Poems, Prayers, Sermons, Anecdotes, Interviews* (New York: Doubleday, 1965), p. 19.
9. *The Way of Life According to Laotzu* (New York: Capricorn Books, 1944), p. 69.
10. *Humanities,* p. 48.
11. *Humanities,* p. 56.
12. *Humanities,* p. 58.
13. Nancy Wilson Ross, *The World of Zen* (New York: Random House, 1960), p. 168.
14. Ross, *Zen,* pp. 169–70.
15. *Humanities,* p. 98.

CURRICULAR PROGRESSION: GRADES K-12

Kindergarten	Early Elementary	Later Elementary	Junior High School	Senior High School
Visual and Tactile Arts	Visual and Tactile Arts	Visual and Tactile Arts	Visual and Tactile Arts	Visual and Tactile Arts
Body Education	Body Education	Body Education	Body Education	Body Education
Music	Music	Music	Music	Music
Drama and Language Arts	Drama and Language Arts	Drama and Language Arts	Drama and Language Arts	Drama and Language Arts
Social Sciences	Social Sciences	Social Sciences	Social Sciences	Social Sciences
	Foreign Languages	Foreign Languages	Foreign Languages	Foreign Languages
		Math and Sciences	Math and Sciences	Math and Sciences
			Industrial Arts	Industrial Arts
			Household Arts	Household Arts
				Philosophy and Religion

Aspects of Religious Influence on Architecture, Painting, and Music

William C. Fenton

To study a history of the fine arts is to study a history of religion and to experience a vast panorama of religious experiences communicated through artistic creations. This article presents a brief description of how three of the fine arts—architecture, painting, and music—convey various expressions of religious experience. Examples are drawn only from Western culture because time and space do not permit expansion into others. One cannot avoid the historical context, for all art is the result of previous experience. Therefore, this essay follows a thread of recorded history.

ARCHITECTURE

The decline of one culture and the ascendancy of another do not occur at a given time or place. Rather, an evolutionary process causes us to move from century to century, from life-style to life-style, from technology to technology. That which is left behind as architecture embodies some of the life and ideals of the culture it represents.

Visibility is an important factor in evaluating the cultural development of mankind. The tombs of ancient Egypt are symbols of the need for the perpetuation of the pharaoh worship which was part of the societal organization in the dynastic periods of Egyptian history. While the pyramids, temples, and palaces were decorated with wall paintings, hieroglyphs, and statuary, they are possibly best remembered as splendid architectural monuments to the Egyptian gods and rulers.

A quite different spirit imbued the aesthetic accomplishments of the Egyptians' neighbors across the Mediterranean Sea, the Greeks. Greek classicism has remained a potent cultural influence on rational

Western cultures since it first appeared. The need for order and balance, coupled with the respect for and admiration of human beauty, gave birth to this lasting influence on the arts. Yet this architecture, too, has religious significance. The temples of ancient Greece were built in homage to a god or goddess, with the god's image (statuary) placed in the interior. They were designed to be visited but not for assembly within. Narrow passageways guaranteed that large gatherings could not take place. These temples were meant to be seen and experienced externally by the populace. Following distinct mathematical proportion, Greek architects managed expertly to relate the presence of gods and goddesses to their society and everyday life. The most outstanding example is the Parthenon, built for the goddess Athena, the patroness of Athens, on the Acropolis, the fortress hill high above the city.

Romans were noted for their borrowing of ideas from other cultures, particularly in architecture. Greek columns and statuary were adopted as decoration, but the Romans developed new engineering to meet their differing needs. Open space for the assembly of multitudes had a priority in their planning. To meet this need, the Romans utilized the rounded arch which enabled their architects to build large, rounded domes supported not by pillars and rafters but by the arch form of the dome itself. In the Roman style, size and practicality played major roles.

This carried over into Roman building for religious purposes, as is so well demonstrated by the Pantheon in Rome. This structure copies the Greek columns and triangular frieze for the portico, but the building proper is a huge assembly hall covered by a dome, opened at the center for a view of the sky. The interior wall allows space for all the Roman gods. As the Greek Parthenon was meant to be appreciated externally, quite the opposite was true of the Roman Pantheon, which accommodated large gatherings of citizens beneath its giant dome.

Roman style in architecture continued to influence design and structure into the early Christian era. In A.D. 313 the Roman Emperor Constantine signed the Edict of Milan, legalizing Christianity throughout the empire. By recognizing Christianity as a legitimate religion, he opened new vistas of activity in the arts. Roman halls of justice, *basilicas,* were converted to Christian use because of their capacity for large gatherings. New basilicas soon were designed, built and furnished as Christian churches. The entrance was moved from the longer side of the rectangle to the end, thereby allowing Christian worshipers to view the raised altar on the opposite end immediately upon entering. By A.D. 380 Christianity had become the state religion of the Roman Empire, thereby increasing the pace of religious architectural activity.

When Constantine moved the capital to Byzantium, the influence of the Orient and Middle East became increasingly strong. The use of multiple colors, mosaics, and lighting effects were some of the obvious characteristics of what was to become known as "Byzantine" art. These new characteristics contributed to an emotional need in the development and support of the concept of immortality. Probably the most outstanding illustration of Byzantine architecture is Hagia Sophia, located in Istanbul. Built in just five years, it was completed in A.D. 537. The church combines features of both the basilica and the Greek cross, and is crowned with an enormous dome that measures 107 feet across. Hagia Sophia truly exemplified the combination of the imperial splendor of the Roman state with the religious feeling of Christianity.

In Western Europe other forces were at work. The Teutonic tribes that overran the empire were converted to Christianity and began to build churches of their own. At first they copied Roman architecture in a style we call Romanesque, but their religious enthusiasm led them to build higher and higher until they developed a whole new architecture, Gothic, and with it one of the finest architectual expressions of religious spirit: the Gothic cathedral. Gothic development flourished during the three centuries from A.D. 1100 to 1400. Many of the outstanding structures of the period remain standing today.

The cathedral became the "outward and visible sign" of the influence of Christianity on the development of the cities. Feudal systems were breaking down and the middle class was expanding. This period also saw the development of early universities in Italy, France, and England. Society was taking hold of its environment and the cathedral played an important role. Ultimately, as the house of God (and the seat of a bishop), it was the place a worshiper could go to seek God. The immense size of the building alone dwarfed all who entered therein. Humility, it would seem, would be almost an immediate response.

But the structural interior of the Gothic cathedral reached skyward, drawing the worshiper's eyes and thought to the heavens and to God.

The Gothic style provides the viewer with vaulted ceilings, flying buttresses, and high, tall windows, all striving heavenward while allowing light to flood the interior. These proportions achieve their intended effect—they inspire an aesthetic and spiritual experience.

Medieval cathedrals were not only religious centers but community centers as well. Often the city owned a major portion of the structure, while the church owned only the sanctuary. Gatherings of all types took place there. Secular buildings were immediately adjacent to cathedrals—indeed, at times, attached. As cathedrals were built in city after city, one cannot but wonder about the political and commercial interest that surely must have been present in the architectural rivalry. But whatever other factors encouraged the construction of these great churches, one can only wonder at the importance of religion to a culture that lavished so much of its wealth on houses of God.

The Middle Ages were, of course, followed by a great flowering of art in the Renaissance during which religious factors exerted a great influence on both painting and music.

PAINTING

As a result of the impact of Christianity, there exists today a heritage of painting that embodies an interpretation of the visual history of the Christian faith. The paintings of the Renaissance visualized for the worshiper almost every phase of the history of Christianity, including the life of Jesus, the Christian miracles, the lives of the saints and of the martyrs, and events from the Old and New Testaments. A well-known example is the ceiling of the Sistine Chapel in Rome, painted by Michelangelo in a period of four years (1508–1512) and dramatically depicting man confronted by the power of God. Additional examples include "The Annunciation" by Albertinelli, "Adoration of the Magi" by Botticelli, "The Alba Madonna" by Raphael, "The Last Supper" by Da Vinci, "The Entombment" by Raphael, "Pieta" by Bartolommeo, "The Transfiguration" by Carracci, and "The Risen Christ with the Four Evangelists" by Bartolommeo.

This is a very small sample of the influence of religion on painting during the Renaissance. As time passed, that influence spread throughout Europe and the civilized world. Today examples of religious art may be found in churches and galleries throughout the world. But few comparable periods of time have had such an impact on visual art as the Renaissance.

MUSIC

Musicians owe a great deal to the Greeks for the mathematical foundation of scale systems, as pointed out by Bronowski in *The Ascent of Man*. However, the musical activities of Greece were centered mainly around the secular drama, where music was combined with speaking choruses, dancing, and poetry.

Early Christian music was written for worship and contemplation, utilizing the single-lined melodic chant for most occasions. The systems of chant-writing, not unlike the Greek modes, became the backbone of early notation in the monasteries of the Roman Catholic church and endured well into the fourteenth and fifteenth centuries.

As the Renaissance evolved, more interest was directed toward polyphony, or the composing of more than one line of music, each interweaving with the other. By the end of the Renaissance, polyphony in choral music had reached a height that prepared composers for entrance into the baroque style.

In this period, the Roman Catholic church demanded much of the composer in the form of motets, masses, and, in the newly organized Protestant churches, hymns and chorales for the congregation. An identifying characteristic of Renaissance polyphony is the harmonic concept utilized by the composer. He concentrated on voice-leading in unison, octaves, fourths, and fifths, allowing his musical ideas to interweave one with the other. One might say that the tonal material was on a single melodic plane, much as the space was organized in an early Renaissance painting. It is worth the observation that both music and painting did, in fact, develop a depth in dimension toward the end of the Renaissance.

Two musical forms dominate this period: the Roman mass and the Lutheran chorale. It is no coincidence that each was often written around the same chant theme of the early church, but for different purposes. A chant theme might evolve into a motet, then into one or more of the movements of the mass. Ultimately, it might even be borrowed by a Protestant composer for a chorale melody.

Borrowing themes was not uncommon, and one could hear secular musical ideas, from time to time, in sacred compositions. At the Council of Trent (1545), one of the aims of the Counter-Reformation was to eliminate the secularism that had developed in the music of the

Church. It seems that some of the mass themes had been copied from chansons and, with the polyphony complicating the text, caused the religious idea to be confused and lost to the ear. The Council instructed the diocesan bishops to implement a directive to avoid everything "impure."

One of the leading composers of his day was Giovanni Pierluigi da Palestrina (1526–1594), who was born near Rome and spent his professional life in that city. First a choirboy, then a student in music, he ultimately came to be choirmaster at St. Peter's in Rome. Several other posts followed, but he was recalled to St. Peter's in 1571 where he remained until his death. His influence was felt throughout the musical world, and his concern for musical purity and nonsecularism was one of his greatest attributes.

Another composer who ranks among the great in this period was the Spaniard, Tomas Luis de Victoria (1549–1611), who never wrote a secular piece. He was a devout monk who had studied in Rome and was undoubtedly influenced by Palestrina in his creative efforts. His style of composition shows more intensity and passion than that of Palestrina. His emotion comes through to the ear of the listener and all to the glory of God.

CONCLUSION

This short article is an attempt to show how a study of architecture, painting, and music may be used to study about religion. Architecture has been stressed because most of the edifices are still visible today and are truly impressive. Not everyone can visit them personally, but the photographer has made that adventure a vicarious possibility. Paintings and musical selections certainly are available, but they do not always carry the impact that a larger-than-life structure may. The ideal experience in this regard would be to walk into a Spanish Renaissance cathedral and listen to a live, reverberating performance of Victoria's beautiful music while viewing some of El Greco's religious paintings. This can be done in Toledo, Spain, but not in the United States. The following unit suggests ways in which this limitation may be partially overcome and how one may conduct religion studies through examining the religious elements in the fine arts.

RESOURCE UNIT ON RELIGIOUS ASPECTS OF GOTHIC AND RENAISSANCE ART

The purpose of this unit is to enhance factual history. It should help to humanize historical events. In addition, it should demonstrate that "time" is a criterion of value in all authentic works of art. Prior to this unit, students should possess some basic knowledge of world history, especially the Middle Ages. The unit is particularly addressed to students in junior and senior high schools. However, with modifications it could be applied to the fourth through sixth grades. Two to three weeks, five periods per week, should be allotted for this unit.

Goals and Objectives

At the conclusion of this unit, there should be a better awareness of artistic resources within both the community and the nation. A better understanding of artistic qualities and of religious influences on art should be apparent. Artistic and intellectual curiosity should be aroused. An appetite for good works of art should begin to surface in the attitudes of most students. A visual "awareness" should develop so that the totality of the local architectural environment should be more apparent.

This unit differs from other areas of study in that it is not only academic but is also dependent on the sensitivity of perception. To the extent that this perception can be sharpened and focused in such a short time, to that same extent will this unit be a success. The unit is visually and aurally oriented. It is filled with the activity of viewing films, slides, and prints and listening to music. All of this leads to discriminating discussion so that after two to three weeks, the student should be more enlightened and aware than he or she was prior to this exposure. The culmination of the activities will be the visits to galleries, museums, and architectural examples that are of superior quality. These visits should increase the perceptive abilities of the students as they take place.

Content

The main generalization stressed in this unit is that human beings express religious and philosophical ideas in artistic ways and that these ideas remain for posterity in the form of objects of art: architectural structure, painting, music, and the other related arts. Religious and

55

philosophical ideas were manifested in Gothic and Renaissance art in a variety of ways: the vaulted ceilings of the Gothic cathedral as the house of God, the emphasis in painting on the power of God over his creatures, and the use of music to enhance the environment of the cathedral to literally attempt to create a heavenly sound. A transition from the Gothic to the Renaissance period might be illustrated as follows: whereas the design of the Gothic cathedral drew an individual humbly to the altar of god in order to transcend everyday life, the revival of classical art forms in the Renaissance represented a re-discovery of humanistic concepts and an affirmation of human fulfillment in history.

Subject-Matter Outline and Related Activities

FIRST WEEK

A. Film: *A Is for Architecture* (14 min.) For sources of this and other items listed on this outline see listings at the end of the article (pp. 59–61).

    Discuss: Leading architectural examples of religious feeling through the centuries. Use additional slides, photos, or prints as needed to enlarge or round out the topic.

B. Film: *Renaissance* (26 min.)

    Discuss: Characteristics of Renaissance period. (See previous discussion in this chapter.)
How many characteristics are illustrated in the film? Are others evident?
List them. How do these characteristics reveal the influence of religion?

    Music: Listen to recording of a short Renaissance choral selection: Victoria, Palestrina, Byrd, Tye.
What music was utilized on the film? Does it differ? If so, how?

C. Paintings: Survey packet from *National Gallery Series One: Looking at Painting: Part I.* Utilize prints for obser-vation and tape for authentic explanation and inter-pretation.

Discuss:	Is there a relationship between these works and what were shown in the film *Renaissance?* Is there often a religious element present?
D. Film:	*Art of the Middle Ages* (30 min.)
Discuss:	Relation of this film to *all that has been seen* by now. To what degree can it be observed (by the teacher) that some discriminating commentary is being developed?

| *E. Visit:* | Arrange for a serious, conscientious tour of either: |

- an art museum;
- an *old* large church or synagogue;
- an authentic cathedral, if possible.

SECOND WEEK

A. Film:	*Chartres Cathedral* (30 min.)
Music:	Play short samples of Gregorian chant.
Discuss:	Does the chant seem appropriate for the image of a cathedral? If so, in what ways? If not, why not? Is it similar to or different from the music in the film? How may it be compared?
	Teacher note: music may be herein described as linear, polyphonic (more than one voice interwoven), unison, melismatic (as in the chant), hymnlike.

B. Film:	Review *Renaissance* (26 min.) Use as a *second* showing.
Discuss:	What was seen *and heard* this time that was not before?
Paintings:	Survey packet from *National Gallery Series Two: Italian Painting.*
Music:	Continue listening to Renaissance composers. (See First Week, B.)

| *C. Discuss:* | No film. No music. Utilize materials from Washington Cathedral (or equivalent). Utilize materials from foreign embassies (or equivalent). Emphasis on distinct characteristics of architectural styles from Egyptian |

structures through the Gothic cathedrals. Final emphasis on place of cathedrals in Medieval society.

D. *Visit:* Arrange for second serious tour of art museum, cathedral, synagogue, or other building that can be authentically described as a copy of Renaissance or Gothic style. What is different about this visit? Are the powers of observation any sharper now? How does this visit support discussions, films, paintings of the past two weeks?

FINAL SESSION

A. *Film:* *Michelangelo and His Art* (16 min.)

Discuss: Sistine Chapel masterpiece. Deeper human dimension effected by utilizing the human form in perspective as contrasted with medieval two-dimensional appearance.

Vocabulary development in this unit should include the correct pronunciation of all artists' and composers' names, all place names, "polyphony," "chorale," "linear" (both visual and musical).

Evaluation

Essay examinations are optional in units that are as short as this. Certain composers, types of music, painters, schools of art, place-names and architectural types all could be organized into some type of written and recognition examination. The effectiveness of the unit can best be measured by the appetite it creates after the fact. If students are still curious and realize that they have merely scratched the surface, then it certainly would prove effective.

Instructional Resources

Reference materials, including books, prints, films, and filmstrips, are listed on pages that follow. Musical recordings have been omitted from any particular list. These may be found in any good community or university library. The writer has found that many private sources are pleased to offer brochures, pamphlets, posters, and the like if one asks for them. For that reason, it is recommended that the following sources be contacted for appropriate material:

National Cathedral, Washington, D.C.
St. Patrick's Cathedral, New York City
Cathedral of St. John The Divine, New York City
St. Peter in Chains Cathedral, Cincinnati, Ohio
Plum Street Temple, Cincinnati, Ohio
National Gallery of Art, Washington, D.C.
Art Institute of Chicago, Chicago, Illinois
Metropolitan Museum of Art, New York City
Foreign embassies in Washington, D.C.—Spain, Portugal, West
Germany, France, Italy, Great Britain, Israel, Egypt. These
embassies will provide the inquirer with literature, posters,
pamphlets, maps, etc., concerning many of the art and architectural
masterpieces in their countries.

RESOURCE MATERIALS

Books

Anson, Peter F. *The Building of Churches*. New York: Hawthorn Books, 1964.

Artz, Frederick B. *From the Renaissance to Romanticism: Trends in Style in Art, Literature and Music, 1300-1830*. Chicago: Univ. of Chicago Press, 1962.

Bailey, Albert E., ed. *The Arts and Religion*. Freeport, N.Y.: BFL Communications, 1943.

Bernen, Satia. *Myth and Religion in European Painting, 1270-1700*. New York: Braziller, 1973.

Bieler, Andre. *Architecture in Worship*. Philadelphia: Westminster, 1965.

Boudet, Jacques. *The Great Works of Mankind*. New York: Golden, 1962.

Bronowski, J. *The Ascent of Man*. Boston: Little, Brown, 1973.

Burland, Cottie A. *Gods and Demons in Primitive Art*. New York: Hamlyn, 1973.

Canaan, Gershon. *Rebuilding the Land of Israel*. New York: Architectural Book, 1954.

Cannon-Brookes, P. *Baroque Churches*. New York: Hamlyn, 1969.

Dineen, Michael P., and Polley, Robert, eds. *Great Art Treasures in American Museums*. Waukesha, Wisc.: Country Beautiful, 1967.

Gedat, Gustav-Adolf. *They Built for Eternity*. Freeport, N.Y.: BFL Communications, 1953.

Gloag, John. *Guide to Western Architecture*. New York: Macmillan, 1958.

Grober, Karl. *Picturesque Palestine, Arabia and Syria*. New York: Brentano's, 1925.

Grout, Donald J. *A History of Western Music*. New York: Norton, 1973.

59

Hammond, Peter. *Liturgy and Architecture.* New York: Columbia Univ. Press, 1962.

Hawgrave-Graham, Robert P. *The Cathedrals of France.* New York: Hastings House, 1959.

Hill, Derek, and Grabar, Oleg. *Islamic Architecture and Its Decoration, A.D. 800–1500.* Chicago: Univ. of Chicago Press, 1965.

Kuran, Aptullah. *The Mosque in Early Ottoman Architecture.* Chicago: Univ. of Chicago Press, 1968.

Lassus, Jean. *The Early Christian and Byzantine World.* New York: McGraw-Hill, 1967.

Lowrie, Walter. *Art in the Early Church.* New York: Norton, 1969.

MacDonald, William. *The Architecture of the Roman Empire.* New Haven, Conn.: Yale Univ. Press, 1965.

——.*Early Christian and Byzantine Architecture.* New York: Braziller, 1963.

Phillips, Lisle M. *The Works of Man.* New York: Philosophical Library, 1951.

Pischel, Gina. *A World History of Art.* New York: Golden, 1968.

Read, Herbert. *Art and Society.* New York: Schocken Books, 1966.

Thiry, Paul. *Churches and Temples.* New York: Van Nostrand Reinhold, 1953.

Van Der Meer, F. *Early Christian Art.* Chicago: Univ. of Chicago Press, 1968.

Van Ess, Donald H., ed. *The Commonwealth of Arts and Man: Readings in the Humanities.* New York: Conn.: Ty Crowell, 1973.

Vogt, Van Ogden. *Art and Religion.* New Haven, Conn.: Yale Univ. Press, 1948.

Von Simson, Otto G. *The Gothic Cathedral: Origins of Gothic Architecture and the Medieval Concept of Order.* New York: Pantheon, 1956.

Wilson, Winefride. *Modern Christian Art.* New York: Hawthorn Books, 1965.

Wold, Milo, and Cykler, Edmund. *An Introduction to Music and Art in the Western World.* Dubuque, Iowa: Wm. C. Brown, 1972.

Wolfflin, Heinrich. *Classic Art: An Introduction to the Italian Renaissance.* London: Phaidon, 1968.

Prints with explanation

The following collections of prints are available from the National Gallery of Art, Washington, D.C. Each packet is accompanied by a tape-cassette explaining the prints. All paintings described in the packets are hanging in the National Gallery and may be seen there.

ART SERIES ONE: National Gallery of Art, Washington, D.C.
Looking at Painting: Part I
Looking at Painting: Part II
French Painting
Portrait Painting
Genre and Still Life
American Painting

ART SERIES TWO: National Gallery of Art, Washington, D.C.
Italian Painting
The Flemish Style and Its Influence in Europe
Rembrandt and Dutch Painting of the 17th Century
English Painting
American Painting, Part II
French Art of the 19th Century

Films

The following films are recommended for junior and senior high school.

A Is for Architecture. 14 min., color, International Film Bureau, Inc., 332 S. Michigan Ave., Chicago, Ill. 60604

Art of the Middle Ages, 30 min., color, Encyclopaedia Britannica Educational Corp., 425 N. Michigan Ave., Chicago, Ill. 60611

Chartres Cathedral. 30 min., color, Encyclopaedia Britannica Educational Corp.

Coming of Christ. 30 min.

I, Leonardo Da Vinci. 54 min., color, McGraw-Hill, 1221 Avenue of the Americas, New York, N.Y. 10020

Michelangelo and His Art. 16 min., color, Coronet, 65 E. South Water St., Chicago, Ill. 60601

Rembrandt and the Bible. 30 min., Graphic Curriculum, Inc., Box 565, Lenox Hill Station, New York, N.Y. 10021

Renaissance. 26 min., color, Encyclopaedia Britannica Educational Corp.

Sound Filmstrips

The following titles are recommended for junior and senior high school. Each title is published by Educational Audio Visual, Inc., Pleasantville, N.Y., 10570.

Baroque Music and Art
Romanticism in Art and Music
Impressionism in Art and Music
Twentieth-Century Artistic Revolutions

Religion Studies in Elementary Language Arts: Beginnings, Mythic and Scientific

Ann M. Hildebrand

"Questions at Night"

Why
Is the sky?

What starts the thunder overhead?
Who makes the crashing noise?
Are the angels falling out of bed?
Are they breaking all their toys?

Why does the sun go down so soon?
Why do the night-clouds crawl
Hungrily up to the new-laid moon
And swallow it, shell and all?

If there's a Bear among the stars
As all the people say,
Won't he jump over those Pasture-bars
And drink up the Milky Way?

Does every star that happens to fall
Turn into a fire-fly?
Can't it ever get back to Heaven at all?
And why
Is the sky?[1]

Louis Untermeyer

Poetry, with its strong images and metaphors, is the natural language of children, and the child's "inner world is made of myth"[2]—humanity's first poetic expression. From the child's first "Why?" poetic, mythic explanations are the natural ones. Because rational explanations are largely irrelevant to them, young children delight in stories about the Man in the Moon and the stork that brings the new baby or, a more modern metaphor, the seed that grows with parents' love and warmth.

When formal education is begun and a child's rationality is consciously developed, such mythic, magic explanations often give way to scientific, measurable ones. The Moon Man is reduced to dimensions of distance and topography, and the good luck stork or the love-nurtured seed lose credence beside diagrams of the reproductive system. In short, scientific, "reasonable" answers to children's wonderings replace metaphoric ones. And when youngsters are ready for the question, not of "Where did I come from?" but of "Where did the world come from?" they too often receive only a scientific explanation, usually a version of Darwin's theory of evolution, presented not as theory but as "truth" and usually not open to question even though the orthodoxies of science can change.

But even more important, children who rely entirely on school for their education are not shown how to pursue another form of "truth" which would extend the measurable limits of science—the truth of the imagination. And to children who already have an answer to the cosmic "Why?" from religious or folk concepts, the sudden injection of science as *the* answer to the cosmos is confusing at best, disturbing at worst.

Introducing mythic or metaphorical explanations of Creation right along with scientific ones in the elementary language arts class not only helps children reconcile seeming contradictions between the new rational reality and the familiar metaphorical reality but also preserves and nurtures the imagination, the best tool in dealing with life's own cosmic problems. "Science flattens, reduces. Art and metaphor fill out and extend."[3] Reduction is sometimes necessary to assess reality, but extension is always necessary to cope with it.

The ideal time to introduce a unit on origins would be at a "beginning"—either the first week of a semester or, paralleling the renewal theme of many Creation myths, at the beginning of the calendar year. This language arts unit should, of course, parallel a similar unit in science or social studies so that the validity of both approaches to beginnings can emerge.

The language of myth is generally simple, direct, and concrete in imagery—all characteristics which reflect its origins in the childhood of humanity. Indeed, since childhood is the time when concrete and imaginative reality are intertwined, children dwell comfortably in the mythic world from their infancy. Fable, Mother Goose, and folktale employ this kind of imagery, which children normally experience long before their formal schooling begins. Then in the early grades, they should read for themselves (or have read to them) fables, short folktales, and perhaps even versions of certain myths. But because science as a separate subject usually begins with the child's increased reasoning abilities and advanced reading skills—grades three to six—the suggestions in this unit are directed toward the upper elementary grades where myths are indeed most needed and least found. Additionally, concepts that require a sense of time long past and a curiosity of matters beyond the self—ideas like "How did the world begin?"—work best with children whose minds are maturing.

Such a unit could take as little as two or three weeks; it could, on the other hand, extend for six weeks if all aspects of Creation, including the coming of human beings, the development of animal differences, the advent of fire, etc., were considered. Indeed the mythic-scientific interest could be pursued through all the upper elementary grades at various points, thereby keeping alive the questioning faculty on both the figurative and literal levels. The idea would not, of course, be to stifle science or reason but to kindle the total thinking process—to extend *while* reducing.

The primary objective, then, in presenting mythic as well as scientific versions of Creation is to give children a reassuring multiplicity of views on the origin of the cosmos while keeping alive the imaginative faculty which is natural and primary to childhood but which, like poetry, tends to become suppressed toward adulthood. And the multiple view is necessary for the child's expanded apprehension of the exterior as well as the interior world. Through a reading of Creation myths, children see individuals in both time and space and gain a respect for civilizations far removed from the present. They learn about the values and needs of many other cultures and gain insights about the peoples who made the myths. They begin to realize that, though the twentieth century with its tendency to measure and quantify may be in its own way the most advanced civilization ever on earth, earlier societies had their own special ways of viewing things which relate in nonquantifying terms a great deal about universal humanity—and thus, about us.

The approach to origins will be made mostly from sources outside the classroom. Textbooks may have effective introductory stories,[4] and surely science books with material on beginnings will be natural starting points. But in the main, students and teachers will have to rely on library sources, some of which are listed in the bibliography following this article. Good readers will be urged to find Creation stories in complex mythologies such as the Greek and Egyptian; simpler, shorter tales from American Indian and African myth will be accessible to the less skilled readers. Even picture books, which use metaphoric language effectively, need not be beneath the dignity of upper elementary youngsters. Many of the best versions of myth are in this form. The teacher may assign specific myths to assure a balance of mythologies and a proper variety of Creation stories, but eager students could very well organize their own discussions. The unit should lead to excited discoveries on the part of the students and be flexible enough to capture their enthusiasm. Overstructuring could suppress the spontaneity that is natural to this subject.

A necessary step in equating stories of beginnings is to establish a broad meaning for "myth." Too often "myth" has the connotation of "lie" and seems especially offensive to people who do not understand that the mythic and the religious are the same. Northrop Frye defines myth as the "union of ritual and symbol, giving action to thought and meaning to action."[5] He illustrates effectively how the stories in the Bible are myths in this sense. Various other explanations of myth should be used as well: "Myths are . . . metaphors that identify aspects of human personality with the natural environment."[6] Or, "Myth is a kind of perspective, a basic way of envisaging experience, a kind of 'first meaning' where no clear-cut ideas of true and false have yet emerged."[7] Perhaps the most useful concept to offer those who misunderstand "myth" is found in George Every's *Christian Mythology:* "[Myth is] an extended sense of a story told to throw light on a mystery that cannot be explained."[8] At the center of all myth is the mysterious, the unaccountable—not entirely accessible, but believed. Even science has its own myths, its own premises based on uncertainties. And to children intrigued with Creation myths, it soon becomes apparent that the beginning stories of all cultures were religious beliefs, stated metaphorically, but no less worthy of respect for that. Calling Genesis 1 a "myth" is, in this context then, acknowledging its connection with the natural environment, its essential "first meaning," its mystery, and its transcendent metaphoric "truth."

Other words will be learned and other concepts broadened. The child will come to recognize a simile, a metapor, an image, and a symbol. After the children have pooled their myth stories, they will learn what motif is; perhaps even "archetype" will arise from the discussions of some children who are keen in seeing the universal patterns in all the Creation myths. The distinction, a valuable one, between figurative and literal language will be made. And in addition, an abundance of new names (of people, animals, places) and new ideas (of chaos, cosmos, Creation, and infinity) will be learned.

Generally, then, such a unit will expand young people's consciousness. Specifically, their consciousness will be touched in many ways. (1) Their knowledge of the diversity in Creation beliefs, both ancient and modern, will be widened, enabling them to respect both myth for its direct way of explaining complex reality and science for its useful measuring of that reality. (2) Their awareness of their own language, through the myths' use of poetic metaphor and imagery, will be refined and expanded, and the language of image will stimulate that mind process called the IMAG-ination. (3) They will see, through discovering motifs, the essential oneness of humankind in its need to define the real world and the forces beyond its control or understanding. (4) They will also gain tolerance for differences in people's mores and learn to respect, rather than fear, cultural attitudes. (5) They will develop a new reverence for the natural world when they study in myths the intensified awareness of human dependence on and origins in nature, in spite of the invention of machines. (6) They will become aware, through myth, of the equality of man and woman and will see that Creation is effected equally by gods and goddesses. (7) They will learn that "scientific method" applies to all areas of learning, and that all sides of a question must be considered before true education can begin, whether about the origins of the world or any other matter. (8) And finally, they will learn that, as early humans searched for answers to the real world through myths, so modern humans do through science, but that both kinds of answers are necessary to explain the beginning of the world. Even Julian Huxley freely admits, "We shall perhaps never know just HOW our planet earth came into being; . . . just how life began may always remain a mystery."[9]

For the child to gain the very important objective of language awareness, reading the actual myths in their fluid, poetic form is essential. Such reading can be done at both the individual and group level, both aloud and to oneself. There can be writing assignments directed toward such linguistic particulars as: What is the central picture (image) of the myth? What metaphors are used to represent concrete reality? How does the language of the Creation myth convey the mystery of Creation (chant, ritual words, refrain)? What, exactly, makes the myth beautiful? How do your senses respond to the mythic images?

In addition to emphasis on language, the content of myths should also be stressed. This may be done best with a guide list that directs the youngsters' reading: What was at the beginning of all? Who was the creator(s)? How did earth and sky come about? What special animals and plants appear in the myth? What does that tell you about the country the myth came from?

Interest in a unit on "beginnings" will be self-generating. Even if not all the children newly exposed to science have had a religious explanation of Creation, certainly enough will have to spark immediate questions and discussion: "But the *Bible* says that God created the world in six days!" It is a short step from this impassioned objection to the fascination of what a Hindu says about Creation or what a Papago Indian might still believe about his or her Creation story or what an ancient Viking thought were the causes of the world of volcano and ice or, indeed, what Charles Darwin believed to be an explanation of Creation compatible with his own Christianity. Children, at the dawn of rational power, need little to prod them into exploration. They are not jaded, and the world of adult explanations (science) is fascinating to them while at the same time they are still enthralled by childhood's explanations (myth). Set side by side, at first seeming antithetic but later seen to be mutually tolerant, the world of myth and the world of science are sure to provide natural soil for real learning.

With this self-generating, natural student interest, myths will continue to fascinate children at each stage of science studies. When, in later grades, they study such natural phenomena as floods, stars, and tides and such social phenomena as laws and language, some of the myths they have read will spring into their minds—or they will go to new myths just to find out what ancient, metaphor-speaking humans had to say. Myth is a way of thinking just as science is a way of thinking, and neither mode of thought should be stifled. Furthermore, the mythic explanations that we associate with the primitive and the childlike are not beneath the appreciation of the civilized adult. No human being should ever reject what Frye calls "an imaginative encyclopedia providing answers to questions of the deepest concern to society."[10] Indeed, the young boy who looks with awe at Mr. Moon is the father of the man who claims the moon for humankind and who sees the essential mystery of life which science alone cannot explain.

After the many different Creation myths have been presented, the children should assess their findings and ask themselves just where the myths coincide and why. They should see where science borders on myth and myth on science and should, by this time, be aware of differences in the kinds of "truths" given by the imaginative and the rational Creation stories. After they have done their own evaluating, children should be evaluated by the teacher, but in keeping with the rather loose structure of the unit.

It is important that the study of Creation myths not devolve into a mere memorization of divine hierarchies or a recitation of creators. The scope of the unit is the forest, not the trees—the cosmos, not the characters. A few names will, of course, be necessary in order for children to be able to articulate their knowledge; so perhaps some form of objective test would not be out of place. Even more valid would be an essay test which would look back to the beginning of the unit when mythic and scientific stories seemed in conflict. In the light of their new learning, youngsters could be expected to show just how the two explanations could exist on different planes of reality (both figurative and literal). Ongoing evaluation would take place as each child presents a Creation story and is questioned by both teacher and peers. Work in a group which perhaps collates Creation accounts from several divergent mythologies should be given credit, just as creative efforts to draw, write, sing, or enact myths should receive not only praise but a plus mark in the grade book. Since the objectives of the unit are mostly behavioral, immediate assessment may not measure the real value of the unit to students. Given time, though, both children and teacher will detect an expanded sense of what is "real" and "true," a new awareness of language, and a tolerance of others' beliefs.

The teacher must strive to be the objective arbiter at all times in this unit. Individual religious persuasion must not enter into the teacher's presentation; an atheistic scientist should be as enthusiastic about this unit as an ardent believer, for the end is not indoctrination but true learning. At no time, of course, should any teacher disparage either the mythic or the scientific stories, but should guide and lead the youngsters in arriving at their own respect for both approaches to reality. In dealing with creators, no attempt should be made to imply the one-God-different-name concept which is in itself a religious point of view; instead, the respect-for-differences attitude which emerges naturally from a wide reading of Creation stories should be stressed. And of course teachers should obtain the approval of their principals before such a *potentially* controversial unit is begun, both to assure their support and to inform and reassure them of unbiased presentation of materials.

SUGGESTED APPROACH FOR A UNIT ON BEGINNINGS, MYTHIC AND SCIENTIFIC

It is assumed that the students, preferably as individuals (although small-group work is viable also), will be reading separate, different myths. The teacher should assign myths from definite, varied cultures of the world (African, Chinese, Pueblo Indian, Greek, Hebrew, Alaskan, etc.) to achieve the desired balance of world-origin stories; three or four scientific "myths" should also be assigned. Student preferences should certainly be considered, especially where a child has a rich ethnic heritage or an acute interest in science, but all regions of the world should be represented in the Creation myths. The teacher may either bring many books to class and distribute one to each student or (a much better way) make a library assignment, alerting local librarians to the unit and its requirements. The bibliography attached will provide more than enough source material for even a modest library. Class time should be given for both reading and discussing; the teacher can determine the extent of out-of-class work (reports, projects, etc.).

Because the unit is part of language arts, the approach should be primarily literary. Myths should be viewed, individually at first, as stories containing all the elements of well-wrought tales (theme, plot, characters, setting, and unique style), and although the teacher may not spell out these elements directly, the class discussions should develop all of them. After the scrutiny of the individual myths, a comparison of all the myths with a sociological-moral-anthropological focus may emerge. But by then the students will have answered, whether they realize it or not, many of the questions that pertain to myths as literature and metaphorical truth.

Since the aim of the unit is to broaden the students' knowledge of, and attitude toward, myth, a good way both to begin and end is to ask the question: What is myth? One measure of the unit's success will be the differences in the "before" and "after" ideas offered by the students.

GUIDELINES FOR DISCUSSION

Introduction to Unit

What is a myth? (Definitions, connotations, cultural impressions.)
What is a creation myth? (Essay definitions may help.)
Who told myths? When were they told? (Origins uncertain.)
What do myths have in common with religion?
What do myths have in common with science? (See end quote.)
Do you know any myths? Which ones? (Greek? *Bible?* Indian?)

Discussion of Individual Myths

Before students begin discussing their individual myths, it might be helpful for them to actually *show* their source, give its title and author, and let fellow students get the "feel" of the book (and see its illustrations if there are any).

THEME

What is the idea behind your myth? (Physical world's beginning, power of a Creator.)
Whose power is strongest in the myth?
What do you believe in the myth? What do you not believe?
Have you ever heard part or all of it before?
Does anything surprise you about the myth? What?

PLOT

Exactly what does your myth tell about? (Brief summary.)
Where does it start? (Chaos? Watery void? Spinning ball?)
How far does it go in the creation of the world? (Man? Animals?)
Is it an exciting story? Why? (Climax, suspense.)
What is your favorite part? Why?
Is the story easy or hard to follow?
Do you think the world began this way? Why?
How does your myth compare with scientific knowledge? Why?

SETTING

What country is your myth from? (Write name of country on board and show geographical locale on globe or map.)

What kind of climate does it have? Vegetation? Wildlife? Geographical formations? (Use encyclopedias or other sources as necessary.)

How does your myth reinforce this physical setting? (Ice? Coyotes? Dry spells? Rugged coastline? Etc.)

CHARACTERS

Within the myth/story: What is the creator's (creators') name?

Is it a man, woman, animal, or force of nature?

What is he, she, or it like? Do you know much about this creator?

If animal(s), does it act like people? What kind of people?

What did the creator do? (Act, speak, or merely think creation?) Did the creator do it alone?

Are there humans in the story? What are they like?

Are there other characters? Do you know much about them?

Outside the myth/story—the mythmakers: What kind of people were they?

What did they value? (Art? War? Adventure? Peace?)

How can you tell?

Are they like people today? How?

How does the creator in their myths fit them as people?

How much of themselves do they project into their myths?

STYLE

Is the myth funny or serious? Is the tone right?

Is it recorded in poetry or prose—or both? (Use quotes from book.)

Is the myth pleasing to read aloud? Why? (Or why not?)

Is there any ritual or chanting in the myth?

Could it be sung? What kind of tune might it have?

What new words did you find? (Names, places, etc.)

What new ideas did you find?

Where is the language literal? Figurative?

Did you find similes? Metaphors? Personifications?

Are any symbols used? What do they symbolize?

Does the language convey any sense of mystery? How?

Could you draw a picture of your myth from the word images?

Could you create a modern myth of your own?

Does your myth answer any of the questions in the poem *Why Is the Sky?* (Poem at the opening of this article.)
Do you know exactly who is telling the myth? When?
Do you know exactly who is *retelling* the myth? When?
Do you think it is a good retelling? Why? (Or why not?)

Discussion of Myths Collectively

Do you find any general similarity in all the myths?
What motifs do you find in many (some) of the myths?
Generally, what is the creator(s) like?
Is the creator(s) a part *of*, or apart *from*, the creation?
What is similar about the makers of myths?
What do myths show about human needs? Worries?
Are the mythmakers' needs and worries different from those of people today? How? Why?
What do the myths show about early people's (the makers of myth) feelings toward nature?
Why are all the myths so bound to the natural world?
Are we still bound to nature today? Do we feel the same way about it as the mythmakers did? Should we?
Do men and women have separate but definite roles in the myths? Why?
How do you account for such simple, "primitive" explanations for the beginning of the world?
Are people much different today than they were when people made these myth-stories? How?
Which time do you think was best, myth-time or modern time? Why? Are there really great differences? What?
Think of a myth idea which science has explained differently.
Think of a myth idea which science still has not answered fully.
How does the study of many myths affect our attitudes towards the beliefs of others? Can we better tolerate what seems strange when we can see the common bond between all cultures?
Would we have science if we did not have myth? (A very broad, culminating question.)

Conclusion

What is a myth? (See Introduction for the full before-after approach.)

What is the place of myth in today's world?
What myths has science yet to deal with? (Open-ended.)

RESOURCES

There are so many excellent versions of myth, simplified religion, and science available to children that the choices become delightful but overwhelming. The bibliography that follows this article does not pretend to be exhaustive but merely representative. Included are retellings that maintain the dignity implicit in myth, and science books that are interesting and well written. There are more myth than science books because the scientific explanation is generally the same. All books are marked for suggested reading level (M for grades three and four; O for grades five and six), but the range is flexible. For adult references, I have suggested books which give a lucid overview from a variety of perspectives.

The study of myth is a life's work devoutly pursued by some of the greatest scholars of our time. All the more reason then to keep the mythic mode alive in a world that encourages the scientific. It is always reassuring for children to remember:

> They stand together, storyteller and scientist, partners in examining the universe around them, sharing the same materials, coming up with answers that are similar and dissimilar.[11]

NOTES

1. *Favorite Poems Old and New,* selected by Helen Ferris (New York: Doubleday, 1957), p. 264.
2. P. L. Travers, "Give the Kid a Bible, for Instance," *Esquire,* vol. 85, no. 3 (March 1976), p. 150.
3. Carl Withers, *The Man in the Moon: Sky Tales from Many Lands* (New York: Holt, 1969), p. 113.
4. "Literary" reading series offer myths at many reading levels. Frances Frost's "The Creation of Man," an Indian myth, is retold in Holt's *Freedom's Ground.* Open Court's *A Magic World* has a science-myth chapter. These are but two series that contain mythic Creation stories.
5. Northrop Frye, *On Teaching Literature* (New York: Harcourt, 1972), p. 31.

6. Northrop Frye, *A Study of English Romanticism* (New York: Random House, 1968), p. 4.
7. Alex Preminger, ed., *Princeton Encyclopedia of Poetry and Poetics,* enlarged ed. (Princeton, N. J.: Princeton Univ. Press, 1974), p. 539.
8. George Every, *Christian Mythology* (New York: Hamlyn, 1970), p. 11.
9. Julian Huxley, *The Wonderful World of Life* (New York: Doubleday, 1959), p. 38.
10. Frye, *On Teaching,* p. 31.
11. Alfred Slote, *Air in Fact and Fancy.* (Cleveland: World, 1968), p. 153.

BIBLIOGRAPHY

For Teachers

Arbuthnot, May Hill, and Sutherland, Zena. *Children and Books.* 4th ed. Glenview, Ill.: Scott-Foresman, 1972. This is especially helpful for its excellent, if not entirely current, bibliography on all kinds of myth.

Coffin, Tristram B., ed. *Indian Tales of North America.* Austin, Tex.: University of Texas Press, 1961.

Eliade, Mircea. *The Sacred and the Profane: The Nature of Religion.* New York: Harper & Row, 1957. The chapter on "Sacred Time and Myths" is illuminating.

Every, George. *Christian Mythology.* New York: Tudor, 1970.

Frye, Northrop. *On Teaching Literature.* New York: Harcourt, 1972. An excellent mytho-poetic approach to teaching literature.

Larousse Encyclopedia of Mythology. London: Hamlyn, 1959. A complete overview of all mythologies.

Marriot, Alice, and Rachlin, Carol. *American Indian Mythology.* New York: Crowell, 1968.

Sheed, Francis J. *Genesis Regained.* New York: Sheed & Ward, 1969. The biblical Creation story is reconciled somewhat with scientific views.

Weigel, James, Jr. *Mythology.* Lincoln, Neb.: Cliffs Notes, 1973. Shorter than the Larousse, but with valuable primary and secondary material.

Wright, Hamilton; Wright, Helen; and Rapport, Samuel. *To the Moon.* New York: Meredith, 1968.

Science Books for Children

Ames, Gerald, and Wyler, Rose. *The First Days of the World.* Illustrated by L. Weisgard. New York: Harper & Row, 1958. Clearly and simply written for the younger reader. (M)

Bendick, Jeanne. *The Shape of the Earth.* Chicago: Rand McNally, 1965. Traces common and differing scientific thought on earth origin. (M)

Branley, Franklin. *The Earth: Planet Number Three.* New York: Crowell, 1966. (O)

Burton, Virginia Lee. *Life Story.* Boston: Houghton, 1962. A dazzlingly illustrated and well-researched book—artistic and scientific. (M)

Carona, Philip B. *Earth Through the Ages.* Chicago: Follett, 1968. Almost an easy reader in its short, simple sentences. (M)

Gallant, Roy. *How Life Began: Creation Versus Evolution.* New York: Four Winds, 1975. Excellent secondary materials on science, myth, and religion—especially helpful to both teachers and students of this unit. (O)

Green, Carla. *How Man Began.* New York: Bobbs-Merrill, 1972. Includes some short myths in a chapter which compares Creation myths with science, though the scientists seem to come out on top. Good chapter questions. (M)

Huxley, Julian. *The Wonderful World of Life: The Study of Evolution.* New York: Doubleday, 1959. Beautifully presented and illustrated by a variety of people and methods. Excellent. (O)

Knight, Charles R. *Life Through the Ages.* New York: Knopf, 1951. (M)

May, Julian. *The First Living Things.* New York: Holiday House, 1970. (M)

Pilkington, Roger. *In the Beginning: The Story of Creation.* New York: Abingdon, 1957. Each chapter begins with a part of the Genesis account and develops into a scientific counterpart. Clear and reasonable. (M)

Reed, W. Maxwell. *The Earth for Sam.* New York: Harcourt, 1960. (O)

Slote, Alfred. *The Moon in Fact and Fancy.* Cleveland: World, 1967. This book, with Slote's *Air in Fact and Fancy,* gives an excellent mixture of myth, science, past, present, and future. Enlightened. (O)

Myths for Children

GENERAL COLLECTIONS—WORLDWIDE SCOPE

Devlin, Harry. *Tales of Thunder and Lightening.* New York: Parents Mag. Press, 1975. Around-the-world myths and tales which stress children's imaginative approach to phenomena. Science-based afterword. (M)

Fahs, Sophia. *Beginnings of Earth and Sky.* Boston: Beacon Press, 1937. Excellent collection of primary sources (including Hebrew Creation) and scientific explanations (including Galileo and Newton). (M)

Leach, Maria. *Beginning: Creation Myths Around the World.* New York: Funk & Wagnalls, 1956. A superior and scholarly (but not too difficult) collection—a tour de force for this unit. (O)

———. *How the People Sang the Mountains Up; How and Why Stories.* New York: Viking, 1967. More excellent world myths. (M)

Lum, Peter. *The Stars in Our Heaven: Myths and Fables.* New York: Pantheon, 1948. Origin of constellations. (O)

McDowell, Robert E., and Lavitt, Edward, eds. *Third World Voices for Children.* New York: Third Press, 1971. Not all myths; some poetry. (M)

Trout, Lawana. *Myth*. New York: Scholastic Book Serv., 1975. An excellent collection of world myths, some on Creation. (O)

Withers, Carl. *The Man in the Moon: Sky Tales from Many Lands*. New York: Holt, 1969. (M)

SPECIALIZED COLLECTIONS

Asch, Scholem. *In the Beginning*. New York: Schocken, 1966. A well-written account of the biblical Creation story. (O)

Asimov, Isaac. *Words from the Myths*. Boston: Houghton, 1961. Greek myths are focus; good for showing myth words and modern cognates. *Words in Genesis* is another helpful work by the same author.

Baker, Betty. *At the Center of the World*. New York: Macmillan, 1973. Pima and Papago Indian Creation myths. (M)

Beals, Carlton. *Stories Told by the Aztecs*. New York: Abelard, 1970. (O)

Belting, Natalia. *The Earth Is on a Fish's Back*. New York: Holt, 1965. Beautiful poetic myths from the American Indians. (M) See also Belting's *Whirlwind Is a Ghost Dancing* (Dutton, 1974) for a stunning visual presentation by Leo and Diane Dillon of more American Indian myth poems. (M)

Benson, Sally. *Stories of the Gods and Heroes*. New York: Dial, 1940. Bullfinch's version of Greek myths, simplified beautifully. (M)

Carpenter, Frances. *People from the Sky: Ainu Tales from Northern Japan*. New York: Doubleday, 1972. (O)

Chetin, Helen. *Tales from an African Drum*. New York: Harcourt, 1970. (M)

Clark, Leonard. *All Things New*. Chester Springs, Pa.: Dufour, 1968. A book of poetry with prose connectives on all kinds of beginnings.

Colum, Padraic. *The Children of Odin*. New York: Macmillan, 1962. A strong, effective retelling of Norse myths. (O)

Coolidge, Olivia. *Greek Myths*. Boston: Houghton, 1949. (O)

Curry, Jane Louise. *Down from the Lonely Mountain: California Indian Tales*. New York: Harcourt, 1965. (M)

Courlander, Harold. *The Piece of Fire and Other Haitian Tales*. New York: Harcourt, 1964. (O)

Daughetry, James. *In the Beginning*. London: Oxford Univ. Press, 1941. A masterful picture book account of Genesis. (M)

D'aulaire, Ingri, and D'aulaire, Edgar Parin. *Norse Gods and Giants*. New York: Doubleday, 1967. This and the D'aulaires' *Book of Greek Myths* (1962) provide valuable picture versions and simple, lucid texts. (M)

Evers, Alf. *In the Beginning*. New York: Macmillan, 1954. Genesis. (M)

Feagles, Anita. *He Who Saw Everything: The Epic of Gilgamesh*. New York: Young Scott, 1966. (M) No actual Creation story but an account of the goddess Aruru creating man. See also Bernarda Bryson's *Gilgamesh: Man's First Story*. New York: Addison-Wesley, 1967. (O)

Fisher, Anne B. *Stories California Indians Told*. Berkeley, Calif.: Parnassus Press, 1957.

Galt, Tom. *The Rise of the Thunderer.* New York: Crowell, 1945. Greek myths simply told. (M)

Glubock, Shirley. *The Art of Ancient Egypt.* New York: Harper & Row, 1962. This and others in *"The Art of"* series give visual dimension to stories of gods and goddesses from African, Indian, Greek, Roman, etc., myth. (M)

Graham, Lorenz. *Every Man Heart Lay Down.* New York: Crowell, 1970. A charming African folk retelling of Genesis, useful especially for its unusual but beautiful language patterns. Picture book. (M)

Green, Roger Lancelyn, ed. *A Book of Myths.* New York: Dutton, 1965. Among others, a rare version of the Egyptian Creation myth. (O)

Hamilton, Edith. *Mythology.* Boston: Little, Brown, 1942. A classic retelling of the Greek myths. (O)

Harman, Humphrey. *Tales Told near a Crocodile.* New York: Viking, 1962. African tribal stories, some of them myths. (M)

Helfman, Elizabeth. *The Bushmen and Their Stories.* New York: Seabury, 1971. Creation stories from the Kalahari Desert. (M)

Hill, Kay. *Glooscap and His Magic.* New York: Dodd, 1963. Myths of the creator of the Wabanaki Indians.

Hodges, Margaret. *The Other World: Myths of the Celts.* New York: Farrar, 1973. (O)

Hosford, Dorothy. *Thunder of the Gods.* New York: Holt, 1952. An excellent version of the Norse myths. (M)

Jagendorf, M. A. *Kwi-Na the Eagle and Other Indian Tales.* Morristown, N. J.: Silver Burdett, 1967. American Indian myths. (M)

Kettelkamp, L. *Religions East and West.* New York: Morrow, 1972. Creation stories from Shinto and Parsee religions and a beautiful hymn to Aton, the Egyptian creator. (M)

Laing, Frederick. *Why Heimdall Blew His Horn: Tales of the Norse Gods.* Morristown, N. J.: Silver Burdett, 1969. An abbreviated account.

Leland, Charles. *The Algonquin Legends of New England.* Boston: Houghton, 1968.

Lewis, Claudia. *Poems of Earth and Space.* New York: Dutton, 1967.

Lewis, C. S. *The Magician's Nephew.* New York: Macmillan, 1955. A beautiful modern literary myth on the Creation of Narnia. A little different from traditional approaches but excellent for this unit. (O)

MacPherson, Jay. *The Four Ages of Man.* New York: St. Martin's, 1962. Greek myths and a chapter, "Creation and the Coming of the Gods." (M)

Maher, Ramona. *The Blind Boy and the Loon and Other Eskimo Myths.* New York: John Day, 1969. Old Woman is suggested as creator. (M)

Marriot, Alice. *Winter Telling Stories.* New York: Crowell, 1969. The creator in these Kiowa Indian tales is Saynday. (M)

Martin, Fran. *Raven-Who-Sets-Things-Right: Indian Tales of the Northwest Coast.* New York: Harper & Row, 1975. (M)

Matson, Emerson. *Longhouse Legends.* New York: Nelson, 1968. Myths of the Shagit Indians. (M)

Nelson, Ralph. *A Tale of Creation and Destruction.* Boston: Houghton, 1976. An ancient Mayan myth. (O)

Newell, Edythe W. *The Rescue of the Sun and Other Tales from the Far North.* Chicago: Whitman, 1970. (M)

Parrinder, Geoffrey. *African Mythology.* New York: Tudor, 1967. (M)

Po, Lee. *The Sycamore Tree and Other African Tales.* New York: Doubleday, 1975. Almost an easy reader in its simplicity. (M)

Reed, Gwendolyn. *Adam and Eve.* New York: Lothrop, 1968. Picture book with striking woodcuts. (M)

Rice, Edward. *The Five Great Religions.* New York: Scholastic Bk. Serv., 1973. Brief accounts of Creation myths from Christianity, Hinduism, Islam, and Buddhism. (M)

Roy, Cal. *Myths of the Mexican World.* New York: Farrar, 1972. (O)

Sechrist, Elizabeth. *Once in the First Times: Folktales from the Philippines.* Philadelphia: Macrae Smith, 1969. (M)

Seed, Jenny. *The Bushman's Dream: African Tales of the Creation.* New York: Bradbury, 1975. Myths involving Mantis. (O)

Southall, Ivan. *The Curse of Cain.* New York: St. Martin's, 1968. A short section of biblical Creation. Well written. (O)

Thompson, Vivian. *In the Time of Deep Darkness: Hawaiian Myths of Earth, Sea, and Sky.* New York: Holiday House, 1966. Poetic prose. (M)

Traven, B. *The Creation of the Sun and the Moon.* New York: Hill & Wang, 1968. Indians of Mexico. (M)

Turner, Philip, ed. *Brian Wildsmith's Illustrated Bible Stories.* New York: Franklin Watts, 1969. Only one of many good versions of Bible myths. (M)

Wolcott, Leonard and Carolyn. *Religion Around the World.* New York: Abingdon, 1967. A good discussion of mythic elements in religion. (M)

Wyndham, Robert. *Tales the People Tell in China.* New York: Messner, 1971. Allusions to Creation and a good flood story. (M)

Religion Studies in Secondary Language Arts

Ruth D. Hallman

Probably no area of the secondary language—indeed of the entire secondary curriculum—exhibits more diversity than the offerings in literature. No general agreement exists on either organization or content. One school decides to structure the study of literature by the different genres; another chooses a chronological approach; yet another elects to offer thematic units. Some schools will combine approaches or provide alternatives. Literature may or may not be organized according to the nationality of the writers (and more recently even the sex of the writers). Furthermore, given some kind of organizational pattern, we find no consensus as to content. We might find that nearly every high school teaches Shakespeare, but which play(s)? Which sonnets? And is this a class for everyone or for just the college-bound? In most instances, moreover, we do not find widespread agreement even as to writers; a "must" in one school is optional or missing in another.

Nevertheless, in the midst of this dissimilarity are some common goals. We seek to pass on a heritage of ideas and experiences, to develop an appreciation for the artistic use of language, to provide our students with the tools for reading subtler, more complex, and more thought-provoking selections than had hitherto been possible for them. We are charged with the responsibility of improving communication; we therefore seek an increased understanding of our associates. Other common goals could be added, but these will suffice.

It is in light of our common goals that I would urge the appropriateness, indeed the necessity, of including religion studies in the language arts. The literature of Western civilization is so infused with biblical allusions that it is impossible to read very far without encountering a reference to some character or event from that context.

Writers in general assume the reader's familiarity with the Bible. Our everyday idiom, too, takes on a richer meaning when we know why someone is referred to as a Jonah, a Judas, or a Jezebel; why we speak of a David-and-Jonathan friendship; why some city is referred to as a Sodom or Gomorrah; or why something is called "manna from heaven." All around us we find the allusions: in paintings, sculptures, and comic strips; in solemn oratorios and modern rock lyrics; in newspaper headlines and billboard advertisements. Furthermore, the legal, ethical, and moral fabric of our society is woven from threads which reach back to the Old Testament. Finally, if we would understand other people, then we must know something of our religious diversity. The ability to communicate effectively may sometimes depend upon our awareness of each other's religious sensitivities.

Even were it not for the arguments cited above, the quality of the literature itself would provide a rationale for giving serious consideration to the inclusion of selections from the Bible in our secondary literature classes. Where would we find a richer source to illustrate the artistic use of language? Suspense, irony, character study, figurative language, word play, variety of genre, style, and tone—all are there in abundance. Many of our greatest writers not only have turned to the Bible as a source of allusions but have consciously imitated its rhythms and its language. Some, like Frost and MacLeish, have even used its stories as the basis for new creations.

The organizational melange of secondary literature which was noted earlier does not really pose a problem for the inclusion of Bible literature; such study can be adapted to almost any approach. In the chronological approach—usually further structured by a division into American, English, and world literature—the Bible appears as a major contribution of the Hebrews (Old Testament) and of the Christians (New Testament) to world literature. In English literature surely some consideration must be given to so influential a work as the King James Version of the Bible. One can hardly study Milton or Bunyan or Shakespeare or Browning, to mention but a few, without going back to the biblical source for so many of the lines. When it comes to American literature, an understanding of those early writers demands some understanding of Calvinism. Whittier's poems lead us into at least a rudimentary knowledge of the Quakers. We surely cannot appreciate the development of Whitman's free-verse style unless we know something of the poetic structure of the Psalms. The biblical allusions, of course, are everywhere.

If our approach is by genre rather than chronology, we can find short stories (Jonah, Ruth, Esther, Judith), epic (Joseph or Saul and David), tragedy (Job), poetry (Psalms or Song of Solomon), parables, fables, and legends. For thematic units the choices are obviously abundant.

The minicourses which have become so popular in recent years offer innumerable opportunities for teaching Bible literature. The most obvious inclusion is the course devoted solely to literature of the Old or New Testament (or a combination of the two). In my course on tragedy, however, I have found that the most successful unit we study is the one comprising the Book of Job, MacLeish's *J. B.,* and Frost's *Masque of Reason.* When I teach the English novel, I use Hardy's *The Mayor of Casterbridge,* which sends us immediately to the story of Saul and David for an appreciation of the constant parallels which Hardy draws with that story. If I use "Rappaccini's Daughter," whether in a study of the short story or in a study of Hawthorne as a part of the chronological development of American literature, I must certainly use the story of Adam and Eve in the Garden of Eden as background material. If I am teaching a class in mythology, there are many biblical parallels which will enrich the course: Pandora and Eve, the Creation accounts, Damon and Pythias compared with the story of David and Jonathan, the story of Deucalion compared with the story of Noah and the flood, etc.

We have looked at some reasons for including Bible literature in the secondary language arts curriculum and have seen ways in which it will fit into various structures. Now let us consider how such material might be taught by taking a look at a possible three-week unit using the first thirty-four chapters of Exodus (abridged) as the core content.

UNIT OUTLINE FOR A STUDY OF EXODUS

This three-week unit, based on the first thirty-four chapters of Exodus, is an example of the multiple ways Bible literature may be used as a teaching tool. The unit allows students to see the use of varied literary forms—point of view, style, and tone; the extension of biblical stories and their statements of the human condition into opera, hymn, and folk song. Familiar themes find expression in painting and sculpture, contemporary novel, and drama. This study supports my contention that the Bible is an integral part of Western culture.

The three-week time frame gives this unit enough flexibility to be used in diverse settings. It could be part of a minicourse on Old Testament Literature, a semester course on The Bible as Literature, or a component of a more traditional year-long literature course. As described, this unit is appropriate for a class of approximately twenty-five tenth-, eleventh-, or twelfth-graders of varied ability.

CONTENT

Before beginning this study of Exodus, the teacher will have decided what portions can be omitted without destroying the continuity and without neglecting sections rich in allusion. (For example, in the first two chapters, I would assign 1:7-14, 22; and 2:1-15, 23-25.) Some parts may be given to the students in summary form, and others—such as the first nine plagues—might be assigned to individuals or small groups who would then report to the entire class.

In addition to the material from Exodus, the class studies an excerpt from Christopher Fry's drama, *The Firstborn,* and excerpts from Samuel Sandmel's *Alone Atop the Mountain.* They also listen to related music, both folk and classical, and look at representations of the characters and events by various artists. In addition, the class will read Arthur Clough's poem "The Latest Decalogue" and an excerpt from Carl Burke's *God Is Beautiful, Man,* entitled "Moses' People Go on a Trip."

GOALS AND OBJECTIVES

This unit has the following performance objectives for the students:

1. Identify allusions to the Moses story.
2. Give examples of oppressed groups who might identify with this story and explain why.
3. Identify characteristics of leadership displayed by Moses.
4. Trace the emergence of Israel as a nation from Abraham to Mount Sinai.
5. Explain the significance of the Jewish Passover.
6. Explain the origin of Christian symbols related to the Passover.

84

7. Demonstrate the ability to utilize each of the following for finding relevant information: a Bible atlas, a Bible dictionary, a concordance, and a Bible commentary.
8. Explain how Fry expands the theme of the Bible story in his play, *The Firstborn.*
9. Write a paraphrase of the Decalogue.
10. Cite examples of irony and explain why they are ironic.
11. Demonstrate an appreciation of the importance of point of view.
12. Present some creative response to the literature (needlework, cartoon, painting, dance, film, drama, music, etc.). This is to be original work from an individual student or a small group of students.

POSSIBLE ACTIVITIES

Prior to this unit the students should have studied the stories in Genesis, so they may begin by reviewing the reason for the Israelites' coming to Egypt and recall the manner in which they were received by the Egyptians. They should also review the idea of "covenant" and look again at the wording of the covenants established with Noah, Abraham, Isaac, and Jacob.

Now the students should be ready to note the changed status of the Israelites as the story begins. From the narrative they should find reasons for that change. They should also be aware of the author's use of the same verbs that were used repeatedly in the convenants just reviewed, perhaps suggesting that those covenants are about to be fulfilled.

The class next examines the author's use of irony as the Pharaoh, having boasted that he will outsmart the Hebrews, is himself outsmarted—first by the Hebrew midwives and then by three other women (Moses' mother, Miriam, and his own daughter). Students notice here, too, how the author has narrowed the focus from the Israelites in general, to one particular family, and hence to Moses.

Little is said of Moses' boyhood. (What might this tell of the author's purpose?) The students can listen to one or two of the incremental stories of Moses which are available on tape cassettes (*The Bible as Literature: Legends, Moses I, II, and III,* Horizon Studies, Inc., 512

Transamerica Building, Tuscon, Ariz., 85701) and can then write their own stories about some imaginary event in Moses' boyhood or adolescence which they feel would be in keeping with what we know from the Bible account. These can be read in small groups with each group choosing the best for sharing with the entire class.

Throughout the unit students are asked to bring in secular examples of allusions to the Exodus story. It is a good idea to have a bulletin board already started with a couple of cartoons, a headline or two, and book jackets from the two science-fiction novels, (*Stranger in a Strange Land,* (Robert A. Heinlein, 1972, New York, Putnam), and *Joshua, Son of None,* (Nancy Freedman, 1973, New York, Delacorte).

Sometime early in the unit students should have an opportunity to examine a newspaper rendition of highlights from Exodus, a format which utilizes a variety of styles in the straight news story, the feature story, the letters to the editor, the editorials, the gossip column, etc. (An excellent source for this is *Chronicles: News of the Past,* Vol. 1, The Reubeni Foundation, P. O. Box 7113, Jerusalem, Israel.) Students can then select a crucial time in the narrative and prepare their own publication to focus on that time.

At appropriate times during the unit listen to excerpts from one or two of the operas based on the Exodus narrative (such as Rossini's *Moses* or Schoenberg's *Moses and Aaron*). The presentation can be prepared with help from the music department or your own background reading. Also sing such folk music as "Let My People Go," "You'll Be a Witness for the Lord," and "I'm Bound for the Promised Land." Listen to and discuss the allusions in such hymns as "Lead, Kindly Light" and "Guide Me, O Thou Great Jehovah."

With help from the art department and the local art museum, arrange for students to see paintings and sculptures that show a variety of responses to this story by different artists.

During the study of the tenth plague, one can arrange for a field trip to a local synagogue, and ask the rabbi there to explain the Jewish celebration of Passover. Here, too, students can see the Torah and become familiar with other aspects of Jewish worship.

After having completed chapter 12, all students but one should be given identity cards designating half of them as Egyptians and half as Israelites and indicating such information as age, occupation, family, etc. The student who received no card will act as a television interviewer, conducting an on-the-spot news interview just after the final plague. Moses, Aaron, and the pharaoh will be among those to be interviewed as well as Egyptian families who have just lost their eldest sons and Israelites who sense that they are about to be freed but who fear the unknown future which awaits them.

When this activity is finished, students should be asked to rewrite chapter 12 as they think it might have been written by an Egyptian. They should be asked to preserve the biblical style as much as possible. The interview activity, coupled with the writing, should provide evidence that students are sensitive to the difference made by the narrator's point of view.

After reading chapter 14 turn to Carl Burke's "Moses' People Go on a Trip" for a change of pace. Students should have no difficulty in seeing how much difference style and tone make. Spend a little time discussing how the difference in style and tone is achieved. Students can be invited to try their hand at retelling a portion of the story using a different style and tone, perhaps retelling it for a small child or using their own modern slang.

Before reaching chapter 20, students should write their own list of "do's and do not's" for an ideal society. Then consider excerpts from Sandmel's *Alone Atop the Mountain* in which Moses meditates on the Israelites' need for law (pp. 121–22) and talks about law with the Egyptian Tat-Rin (pp. 129–33).

After reading chapter 20, one can see how many of the "laws" written by the students fit into the ten given to the Israelites. Note the different numbering of the commandments by people of different religious faiths and discuss other notes relevant to this chapter as found in *The Bible Reader* (pp. 94–97). Then read the account of the giving of the Law in Sandmel's novel (pp. 154–57). Students should be asked to write a paraphrase of the Decalogue (a word to be introduced at this time) to be sure that they understand what is being said.

Much of the remainder of the book can be given in summary form, but some time should be spent with the incident of the golden calf and the breaking of the tablets. Be sure the students are familiar with the terms "tabernacle," "ark of the covenant," "mercy seat," "holy of holies" (noting here the Hebrew forming of the superlative), and "inner sanctum."

Students will have been working for some time now on their own creative responses to the Exodus narrative. However, before engaging in the "show and tell" that will cap the unit, students should be asked to present a reading of an excerpt from Christopher Fry's *The Firstborn*. (I like to use the final scene, so I prepare a summary of the play to that point and assign a narrator to read the summary before the final scene is presented.) In discussing this last scene, after student readers have presented it, the class should be able to see how writers use the basic elements of a well-known story such as this one (or as Greek dramatists did with the myths) to make additional statements about the human condition or to raise new questions about human beings and their relation to God.

EVALUATION

The class discussions, writing activities, contributions to the bulletin board, and final sharing of creative work will provide most of the basis for evaluating this unit. A short written test might concentrate on objectives 4, 5, and 6. As a final challenge, ask the students to explain the allusion in four lines from Elizabeth Browning's "Aurora Leigh":

> Earth's crammed with heaven,
> And every common bush afire with God;
> And only he who sees takes off his shoes;
> The rest sit around it and pluck blackberries.

BIBLIOGRAPHY

For Students

Abbot, Walter M. et al. *The Bible Reader: An Interfaith Interpretation.* Beverly Hills, Calif.: Bruce, 1969. Helpful and readable notes prepared by Catholic, Protestant, and Jewish clergymen.

Avi-Yonah, Michael, and Kraeling, Emil G. *Our Living Bible.* New York: McGraw-Hill. Beautifully illustrated and easy to read. Recounts many of the Bible narratives with added insights from archaeological finds.

Burke, Carl F. *God Is Beautiful, Man.* New York: Association Press. Kids from the city streets retell stories from the Bible in their own language and from their own perspective.

Chase, Mary Ellen. *The Bible and the Common Reader.* Rev. ed. New York: Macmillan, 1962. The two sections on the Hebrew people as well as the short section on Moses should be helpful.

Fry, Christopher. "The Firstborn" in *Three Plays.* New York: Oxford Univ. Press, 1965. Verse drama based on the Exodus story.

Reader's Digest Great People of the Bible and How They Lived. Pleasantville, N.Y.: Reader's Digest Assoc. Excellent illustrations and easy reading. The section on Moses should be useful so long as students understand that added details are not necessarily factual but are based on what we know of life in that time.

Sandmel, Samuel. *Alone Atop the Mountain.* New York: Doubleday, 1973. A novel based on the biblical account of Moses, told as if Moses were writing his memoirs. Good character studies, touches of humor. Most high school students should be able to read this one.

————. *The Enjoyment of Scripture.* New York: Oxford Univ. Press, 1972. Considers the Bible primarily from a literary point of view.

Shippen, Katherine B. *Moses.* New York: Harper & Row, 1949. An easy-to-read biography emphasizing Moses' dedication and his singleness of purpose.

For The Teacher

Ackerman, James S. et al. *Teaching the Old Testament in English Classes.* Bloomington: Indiana Univ. Press, 1973. Invaluable in providing background information and helpful suggestions. Top priority.

Chamberlin, Roy B., and Feldman, Herman, eds. *The Dartmouth Bible.* Sentry paperback. Boston: Houghton, 1965. Notes and commentary make this especially helpful to the teacher.

Gros, Louis, Kenneth R. R. et al. eds. *Literary Interpretations of Biblical Narratives.* Nashville, Tenn: Abingdon, 1974. Two excellent chapters on the Moses story, emphasizing the literary qualities. Very useful.

Wright, G. Ernest, and Fuller, Reginald H. *The Book of the Acts of God: An Introduction to the Bible.* New York: Doubleday, 1957. Written for the layman. Combines Bible scholarship and knowledge of archaeology to provide excellent background for teaching about the Bible.

Records

Rossini, *Moses in Egypt.* Phillips Records.

Schoenberg, *Moses and Aaron.* Phillips Records.

The Living Bible. Mercury Records. Outstanding readings of the Bible text with appropriate musical background. Reproductions of famous paintings relevant to the particular stories are on the record jackets.

The Bible as/in Literature

Thayer S. Warshaw

Teaching The Bible as/in Literature does not mean teaching The Bible as a Religious Document. In a public school literature course, "teaching about religion" should not be a main purpose, expressed or not. Such a primary focus is the business of a social studies class, not a language arts class.

Agreed, the two disciplines are not completely separate, especially when the literature examined in both cases is from the Bible. While a social studies teacher often ignores the Bible's literary form, a literature course rarely ignores the Bible's religious content. The Bible is a religious document—not only because it is sacred to many people but also because of its subject matter: its main character is God; its themes are theological and moral, and they are closely related. The themes and values of any piece of literature are legitimate subjects for discussion in a language arts class.

In some cases a teacher of literature may skirt themes and moral issues. He or she may be interested only in the students' acquaintance with a story for purposes of background necessary for understanding another piece of literature that was inspired by it. For example, students need to know Greek mythology to appreciate the creative achievement of Racine in *Phaedre* and similarly need to know about Job for MacLeish's *J. B.* Again, the teacher may choose to de-emphasize theme and focus the students' attention exclusively on the work's craftsmanship, concentrating on reading and writing skills. More often, however, the teacher asks students to consider the appropriateness of that craftsmanship—its literary technique—to its content. How well do the imagery, setting, characterization, and narrative devices of a piece of fiction suit the events of the story and the issues they illustrate? Do manner and matter fuse into a work of art?

Furthermore, most teachers ask students to relate the issues raised by a piece of literature to their own experiences, insights, and values. Some teachers do so in order that the students may participate more fully in the literary experience. Some offer another justification for the activity. They say that beyond the specific obligations of language arts teachers to focus on the facts and skills of literature, composition, and language, all teachers in all disciplines have the responsibility of asking their students to confront questions of ethical values. That this activity presents special problems to the teacher of literature in a public secondary school when the selections are from the Bible will be obvious to every reader. This chapter will mention only a few.[1]

The Bible as a Religious Document in a social studies class and The Bible as/in Literature in a language arts class, therefore, are not entirely separate. A language arts class may, like a social studies class, examine the religious aspects of the Bible, its theology and moral values. Yet the two courses are different, and the difference lies in approach and emphasis. A social studies class may approach the Bible from an interest in ancient history and ancient civilizations, cross-cultural themes in society, backgrounds to modern problems and institutions, comparative religions, or whatever. In most cases its emphasis will be on the values expressed or implied in the Bible through its teachings or as exhibited by the people and events of the stories—on its personal and societal ethics, its theology and its "view of life."

A literature class, on the other hand, may approach the biblical text as a work of literary art itself (The Bible *as* Literature), as an influence upon other literature (The Bible *in* Literature), or as a special instance of a genre or a theme that ties together many otherwise unrelated pieces of literature (The Bible *and* Literature). These alternatives are discussed more fully below; here the main interest is in literary analysis. How are biblical and secular literature written? To what extent does the story or theme justify the literary devices and techniques? To what extent do the literary devices and techniques develop—support, enhance, reinforce—the major themes of the story? How well is it written?

The amount that students learn about religion in a Bible as/in Literature course will depend on the approach used by the teacher. The question is, to borrow a phrase: What is the "primary purpose and effect" of the course? A secondary school teacher whose principal emphasis lies in teaching about the theological and moral values in or related to the Bible is at best neglecting the discipline's mandate to teach reading and writing skills. At worst, the teacher may be in danger of pursuing an unacknowledged goal—religious indoctrination. Our first point, then: the teacher should recognize the distinction between teaching The Bible as/in Literature and teaching The Bible as a Religious Document.

In the second place, there is no *best* approach, method, or materials for all courses in The Bible as/in Literature. There are only choices— which may be either conscious or haphazard, theoretically valid or inappropriate (for the Bible and for a literature class), viable or impractical for this particular class, this particular school and community, or this particular teacher.

In developing the most appropriate unit or course on the Bible, the teacher will have to think through the following questions: What information, skills, and dispositions does the teacher want the students to learn, and what are the alternatives? Is this to be a two-week unit, a nine-week minicourse, a semester or full-year course, and how much can be covered realistically? What materials and methods are available in the field and at school, and how much leeway does the teacher have in choosing? How much does the teacher know about the subject matter and about the attitudes and assumptions concerning the historicity and authority of the Bible that may be found among the students, within the community, and in the teacher's own self? How much does the teacher know about alternative sensibilities not represented or acknowledged in this particular classroom or community? These are a few of the considerations that shape, overtly or without examination, what will go on in the classroom. It is important to face them in advance and even more important to keep them in mind while teaching. For classroom situations are unpredictable; and, like their students, teachers learn from experience.

Let us now briefly review some of the possible approaches to The Bible as/in Literature, a title taken from our textbook.[2] To approach The Bible *as* Literature means to subject biblical passages to the kind of literary analysis that one uses with any secular poem or short story. One finds, for example, that Psalm 23 and the story of the tower of Babel are very carefully crafted.[3] To approach The Bible *in* Literature is to examine biblical images in secular literature.[4] A third kind of approach may be called The Bible *and* Literature. Here a biblical selection is included in a literature unit that is unified by genre (a psalm among the poetry, the Book of Ruth among the short stories) or theme (unmerited suffering in Job and *Candide*).

Within these three large categories are subdivisions among which the teacher may select, mix, and match. Under the rubric of The Bible *as* Literature, the alternatives have already been suggested. First, there may be very little literary analysis of the Bible selection itself because it is being read only to see its relevance to other pieces of literature. What did a secular author (or painter or musician) do with the story? How did someone else treat a similar theme? Second, literary analysis may be limited to the craftsmanship of the biblical passage: concrete imagery, balanced sentences in Hebrew poetry (both Old and New Testaments); verbal and situational irony in Job; structure and recurrent motifs in the Joseph story. Third, literary analysis of a biblical selection may extend to the appropriateness of the craftsmanship to the themes, of manner to matter. How do the underlying themes of preservation and conservation account for the recurrent images and surface structure in the Joseph story?[5] How does Psalm 23's shift in person ("the Lord" to "Thou" back to "the Lord") and in controlling metaphor (from sheep/pastures to man/house of the Lord) reflect the movement and changing mood of trust?[6]

These are three of the common ways of treating a piece of literature within a secondary school language arts class. In approaching The Bible *as* Literature, the last is the most difficult and the most rewarding. Teachers can expect little help from early writers on the Bible as literature, but contemporary scholars with competence in both biblical studies and literary criticism are increasingly turning their attention to this kind of analysis. Even so, teachers may have to work out, with their students or alone, workable classroom exercises in literary analysis of biblical selections.

The Bible *in* Literature is more commonly used than literary analysis of the Bible itself as an approach to the Bible in secondary school language arts classes. Basically, the biblical passage and its related secular literature are chosen to be read together, with an emphasis on the latter. Again there are several options for the teacher, not only as to how to treat the Bible passage but also as to what criteria to use for selecting the related literature. In the first instance, the teacher must decide whether to read the Bible selection first or last and how thoroughly it is to be analyzed as a work of art per se. In the second, decisions about which secular pieces to include may be based on how they are related to the Bible selection. That relationship may be of many different kinds, some of which we will now examine.

The secular Bible-related literature may "fill in" the Bible story. In the manner of Shakespeare reworking Holinshed or North's Plutarch, the modern author sketches in the setting, depicts the consciousness of the biblical characters, furnishes dialogue, invents new actions and even new characters. The resultant poem, play, or prose fiction is the author's imaginative response to the Bible story and to the issues it raises. The modern piece of literature may give the reader new insight into the original meaning of the biblical story, or it may ironically reverse that meaning. Thus we have both Milton's *Paradise Lost* and Twain's *Extracts from Adam's Diary*.[7]

A somewhat similar device is to "modernize" the Bible story. Just as Joyce replaces Odysseus and Telemachus with Leopold Bloom and Stephen Dedalus, the secular writer retells the Bible story in a modern context. The parallel between the biblical account and the modern setting, characters, and events may be quite allegorical or only partial; it may be obvious or unobtrusive; but the Bible story or teaching is, in these instances, central to the modern work. Farfrae and Henshard subtly replicate the story of David and Saul in Hardy's *The Mayor of Casterbridge*. Santiago reenacts elements of the passion in Hemingway's *The Old Man and the Sea*. The theme of Cain and Abel pervades Steinbeck's *East of Eden*. So closely is the modern piece of literature tied to the biblical original that it represents an almost exact counterpart of the filling-in technique described above.

The teacher may also approach The Bible *in* Literature by choosing secular pieces in which the biblical theme or image is less central or pervasive, yet important to a full appreciation of the author's intention. Such a modern work alludes to the Bible either at key points or now and then in such a manner that the biblical resonances cause the secular literature to acquire overtones of deeper meaning. Keats is forlorn when he hears the nightingale; the depth of his feeling is enchanced for the reader by the memorable reference to "the sad heart of Ruth, when, sick for home, she stood in tears amid the alien corn." Hamlet, in calling Polonius "Jephthah," helps (or confuses) us as we try to solve the mystery of Hamlet's true feelings toward Ophelia.

Further, The Bible *in* Literature may move in the direction of the humanities. Western art abounds in pictures, sculpture, and architecture inspired by the Bible. Rembrandt's paintings, Dürer's drawings, Michelangelo's sculptures, cruciform churches and their murals and carvings, all reinforce the students' knowledge of the Bible and enrich their understanding of the artists' creative response to its stories. Biblical texts and allusions occur in every kind of choral music, from majestic masses and oratorios to country-and-western songs. Popular culture shows the influence of the Bible in movies, political and humorous cartoons, advertising, and cliches of everyday language.

As an alternative or in addition to approaching The Bible *as* Literature and The Bible *in* Literature, the teacher may choose to follow the path of The Bible *and* Literature. Here the secular selections are related to the Bible merely by sharing a common genre or theme. The list of possibilities within this category is long and varied. The most common division of literature into genres distinguishes poetry, drama, prose fiction, and nonfiction. Teachers may include a psalm with the poetry, excerpts from Job or the Song of Solomon with drama, Jonah with short stories, Paul's sermon on love with the nonfiction. School anthologies increasingly include biblical selections within these categories.

Thematic organization of a literature course may fit inside the genre structure or cut across it. Sibling rivalry, rites of passage and the fall from innocence, social justice and ethnic prejudice, women in society, creativity and the thirst for knowledge—all these themes that interest secondary school students and that appear in their regular reading—are exemplified in the Bible.

Beyond these traditional ways of organizing the study of literature are others—some recently elevated to the status of elective courses—for which the Bible has relevance. For example, the first eleven chapters of Genesis go well with the epic of Gilgamesh, which also contains motifs of Creation, the loss of paradise and peace, the temptress, the evils of civilization, a flood—all common threads within the traditions of nearly every culture. The teacher may append some of these stories to a Bible *in* Literature course. Alternatively, a mythology unit or course might include the Bible stories provided, of course, that they are distinguised from "pagan myths" to protect religious sensibilities.

Mythology suggests the genres of legend and folklore. Tales of legendary heroes go well with the exploits of the Judges, David, and Judith. Folktales contain many stories similar in kind or purpose to biblical parables and fables. Rabbinic and Christian legends that embellish the Bible stories also may be included.

Similarly, some of the more thoughtful science fiction is apocalyptic. Visions of a world doom, beasts and dragons, prophecies of judgment with revenge against the evil ones and salvation for the elect, predictions of a new world are themes of science fiction found also in the Bible, most typically in the Book of Revelation. Utopias (and dystopias) may also make up a distinct genre or theme for a literature unit or course. The Bible includes many variations: physical and spiritual quests for God's kingdom; old men's dreams and young men's visions.

There are still other approaches to The Bible *and* Literature. One may fit the story of Saul into a unit or course on tragedy, Jonah with satire, Kings and Chronicles with history, Judith with romance, Jacob with epic cycles, and Proverbs and Ecclesiastes with wisdom literature. Whatever criterion the teacher uses to organize the literature course, the secular pieces in all these cases do not depend on biblical imagery, as they do within the rubric of The Bible *in* Literature. The link is genre or theme, terms that have many dimensions. Within each, biblical selections are appropriate.

Thus we have three kinds of approaches to the Bible—*as* Literature, *in* Literature, *and* Literature. Each has several options that may form the core of a course or unit, or may be combined in an infinite number of ways.

The Bible Literature course at Newton (Massachusetts) North High School has developed and changed over its fifteen-year history. Most recently it has used the textbook, *The Bible as/in Literature,* that grew out of the course and out of the Indiana University Institute on Teaching the Bible. What follows is a discussion of some aspects of our semester elective using our textbook, with special attention to one typical unit.

Three introductory observations are necessary. First, let it be acknowledged that the textbook contains too much to cover adequately in one semester but not enough to satisfy a creative teacher and inquiring students. The latter problem exacerbates the former. The more outside reading, audiovisual materials, and activities the teacher wants to add and the more leeway the students are given to ask questions, make comments, and contribute materials, the more difficult it is to cover everything in the book. The first practical problem for the less experienced teacher, with this book or any other curriculum, is to decide how intensively and extensively to treat each Bible-centered unit, how many units to insist on as a bare minimum, and which ones (alas!) to omit. One may have to be ruthless.

Second, in addition to some favorite biblical passages and much worthy secular literature that were reluctantly omitted from the textbook for lack of space, the teacher will find other holes to fill. One needs to acquire sufficient information and perspective to present the material properly, to answer student questions, and to preside with some assurance over classroom discussions, taking into consideration potential problem areas. The *Teacher's Resource Book* offers some help in literary analysis, minimal notes of scholarly background, and some general hints about classroom procedures. The teacher should also be familiar with the recommended references—Bible versions, commentaries, study Bibles, dictionaries, concordances, atlases, and literary studies—and have them available in the classroom and/or in the school library.[8] These books can provide some background for the teacher in both critical scholarship and various mainstream religious traditions. They are valuable in developing both knowledge and sensitivity, so necessary in our pluralistic society.[9]

Third, it is necessary to clarify the format of the textbook. Biblical selections are followed in most cases by related secular literature, and both have student aids. Student aids are of three kinds: (1) *For close reading*—factual questions to help the student focus upon and grasp important or subtle details. The answers may be found by simply rereading the relevant portions of the text or, in a few instances, by consulting a dictionary or simple encyclopedia. (2) *For thought and discussion*—open-ended questions whose answers are meant to be judged not as either "right" or "wrong" but as "more appropriate" and "less appropriate." In many cases these questions ask students to act upon the facts elicited in the close-reading questions. (3) *Activities*—suggestions for imaginative responses to the text. Those suggested for any one selection can usually be adapted for others throughout the book. They are intended to provide a wide variety of alternatives: for individuals or groups, oral or written, verbal or nonverbal, short- or long-term.[10]

It has been customary in our course for the students to produce one long-term project, approved by the teacher and with progress conferences, for presentation to the class at the end of the course. Here students have the option of making some sort of creative connection between a Bible story or theme and one or more of the following fields: art, music, literature, mythology, ancient history, or current events. At the presentation each student explains, or answers class questions about, how and why the project was created.

Both the fact questions and the discussion questions have two purposes, however imperfectly achieved in some instances. First, they try to help the students recognize and analyze the literary craftsmanship of the biblical and secular selections. Second, they ask students to think about the themes—in terms of their own experiences and ingenuity—treated in an individual selection or in several pieces of thematically related literature taken together.

Examination of The Bible *as* Literature, at least as defined above, may be a less familiar pursuit to most teachers than critical analysis of The Bible *in* Literature. Therefore, for our necessarily limited example, let us take an instance of The Bible *as* Literature, the textbook's treatment of Genesis 1–3. This block of material is broken down into three passages: Part One of the Creation story (1:1–2: 4a), Part Two of the Creation story (2:4b–2:25), and the Eden story (3:1–3:24). The two accounts of Creation are called "parts" to avoid commitment either to the two-source theorists or to traditionalists, for whom source theory is objectionable. The controversy, however interesting, is not vital to a purely literary analysis of the text, at least for a public secondary school class (although not necessarily to be avoided for that reason when a student raises the question).

The Creation story is separated from the Eden story for purely practical reasons. The Eden story abounds with so many provocative themes and literary techniques and has inspired so many excellent pieces of secular literature that students ought to be allowed to consider it separately. True, most scholars regard it as a continuation of the second (part of the) Creation story. But that connection can be made effectively at the proper time.

The insights into the Creation story that had the strongest influence on the textbook questions concerned with literary analysis are derived from Gros Louis.[11] Among other observations, he calls attention to the language and structure of the first part of the Creation story: the kinds of verbs whose subject is the word "God," the formulaic repetition of words, the parallels and the progressions of the days of Creation. The point is made that *the orderliness of the Creation process is reflected in and reinforced by the orderliness of the form in which Creation is presented,* and both enhance the picture of an orderly God. God is transcendent, omniscient, omnipotent, majestic; his universe is previously thought out, patterned, and hierarchical. Humankind, his vice-regent made in God's image, should be orderly and conservative. Thus we go from an examination of the literary devices present in the text to a recognition of the close relationship between those devices and the content and themes, and we gain appreciation of the literary artistry of the story. The themes turn out to be nothing less than the nature of God, the nature of the universe, and the nature and purpose of humankind.

Our textbook's fact and discussion questions include several that point the students toward these insights—though there are enough other questions to avoid limiting the imagination. Some of the close-reading questions ask students to make lists of each day's creations, repetitive phrases, and verbs describing God's actions. Certain thought-and-discussion questions ask students to speculate about these lists: Is there any logic to the order, the repetitions, the parallels? Other discussion questions ask students to draw inferences about the nature of God, about his relation to the world and its creatures, and about what it means to be created in God's image.

In the second part of the Creation story, the Lord God is not depicted as a remote, disembodied voice; he is described in human metaphors. The Lord God creates a world in which he is immanent, a world in which the rationale of Creation seems to be the satisfying of the human being's needs as they become evident in time. He experiments and allows Adam to participate in the experiment by giving names to the creatures. (In the Eden story the Lord God questions both the woman and the man, asking them to assume responsibility for their actions.) By analogy, human beings not only must be orderly and conservative but must also question and experiment—responsibly.

In the textbook this passage follows the first without intervening secular pieces, in order to emphasize the relationship between the two parts of the Creation story. Once again, the textbook's questions ask for lists and for inferences from them: about the order of Creation, the nature of God and his world, and the role of human beings. Finally, the student is asked to contrast the two parts of the Creation story: What are the differences and how might one explain them? The last part of this question is completely open-ended and permits answers from all kinds of religious traditions and at all levels of maturity, knowledge, and intellectual and imaginative ability. How far the teacher chooses to lead students to a really sophisticated literary analysis will vary. Perhaps all but the top students may need help in seeing that the way the story is told in each case is suited to what is being told and what is being implied, that we have two excellent and complementary works of literary art. The structure and style of the first reflect the theme of the conservative orderliness of God, the universe, and humankind; the contrasting structure and style of the second help elaborate the theme of the dynamic potential for change.

As noted above, the Eden story may be considered a continuation of the second part of the Creation story. The setting, especially the tree, ties them together; more important, the picture of human beings, of God, and of their relationship to each other is similar, and quite different from what is presented in the first chapter of Genesis. (The story of the Fall also looks ahead: it is the first step in an increasing alienation of humankind from God that ends with Babel.) The Eden story has its own multiple themes and literary devices. Let us consider one already hinted at.

The serpent (whether Satan, as in the Christian tradition, or not) is the creature that pulls Eve (and Adam) away from the Lord God. The polar relationship between the serpent and the Lord God is reinforced by the fact that both of them ask questions of the human beings, questions to which the questioner already knows the answer. In both cases the purpose of the questions is to involve the people, to force them to accept responsibility. These similarities in manner and purpose of address emphasize their differences. The serpent wants Eve to be responsible for the decision to disobey the Lord God, and he is successful. The Lord God, rather than lecture Adam and Eve, wants them to *admit* their responsibility for their action; but he gets evasive answers. Failing this more important moral test, Adam and Eve must learn the hard way and feel the consequences: physical pain and banishment from the paradise they do not deserve. A thought-and-discussion question in the textbook directs students' attention toward this kind of literary analysis of The Bible *as* Literature, helping them uncover the literary artistry of the passage, in which content is wedded to form.

These examples, taken from our high school's Bible elective and its textbook, have dealt with The Bible *as* Literature. Beyond that, the course uses Bible-related literature, reinforced and enriched with hundreds of slides and tapes illustrating the influence of the Bible on our artistic culture and everyday life. The main purposes of the course are to familiarize the students with the Bible, to improve their reading skills by close attention to good literature, and to help them grow through the experience.

NOTES

1. For a more detailed discussion of such problems, see the forthcoming *Teacher's Handbook* by Thayer S. Warshaw and James S. Ackerman (Nashville, Tenn.: Abingdon), on which the present chapter is based.

2. James S. Ackerman and Thayer S. Warshaw, *The Bible as/in Literature* (Glenview, Ill.: Scott, Foresman, 1976). See also the accompanying *Teacher's Resource Book*.

3. For a fuller discussion and examples of The Bible *as* Literature, see Kenneth R. R., Gros Louis et al., *Literary Interpretations of Biblical Narratives* (Nashville, Tenn.: Abingdon, 1974).

4. For examples of such analyses to be used with secondary school students, see Roland Bartel, et al., *Biblical Images in Literature* (Nashville, Tenn.: Abingdon, 1975).

5. See Donald A. Seybold, "Paradox and Symmetry in the Joseph Narrative" in Gros Louis, *Literary Interpretations,* chap. V.

6. An extended analysis appears in the Warshaw and Ackerman *Teacher's Handbook*.

7. For suggestions about literature and other resources appropriate for secondary school classes, listed according to biblical passages, see Thayer S. Warshaw et al., *Bible-Related Curriculum Materials: A Bibliography* (Nashville, Tenn.: Abington, 1976).

8. The following items should be added to the list of recommended reference materials:

   Bratcher, Robert G., ed. *Good News Bible.* New York: American Bible Soc., 1976. The easily understood and scholarly Today's English Version.

   Brodsky, Marvin A., ed. *The Family Bible Encyclopedia.* 22 vols. New York: Curtis

Books, 1972. Illustrated, with vocabulary and format suitable for secondary school students, representing critical scholarship.

Burren, Marjorie, prod. *The Bible: A Study in Literature.* Pleasantville, N.Y.: Guidance Assoc., 1975. A two-part sound filmstrip.

Juel, Donald, et al. *Teaching the New Testament in English Classes.* Nashville, Tenn.: Abingdon, 1977. A companion book to Ackerman's volume on the Old Testament.

Lindsell, Harold, ed. *Harper Study Bible.* Grand Rapids, Mich.: Zondervan, 1972. The RSV text with critical notes representing conservative Evangelical Protestant scholarship.

Sandmel, Samuel, ed. *The New English Bible with the Apocrypha: Oxford Study Edition.* New York: Oxford Univ. Press, 1976. With notes representing liberal interfaith scholarship.

9. Teachers, administrators, and members of the community may be interested in a forthcoming book: Thayer S. Warshaw and James S. Ackerman, *Religion, Public Education, and the Supreme Court* (Nashville: Abingdon).

10. For a list of suggestions, see the Warshaw and Ackerman *Teacher's Handbook.*

11. Op. cit., chapter 3.

Part 3

Religion Studies in the Social Studies

Learning about Religions through the Elementary Social Studies Program

Joan G. Dye

A cross-cultural approach to learning about religions lends powerful assistance to the realization of the acknowledged aims of the elementary social studies curriculum. Public school programs of social studies education center on such concepts and understandings as: social and personal goals, social interaction, the nature of social institutions, acculturation, belief systems, and the forces of social change. In addition, these programs are concerned with a host of contemporary social issues such as: the role of women in society, ethnicity, environmental protection, the energy crisis, honesty in government, and world hunger. The study of the religious dimensions of these ideas and issues provides the grade school child with a sound academic and social preparation for living in our multireligious society.

Religion studies can be incorporated into the social studies program in three ways: as a special course, as a special unit, or by the program infusion method.

The special course method is more appropriate at the high school level, where students may elect certain courses in fulfillment of social studies requirements and where teachers are more likely to prepare for a particular content area. Elementary teachers are under increasing pressure to emphasize the teaching of basic skills related to the language arts and mathematics. It is unrealistic to expect that time and resources would be allotted for a year or half-year course on religion as a separate subject at the elementary level.

In the past, religion studies in the public elementary school setting has most often been implemented as a special unit. At the primary level it is quite likely that the child's only in-school exposure to religion studies will occur as part of a holiday pageant during the Christmas season. The resulting learning often leaves the lasting misconception that Christmas (rather than Easter) and Hanukkah (rather than Rosh Hashanah and Yom Kippur) are the highest holy days for Christians and Jews respectively. At the intermediate level, this annual event may be supplemented by a unit on "Religious Holidays and Festivals" or by a unit on "Religious Music and Art." Units on "Religious Literature" or on "World Religions" occur infrequently. This fragmented approach lacks continuity from level to level. Learning about religions becomes compartmentalized rather than integrated with other areas of the curriculum.

The curriculum-infusion method has clear advantages at the elementary level. Several practical considerations are attractive to the elementary teacher. With the curriculum-infusion method, learning about religions need not be viewed as an additional subject. As an integral part of the year-long social studies program, many of the same activities which are used in elementary programs of basic skills can be used for learning about religions. In addition, the teacher is not presented with problems of scheduling and classroom organization.

The curriculum-infusion method complements current inter-disciplinary social studies programs. These programs integrate key concepts and inquiry skills from the various disciplines—anthropology, sociology, economics, history, political science, and geography. Such integrated studies provide a balance between the study of each discipline separately and in context with the other disciplines. For example, religion might be "separated out" for special emphasis in two or more units during the year-long social studies program. In these units, key concepts, ideas, and sensitivities related to religion would be systematically studied. In the other units these learnings about religions would be "placed in context" with the other disciplines.

To provide the necessary continuity for incremental learning, it is essential that major objectives for the entire elementary social studies program, K–6, be established. These objectives should be directed toward the development of key concepts, understandings, and sensitivities for each discipline. In keeping with research by Piaget and Kohlberg[1] on the child's cognitive and moral development, concepts and understandings should be introduced in simple form at early levels and increase in difficulty at subsequent levels. One of the primary tasks of the Religion in Elementary Social Studies Project at Florida State University was to work with religious scholars and educators in the development of the following major objectives for learning about religions in public school programs of social studies education.

MAJOR OBJECTIVES

The result of the project is the six-level *Learning about Religion/Social Studies (LAR/SS)* program, which has as its purpose the development of the following concepts, main ideas, and sensitivities:[2]

Concepts

world view (story), life-style (way)

sacred/profane: time, space, literature, objects, symbols, celebrations, myth

religious/secular: traditions, communities, institutions, leaders, adherents

diversity, acculturation, interaction, change

Main Ideas

1. The religious dimension has to do with world view and life-style.
2. World view is a sense of reality from which a person and/or a community makes sense of life; this sense of reality is a belief about *what is* and a commitment as to *what ought to be.*
3. Life-style is the way in which a person or a community moves, acts, and lives; life-style reflects world view.
4. The religious dimension is manifest in both religious and nonreligious traditions.
5. Religious traditions develop out of the interaction of the adherents with the sacred, in time and space.
6. A religious tradition is a pattern of thinking, feeling, valuing, and acting preserved by a community in symbols, events, persons, documents, artifacts, rites, customs, beliefs, and ideas.
7. Religious communication is symbolic; it points beyond itself.
8. The religious dimension is universally manifest in human societies.
9. The religious dimension is both a personal and a community experience.
10. The religious dimension and culture are mutually interdependent.

11. Religious experiences and expressions change over time.
12. The study of the religious dimension and of religious traditions is an integral part of the study of humankind.

Sensitivities

Developing self-concept:

Feeling free to make appropriate references to and statements about one's own world view, life-style, and religious or secular tradition.

Living openly by the commitments which one's world view and life-style entail.

Developing empathy for others:

Appreciating the diversity of world views and life-styles in human societies.

Supporting people in their beliefs and behaviors which are unique to their secular or religious traditions.

Being willing to negotiate accommodations for persons in the living out of their traditions and beliefs.

Considering the values of particular traditions which might be involved in a problem-solving situation.

The following unit on Java seeks to illustrate how these major objectives may be fulfilled.

UNIT ON JAVA

Learning About Religions/Social Studies[3]
Second Level: Community Studies

Community interaction in both its sacred and secular dimensions provides the theme—and the key concept—for the entire second level of the *LAR/SS* program. This theme correlates well with cross-cultural studies of the community in conventional second grade social studies curricula. The unit on Java is the second of three sequential units in which religion is systematically studied. The three units should be spaced at intervals spanning the entire academic year so that the learning may be continuously integrated with other areas of the social studies program.

The first unit, on the prehistoric society of Indian Mound Builders near central Georgia, introduced the concept of community interaction in a simple society with limited contact outside its own culture. Children learned that the ritual life of the community was integrated with its economic, political, and social life, and that people depended on one another to fulfill clearly differentiated roles in each of these vital areas.

The unit on Java continues the development of these understandings at a more complex level of understanding. Java was selected as a content sample for a variety of reasons. Religious ritual in the village life of present-day Java is readily observable. Java's history of continuous outside cultural contact and assimilation provides a background of understanding for later studies of diversity and change in our society. The study of Java also provides a preconceptual introduction to non-Western religions early in the child's education. Of primary importance in the development of the curriculum, the work of noted anthropologist Clifford Geertz provided an extensive, authoritative base of information and insight.[4]

The final second-level unit provides the opportunity to apply the learning to a study of the children's own community in a society of religious pluralism. Again, the level of difficulty is increased. Unlike the Mound Builders' homogeneous society, our society is heterogeneous and rapidly changing. Unlike the communally shared religious syncretism of Java, religious adherents in our society usually feel a sense of primary membership in a single religious tradition. Students begin to form simple generalizations: there is a plurality of religions; religious traditions allow significant differences within them; these traditions change in response to new social situations; a person's religion is not entirely separate from his or her economic, political, and social life; sensitivity to the religious values and beliefs of others prepares one for living in our multireligious society.

Multimedia materials developed for the unit on Java include a read-along book, filmstrips, audiocassette, an activity book, and a detailed teacher's guide. The teacher and class would take about three weeks to complete the basic lessons in this unit, but this may be lengthened considerably by the use of the suggested extending activities.

Content

Concepts for the unit include: community interaction, celebration, acculturation, change, diversity, myth, symbols, sacred space. Main ideas 5, 6, 9, and 10 receive key development in this unit. Main ideas 1, 2, and 3, introduced at the program's first-grade level, receive continuing development.

Outline of Content

Lesson 1: "The *Slametan*"—a communal feast as the core ritual in which benefits increase in proportion to the number of participants.

Lesson 2: "A Mixture of Spices"—relationship of culture contact through trading to the assimilation of ideas from many different religious traditions.

Lesson 3: "A Visit to the Shrines"—religious heritage of Java preserved in ancient Hindu and Buddhist shrines near Jogjakarta, the cultural center of Java.

Lesson 4: "A Javanese Shadow Puppet Play: The Story of Rama and Sita"—theater as a communal celebration of religious story and cultural values.

Lesson 5: "Rijaja"—a national holiday incorporating elements of Islam (the official national religion), Hinduism, Buddhism, and native animism and repeating the theme of mutual benefits deriving from communal participation.

Behavioral Objectives

Specific objectives for each lesson are stated in behavioral terms. They relate to the concepts, organizing ideas, and sensitivites which are stressed in the particular lesson. The objectives often require prepared materials such as paired drawings, maps, and charts, which are compiled in a student activity book. For example:

Lesson 1: The child will be able to pair drawings of community helpers with drawings of the actions performed by the helpers in secular and sacred ways of curing. The child will also be able to sort drawings of celebrations, symbols, and community helpers into two categories—the Mound Builders and the Javanese.

Lesson 2: Given a desk copy of a world map labeled "The Spice Trade" and a list of three religious traditions (Islam, Hinduism, and Buddhism), the child will be able to write the name of each tradition in the geographic region of its origin. He or she will then be able to draw an arrow representing the trade route from that region to Java.

Lesson 3. Given a list of vocabulary words from this unit and from the preceding unit, the child will be able to chart information about the cultures of the Mound Builders and the Javanese and use this information to hypothesize about similar phenomena in their own society. The vocabulary words from the unit on Java are: Java, slametan, dukun, Islam; Hinduism, Buddhism, shrine, mosque, Rijaja.

Learning Activities

The study of Java lends itself well to active, experiential learning. The introduction to each lesson begins with an "opener" designed to relate the area of study to the child's prior knowledge and experience or to provide an initial experience. The following opening activities involve the senses of tasting, touching, and smelling, as well as hearing and seeing:

> Set the stage for a simulated *slametan.* Burn some incense in the room. Turn on a recording of authentic *gamelan* music. (See Resources.) Give the children a few minutes to discuss their reactions to the odor of the incense and the sound of the music, then turn off the lights and present the opening filmstrip, *The Name-Changing Slametan.* (Children will learn that the odor of incense is an important spirit offering in the Javanese tradition).
>
> Arrange a spice-tasting and smelling tray with boxes of cinnamon, nutmeg, mace, and pepper. Provide each child with a plastic spoon and a small paper cup of applesauce on which to sample the various spices. After some experimenting, they might try to identify the spices by taste alone, then by smell alone. (The odor of spices is also regarded as a spirit offering by the Javanese.)
>
> Turn off the lights and use the filmstrip-projector lamp to make shadows. Children may take turns casting their own shadows on a projection screen. Ask: "How is your shadow like you? How is your shadow not like you?" (The famous Javanese shadow puppet plays are a ritual art form in which the spirits of the characters from the Hindu Ramayana tales are believed to be present in the shadows cast by the puppets.)

The major portion of each lesson is the *development.* It involves the employment of academic and social skills in a sequential series of investigative and analytic tasks. Some of the following activities are drawn from learning sequences which are an integral part of a lesson. Others are from the optional extending activities, which provide enrichment or further development:

Use globes to discover the location of Indonesia in relation to the students' community. Have several primary-level globes available. Divide the class into as many groups as there are globes. Members of each group should work together to locate their own country and Indonesia. Use a string to find the shortest route between these two points.

Role-play a name-changing *slametan.* Assign the various roles (Islamic prayer chanter, father, mother, guests). Prepare some simple Javanese rice dishes (recipes for which are provided in the teacher's guide). Children should sit in a circle on the floor. They should choose new names for one another based on personal tastes or interests. Each child must agree to his or her new name, for in Java it is believed that one's name should "fit" a person. (More detailed role-playing instructions are in the teachers' guide.)

Discuss the uses of incense which children might have encountered in our society, either in the home or as part of a religious celebration.

Read and discuss *The Story of Rama and Sita,* adapted from the Hindu Ramayana tales. Ask: "Who was the hero? What did you like about him? Who was the heroine? What did you like about her? What does the story tell us about the ideal man in the Javanese tradition? About the ideal woman?"

Stage a shadow puppet play telling the story of Rama and Sita. Make puppets out of cardboard characters mounted on sticks. The stories in the *LAR/SS* student booklet may be used as a narration or as a basis for a script. Emphasize again the importance of community participation in the shadow puppet play as part of a ritual celebration benefiting those in attendance.

Discuss secular and sacred examples of fasting in our society in order to understand the national holiday, *Rijaja,* as a celebration ending the Muslim month of fast.

Have the children make *Rijaja* greeting cards. The message inside the card should be a traditional Javanese request for forgiveness—*latir batin,* "I humbly beg your forgiveness." Discuss secular and sacred ways of seeking forgiveness in our society— Yom Kippur, Christian reconciliation rites, apologies.

From the information in the LAR/SS student booklet, have the children role-play the celebration of *Rijaja*. the role-playing activities would include; going to the mosque to pray, watching a shadow puppet play, attending a *slametan*, giving money to the poor, and visiting neighbors in order to ask forgiveness for any intentional or unintentional offenses, and to receive a treat, usually a sweet.

The culminating activities provide an opportunity for the students to internalize the learnings and to apply or synthesize them. The final unit for the second-level program is a study of the religious dimension of the child's own community. As a major culminating activity for that unit, provide students with large activity posters—one poster for each group of four children. The posters suggest, with simple line drawings, the many services found in most communities—hospitals, schools, homes for the aged, churches, day camps, parks, and so forth. Students fill in and add to the posters names, drawings, and photos of organizations which provide for the various needs of the community. In so doing, they discover that religious and nonreligious individuals work together to make the community a better place in which to live.

Evaluation

The behavioral objectives provide evaluative checks through the activities and the anticipated outcomes stated in those objectives. In addition, a six-week study at the Florida State University's Developmental Research School has evaluated the second-level program for its impact on attitudes of prejudice. The study concluded that the program, the classroom atmosphere, the teacher as a role model, and the influence of peer pressure through group discussion combined to result in higher religious-tolerance scores for the exposed group of children.[5]

NOTES

1. Ronald Duska and Marjellen Whelan, *Moral Development; A Guide to Piaget and Kohlberg* (New York: Paulist Press, 1975).
2. Joan G. Dye, Robert A. Spivey, and Rodney F. Allen, *Learning About Religions/Social Studies* (Niles, Ill.: Argus Communications, 1976). *LAR/SS* was developed

by the Religion in Elementary Social Studies Project at Florida State University. The program also includes the teaching of skills.

3. Ibid.

4. Clifford Geertz, *The Religion of Java* (New York: The Free Press, 1960).

INSTRUCTIONAL RESOURCES

Capsuled background information is inserted in the teacher's guide at points where it is most convenient for quick reference. Earlier prototypes of the teacher's guide listed the following references for the religion scholars and educators who were reviewing the program during its development:

Geertz, Clifford. *Islam Observed: Religious Development in Morocco and Indonesia.* New Haven, Conn: Yale Univ. Press, 1968. See chap. 4, "The Struggle for the Real."

————. *The Religion of Java.* New York: The Free Press, 1960. A descriptive monograph by a noted anthropologist. Describes contemporary life in an actual place in east-central Java. Chapters which relate directly to this unit are: chap. 1, "The Slametan: Communal Feast as a Core Ritual"; chap. 2, "Spirit Beliefs"; chap. 7, "The Slametan Cycles: Calendrical, Village, and Intermittent Slametans"; chap. 8, "Curing, Sorcery, and Magic"; chap. 11, "The Development of Islam in Modjokuto"; chap. 16, "The Santri Ritual Pattern"; chap. 18, "The Role of Classical Art"; and chap. 22, "Conflict and Integration" (section entitled "Rijaja: The End of the Fast Holiday").

Moebirman. *Wayang Purwa: The Shadow Play of Indonesia.* The Hague, Nether.: Van Deventer-Maastichting, 1960. A description of the popular folk-art shadow theater of Indonesia—its origins, meaning, and artistic value.

Scott-Kemball, Jeune. *Javanese Shadow Puppets: The Raffles Collection in the British Museum.* London: Trustees of the British Museum, 1970. Many beautiful color plates. Describes the Javanese shadow plays as more than mere entertainment.

Stutterheim, William F. *Studies in Indonesian Archaeology.* The Hague, Nether.: Martinus Nijhoff, 1956. Because of Indonesia's period under Dutch rule, many studies of its culture have been done by Dutch scholars. This book is a translation of a selection from the work of the late Dr. W. F. Stutterheim, art historian and archaeologist, who exerted a revivifying influence on archaeological research in Indonesia.

Ulbricht, H. *Wayang Purwa: Shadows of the Past.* New York: Oxford Univ. Press, 1970. Accurate information and illustrations on Javanese shadow puppet plays as a religious art form.

The following instructional resources are listed in the teacher's guide:

Books

Bro, Marguerite Harmon. *How the Mouse Deer Became King.* New York: Doubleday, 1966. An illustrated series of adventures in which Kantchil, the folk hero of Indonesia, becomes king of the jungle.

Bulla, Clyde R. *What Makes a Shadow?* Paperback. Illustrated by Adams. New York: Ty Crowell, 1962. Easy-to-read picture book of shadows—their sources, different sizes and shapes—in terms young children will understand and enjoy.

Choudhury, Bani Roy. *The Story of Ramayan: The Epic Tale of India.* Thompson, Conn.: Inter-Culture, 1970.

Courlander, Harold, and Kane, Robert, *Kantchil's Lime Pit and Other Stories from Indonesia.* Illustrated by Robert Kane. New York: Harcourt, 1950. This is an unusual collection of folktales about wise and foolish men, rajahs, and heroes, animals of the forest, grassland, and river—and, most loved of all, Kantchil, the tiny mouse deer.

DeLeeuw, Adele. *Indonesian Legends and Folk Tales.* Illustrated by Ronni Solbert. Nashville, Tenn.: Nelson, 1961. The *kris* (sword), the growing of rice, the snakes, buffalo, water jars, and the mouse deer are all subjects of these stories, which are so much a part of Indonesia. Glossary with pronunciation appended.

Dolch, Edward W., and Dolch, Marguerite P. *Stories from India: Folklore of the World.* Illustrated by Gordon Laite. Champaign, Ill.: Garrard, 1961. "Young Rama," "Rama and Sita," and "Ravana, King of the Rakshasas" relate to this unit.

———, and Jackson, Beulah F. "The Maker of Puppets" in *Far East Stories.* Illustrated by Marguerite Dolch. Champaign, Ill.: Garrard, 1953. This story of an Indonesian puppet maker is written at the third-grade level.

Flagg, William, ed. *The Raffles Gamelan: A Historical Note.* London: Trustees of the British Museum, 1970. Photos of the percussion instruments used in the *gamelan.*

Guillaume, Jeannette, and Bachmann, Mary Lee. *Amat and the Water Buffalo.* Illustrated by Kurt Wiese. New York: Coward-McCann, 1962. Picture book of home, food, markets, and life of an Indonesian country boy. Glossary.

Joseph, Joan. *Folk Toys Around the World and How to Make Them.* Illustrated by Mel Furukawa. New York: Parents Mag. Press (in cooperation with the U.S. Committee for UNICEF), 1972. Provides a pattern and directions for making Javanese shadow puppets.

Kalish, Betty McKelvey. *Siti's Summer.* Illustrated by Ipe Maaroef. New York: Macmillan, 1963. Because her mother is ill and her father is in the army, Siti leaves her city home in Indonesia to live with her great-grandfather in a tiny village near the jungle. Woven into the story are Muslim customs and everyday life of the village. Intermediate-grade reading level, but the teacher might read excerpts.

Kimishima, Hisako. *The Princess of the Rice Fields: An Indonesian Folktale.* Illustrated by Sumiko Mizushi. New York: Walker-Weatherhill, 1971. Beautifully illustrated, this Indonesian folktale is about a princess of the sky who fell in love with a young rice farmer. Her irate father refused to permit her to marry her earthly lover, and changed them both into rice plants that "swayed and danced in the wind."

Klagsburn, Francine. *The First Book of Spices.* New York: Franklin Watts, 1968. Provides information about tasting and smelling activities with spices.

Meyers, Bernice. *Come Out Shadow Wherever You Are.* Englewood Cliffs, N.J.: Reader's Choice, Scholastic Book Serv., 1971. Delightful, instructive story of a boy's shadow and what happens to it as the day progresses.

Rao, Shanta Rameshwar. *The Children's Mahabharata.* Thompson, Conn.: Inter-Culture, 1968.

Taylor, Carl. *Getting to Know Indonesia.* Illustrated by Eleanor Mill. New York: Coward-McCann, 1961. Introduction to geography and history of Indonesia. Pronunciation glossary and chronology of Indonesian history.

Filmstrip

Religions Around the World. "Understanding Shintoism," "Understanding Islamism," "Understanding Buddhism," "Understanding Hinduism." Society for Visual Education, Chicago, Ill. Each of the four filmstrips (available with either records or cassettes) centers around the everyday life of an elementary-school-age child in a contemporary setting.

Record

Indonesia, Its Music and Its People. 33⅓ rpm recording. Desto Records.

Religion Studies
in Secondary Social Studies

Geraldine H. Rosenthal

For a knowledgeable social studies teacher, the field of religion is an automatic part of every social studies course taught. Religion is so intertwined with all facets of life that it is not necessary to search for connections—they present themselves constantly in the context of anthropology, economics, geography, history, political science, psychology, and sociology. This article provides a number of exemplary ways religion studies interrelates with the varied disciplines included in the social studies. Also, specific proposals are developed for American Government and American History courses. Finally, a World History course outline is presented in some detail. Before the actual *content* of possible studies is considered, I would like to touch on several issues related to the *context* in which religion studies may be included in the social studies.

THE CONTEXT FOR RELIGION STUDIES

The teacher's attitude is important in every subject taught. It is, however, even more crucial in teaching about religion, because religious affiliation and religious values reflect the basic core of the individual's philosophy and commitment. A teacher who disturbs the religious sensibilities of a student is striking at the very foundation of that student's personhood. The teacher presenting religion as an academic subject must therefore be scrupulously careful not to be judgmental about the religions studied. Although students may express distaste for various religious ideas or practices foreign to their own, the teacher must carefully neutralize such expressions. The job of the teacher is to present objectively the practices and overall viewpoint of the religion under consideration and to indicate the historic influences which shaped the religion's ideas. This is not to suggest that either the teacher or the student of academic religion studies cannot be firmly committed to his or her own religion. Both individuals who are ardent practitioners of their own religious faith and those who are adherents of no religion whatever can show respect for and understanding of the variety of religious expressions found in the human experience.

It is well to be honest, however, and to admit that the academic study of religion as espoused here will be disturbing to some students. They do not want an atmosphere in which all religions are considered equally. Acceptance of religions other than their own as valid is contrary to their religious beliefs. They want documentation that their own religious persuasion has all truth. It would not only be unsuccessful but also counterproductive to argue with this viewpoint on religious grounds. The only appropriate response to this position is an affirmation of our Supreme Court's prohibition of partisan indoctrination of religion in a public school setting but support for the study of religions' impact on society and the individual.

The social studies teacher is not in a position to develop a checklist of acceptable moral postures based on our religious heritage. Deeply religious people can be found on both sides of the abortion issue, family-planning, imbibing of alcoholic beverages, and so on. Needless to say, the class considers such topics when they are brought in by the students, but it does not attempt to answer them. The teacher must play the role of the devil's advocate, raising opposing arguments and alternative viewpoints if the students bring out only one side of an issue, always attempting to clarify and to expand the students' perception of the issue. The teacher needs to encourage students to develop respect for the legitimacy of differing interpretations of the religious conscience and to help them learn how to put their decision-making role as citizens within the context of separation of church and state. They must begin to wrestle with the question of which decisions are religious—to be made by the individual in private life, and which are civic—to be made by the body politic for all.

CONTENT FOR RELIGION STUDIES

Social studies in American education has come to be an all-inclusive term incorporating insights and methods from many academic disciplines. Therefore, many of the following ideas can be studied under a variety of course labels. How these topics are incorporated may be determined by the interaction of a variety of factors—the curricular-organizational pattern of a particular teacher. Thus, many of the ideas suggested in one of the sections to follow might be used under one rubric as well as another. Some topics might be utilized for student research topics or individualized learning projects. There is nothing sacred about subject matter separations: the goal of the teaching is to bring students into contact with the full richness of the religious dimension in human life.

A number of these ideas are presented below in the form of questions or issues. Questions do not, of course, make a curriculum. They are presented in this way in order to emphasize student involvement in analyzing and synthesizing data. Students are much more likely to understand the role of religion in human life if they must develop the avenues leading to this conclusion than if they are simply "told." Thus, the issues raised create problems which require the student to weigh the complexities of the issues in a process of personal reasoning.

Geography provides a number of opportunities to explore the interaction between physical circumstances and religious develop-ment. For example: What has been the geographical influence upon the routes of religious penetration and conquest? The role of the wastelands of Arabia as a barrier to the migrations of the patriarchs of Judaism and yet as an open door for the early efforts of Muhammad and his followers is a fascinating study of changing time and place. The high mountain passes of Asia were the conduits not only for armies but for religion; the watering holes of the Near East have shown modern archaeologists the routes of biblical adventure; the river valleys and sealanes of the European and Asiatic ecumene trace the development of religious migration.

Psychology, geography, and religion converge to deal with the question: What is the influence of geographic location upon religious inspiration? The impact of the Judean hills, the heights of the Sinaitic mountains, the sands of Arabia, and the forests of northern India on religious ideas might be discussed. Likewise, what is the effect of solitude in nature upon the individual religious genuis? What is the importance of the clash of cultures in the marketplace of ideas in trade centers upon the development of institutionalized religion? How do such diverse forces play against each other?

In economics, consideration can be given to the impact of the tax-exempt status of religious properties upon the tax base of local governments. What are local community attitudes toward such exemptions for houses of worship, the homes of clergymen, income-producing properties owned by religious bodies? What is the rationale for such tax exemption? What are community values regarding what should be taxed? What is the impact of such tax-exempt status on an urban metropolis like New York City? What is the thinking behind the decision by the national bodies of some religious groups to encourage their local affiliates to offer contributions to local governmental bodies in lieu of the taxes they are not assessed?

Economic systems are analyzed as making their decisions on the basis of tradition, command, the market, or some combination of such constructs. It is valuable to investigate the role of organized religion in communities functioning under these differing conditions. Do status and power stem from political, social, or economic position under these differing systems? What is the relationship of religious leadership to such decision-making groups? What influence do religious attitudes toward economic activity have upon the level of economic development in a society? What is the impact of economic development upon traditional religious values?

The interrelationship between economic success and religions provides a fertile area of study. What is the attitude of a religion toward the poor? Toward the wealthy? Does the religion indicate that economic inadequacy on the part of a family is a problem which should be responded to by governmental action, individual acts of charity, or group religious activity? Does the religion hold that economic competence is a sign of God's favor, a healthy economy, or personal ability? How have basic religious attitudes toward economic activity influenced economic development (not only the usual Protestant ethic of the West, but for example, India today)?

Religion is one of the five basic institutions studied in sociology. Every text in the field has a section on this topic. Several facets of study which can be fruitfully developed, however, have been largely ignored in the regular material. Is there a difference in the stability of families which are "religious" and those which are not? Is a religious family defined as one which has ties to organized religion, or one which sets normative religious values as its basic operating procedure or a combination of both?

Another avenue which can expand consideration of religion in sociology or anthropology is the cross-cultural approach. What have been the kinds of relationships of religion to government? Is religion more or less free, government more or less responsive to its citizens, under differing arrangements? (This will be considered more fully in the sections on government and history.) Quite apart from an analysis of how institutionalized religion is organized, how does it affect the daily relationships of individuals with each other and of groups with each other? May they eat together? Attend school together? Work together? Live next to each other? Marry each other?[1] Why do such taboos break down in urban, industrialized societies, yet remain strong in rural, handcraft societies? How do such phenomena contribute to the tension between urban and rural residents in technologically advanced societies? What stresses does it cause in technologically developing societies, such as the caste system is doing in India today?

Sociology and anthropology can also be used to analyze the relationship of the religious role to other areas of leadership. What is the pecking order of religious, military, political-social leadership in tribal societies and how does it apply to economic leadership in more complex societies, ancient and modern? How does it change when moving from a largely face-to-face society to one where anonymity is the norm?

The secondary school classroom can concern itself with the needs of humankind reflected in the presence of religion in every culture in the world, ranging from simple, tribal societies in which religion gives each person an assigned place, to complex, urban-industrial societies in which it provides each person with perhaps the only place where he or she is an individual apart from the mass. After the psychological and social needs fulfilled by religion have been delineated, they can be used as a checklist to analyze a variety of supposedly nonreligious value systems. For example, one of the great ironies of the contemporary world is that the officially atheistic, antireligious, political-economic-philosophical system known as "communism" has found it necessary to provide as its legitimizing authority sacred founders, sacred writings, a sacred place of pilgrimage, sacral communal experiences replete with pageantry centering on a sacred calendar, centers where the "revealed" dogma is taught, rules for achieving membership which are guarded by the already-elect, initiatory rites, and symbols of membership.

Government and religion offer many thought-provoking issues for study. What is the dynamic of the relationship between religion and government? Do American voters, either consciously or in their collective unconscious, identify with certain religious postures? Why the long history of conservatives fearing the nomination of a Roman Catholic for President or liberals fearing a practicing Southern Baptist as President? Why the widely held assumption that a Jew would add no strength to a national ticket which would not be more than offset by the weakness? Why is the Supreme Court decision on prayer and religious observance in public schools so widely ignored and even more widely resented? Why do some Americans believe it is necessary for all to share and participate in a common civil religion in school which is believed to provide the glue holding society together, while others believe Americans can owe allegiance to widely divergent religious traditions which are not celebrated in public schools, the glue holding society together being the protection afforded all by our constitutional safeguards?

In the study of government, many religious avenues can be explored. One possibility is to contrast the basic view of human nature inherent in a government based on the divine right of kings with one based upon the social contract. Another is to study the great political philosophers of the seventeenth and eighteenth centuries and to become familiar with their arguments for separation of church and state. This study leads directly to the background of the role of the First Amendment in establishing the right to personal privacy in many areas, including that of religion.

What is the dynamic tension in the relationship between church and state? How far may the state go in controlling individual religious beliefs and practices? Perhaps the most important arena of study for the secondary school student in a government course should be the watershed Supreme Court decisions relating to religious freedom. The First Amendment statement, "Congress shall make no law respecting an establishment of religion, or prohibiting the free exercise thereof," appears to serve as a double prohibition against positive and negative action by Congress. Some have thought this phrase was an absolute prohibition of any government action affecting religious life.

However, the *Reynolds* decision, the critical Mormon polygamy case of 1879, demonstrated that government can legislate in areas affecting religious life. The student must understand that because some religious practices threaten the accepted social fabric of our society (in this case marriage and the family), the Court must uphold the interest of the state as primary.

The flag salute cases of the Jehovah's Witnesses in 1940 and 1943, in which the Supreme Court reversed itself in the short span of three years, is another case in point. At a time when we as a nation were engaged in a contest for global survival, the issue of primary allegiance to God or Caesar was raised by the refusal of Jehovah's Witnesses to pledge allegiance to the flag, which they regarded as a public declaration of reverence for a material symbol. The decision of the Court honoring their religious position acknowledged the transcendence of religious commitment.

The most difficult decision for many teachers and students to understand was rendered in the twin cases of *Murray* and *Schempp* in 1963. Its study needs to be prefaced by a clarification of the question, Whom does the Bill of Rights protect? Not the majority, because the majority is presumed capable of protecting itself through the normal processes of democratic government. They do, after all, have the vote and social pressure on their side. The Bill of Rights, therefore, is to protect the minority from the majority. Both the *Murray* and *Schempp* cases exemplify this concept. In both cases children from religious backgrounds different from the prevailing religious views of their community were subjected to pressure to participate in school-sponsored and -sanctioned religious activities alien to their own belief. The point of the *Murray* and *Schempp* decision was that no government official has the right to prescribe a child's religious activity. The principle of separation of church and state must be upheld in the defense of the minority. Helping students who themselves are a part of the majority understand that this position ultimately serves the good of all is a sensitive and necessary task.

In American Government classes, the role of the courts is frequently studied through an examination of the Civil Rights movement. There are two ways in which this topic lends itself to the academic study about religion. The first emphasis is to make explicit the bases on which the great judges in our history have made their seminal decisions.[2] To encapsulate only too briefly: the plaintiff must convince the court that a contested action was illegal. The action may have been legal according to statute, but illegal according to the Constitution. The Constitution, of course, takes precedence over a statute. A state may pass a statute in a new area of law, and it may be challenged as unconstitutional. Its supporters contend that although it is not specifically mentioned, either by permission or prohibition in the Constitution, it is within our cultural-legal framework. The judges will then look to the common law of our Anglo-American heritage and previous judicial decisions for guidance. But what if this avenue is not sufficient for the jurists to use as bedrock? Then where do they look? To the moral law. It is to this moral law, stemming from the Judeo-Christian ethic undergirding Western civilization, that the justices of the Supreme Court of the United States looked when wrestling with the injustices of racial segregation. The specifics of overcoming these injustices are still in contention and will be for many years, perhaps another generation. But the illegality of segregation ultimately was determined on the basis of moral law.

A second approach is to investigate how the Civil Rights movement, after a century of failure, became the dominant motif in recent American life. The primary role of religious leadership is at once obvious. The issue, despite its political, economic, psychological, and social overtones, became a moral issue for the American people. This major movement in American history was dominated by leadership—ecumenical and both clerical and lay—which, in large part, identified itself as religiously inspired. A case study of the Civil Rights movement from this perspective can be most instructive as to the constitutionally permitted role of religion in American life.[3]

In a history course there are two basic approaches to the study of religion. One is to study a religion in terms of its own dynamics; the other is to study its influence upon the circumstances of life surrounding it and the impact of such circumstances on a particular religion or on religion generally. Both approaches are suggested here for World History, the second for United States History.

Every human institution has both positive and negative features. In an academic study of any social studies discipline, arguments on all sides of a question are investigated. It is hoped that the same would apply to the study of religious influence in American history.[4] This writer views United States history as the unfolding of ways to increasingly protect individual rights—political, economic, social, cultural, and religious. On the basis of this interpretation, the study of American history would be organized around competing trends toward elitism and toward democracy in all of American life. There have been similar competing trends in American religious history between authoritarianism and individualized expression. It would seem instructive for students to understand why the Puritans, as one example, feared religious individuality and how the American experience shifted the balance in favor of it. The colonial experience with official religion and its disenchantment with permutations of public control of religion; the contribution of the frontier church to the social as well as spiritual life of the people; the intellectual leadership of the clergy in the nineteenth century; the role of the church on both sides during the Civil War; the Christian Socialist movement around the turn of the century; the *pro forma* indentification of Americans as Catholic, Protestant, or Jewish in the twentieth century, accompanied by political, economic, and social expressions of religious bigotry; the role of the clergy in the Civil Rights movement; the War on Poverty; the anti-Vietnam involvement in the 1960s—all indicate the real influence of religion on questions of public morality in secular America. The questions could be raised: Why has American religion mobilized itself so well in fighting the aforementioned problems, but not those of family stability, crime, alienation? What does it mean for a society to be secular, considering the vast influence of religion on American life? Such investigations might help students understand how religion can or cannot operate in a free society. Such analysis would seem to bring young people to grips with religious questions in a way which is constitutionally permissible and personally productive. Finally, the Supreme Court decisions on religious practice in public schools should be given some attention.

The exemplary unit for a World History course which follows incorporates both the study of particular religions in terms of their own dynamics as well as a consideration of the interactive impact of religion and its cultural milieus.

INTRODUCTORY UNIT FOR WORLD HISTORY WITH EMPHASIS ON RELIGION

The writer of this article developed and taught a two-semester course in senior high school on World History with Emphasis on

Religion.[5] The textbooks which have begun to be offered in this field usually present the five or six or seven "great" religions of the world. (The value judgment made in such titles is open to serious question.) In the aforementioned course, however, the first nine weeks was spent on prehistory and the rise of civilization in the Tigris-Euphrates Valley. The study of religions no longer competing for adherents in today's world provides the most emotion-free atmosphere in which to learn how to analyze the reciprocal forces at play amongst political, economic, social, cultural, and religious developments. It was during this introductory quarter that students learned to apply Parts I and II of the following analysis.

Goals and Objectives

Although the teacher had firmly in mind what needed to be studied, Part I of the outline was developed the first day by each class brainstorming what it felt would be necessary for one to know about a religion in order to understand it. Each class worded the items somewhat differently, but as long as the same data and attitudes were explored, this made no difference. In some classes the teacher needed to suggest some of the items. It was made explicit that the religions would not be evaluated, either internally or against each other. It was stated that since religious commitment and attitudes are significant elements of a person's identity, every effort would be made to respect the sensibilities of all. Hence the goal was to understand the roles of religion in individual and corporate life and the variety of religious expression in the world.

After this first day, one, two, or three students might ask to transfer from the course; they wanted a study which would vindicate their personal religious beliefs and were unwilling to engage in an academic study of religion. They were, of course, helped to transfer. Even among those electing to remain in the course, frustration at the long history of religious development antedating Christianity was experienced. Many students do not have a historic sense of the origin, growth, and development of religions. The religious dimensions of their knowledge are bounded by their own church affiliation. They view human religious history as if it had begun shortly before Jesus, with a very short interval between Jesus' time and their own.

Content

I. Analysis of a religion.

    A. Complete, accurate, formal bibliography. Reflect as many points as possible.

    B. What was the central pillar from which all else developed? (What did the adherent get from belonging to the religion? What would the adherent have been denied if he or she had not been a member of the religion?)

    C. How did an adherent achieve the central pillar?

    D. How did the religion start? Why? What was the world like where it first grew? If there was a founder, what was the founder's personality and role?

    E. What were the holy writings?

        1. Written, revealed? Oral traditions?

        2. What did they say? (Class may decide on a partial list of items from the writings for which they will ascertain positions.)

    F. Were there sacraments?

    G. What were the ceremonies of the religion?

        1. Personal.

        2. Group.

        3. Daily, weekly, seasonal, yearly.

        4. At special times in life.

    H. What kinds of religious leadership did the religion have? How was the faith propagated?

        1. Priesthood: special powers.

        2. Medicine man or shaman: special knowledge.

        3. Teachers.

        4. Exemplars of behavior.

    I. What was the role of myth (a traditional story, authenticity not relevant) or magic (ritual to control the god)?

    J. How did this religion influence the culture of the people by whom it was practiced, and how did the culture (including other religions) influence the religion?

        1. Political.

        2. Economic.

        3. Social.

        4. Cultural: music, art, literature, dance, architecture, crafts.

K. How did the religion influence the daily life of its adherents?
1. Did it give emotional peace, a feeling of well-being (insisted upon by students as an item for study)?
2. Did it influence behavior toward other individuals or groups (insisted upon by the teacher)?
L. Where is the religion practiced today? By how many?
M. What was (is) the attitude of the religion toward members of other religions?
1. Actual belief.
2. Actual practice.
N. What changes have taken place in the religion during its history? (Students generally think of religion as static rather than dynamic.)
O. Anything else you consider to be of importance. (Students frequently show a real grasp of the religion when free to answer this item.)

II. Analysis of a problem in church-state relationships.
A. Complete bibliographical data in correct form. Reflect as many points of view in your sources as possible.
B. Relation of church and state.
1. Did the political leaders control the religious system?
2. Did the religious leaders control the political system?
3. Did the two systems work together without actual control by either? How?
C. General Atmosphere.
1. How much political, religious, artistic freedom was there?
2. How much social mobility or rigidity was there?
3. How much fundamental change in life was taking place through legal means?
4. How much fundamental change in life was taking place as a pragmatic response to changes in economic organization?
5. How much religious tolerance, acceptance, prejudice was exhibited in the society? In what way?
D. What was at stake in the church-state problem?
1. With what political-economic-social-cultural forces were the various antagonists aligned?
2. What political-economic-social-cultural advantage would accrue to the various antagonists by winning?

3. What would be denied them if they lost?
E. Effects: What happens when political-economic-social-cultural-religious powers are in the same hands?
  1. To the religious institutions, religious organizations, or individual members of a religion?
  2. To the quality of freedom in all areas of life?

Activities

The second day of class, the teacher developed Part II of the outline with each class and passed out a list of about thirty religions from which the students could choose their individual research projects. These would be presented to the class when it would be a normal part of study during the year. The branches of Islam, Hinduism, and Buddhism; religion in the Old-Middle-New Kingdoms of Egypt as well as the many other religions in the ancient world; religions of the American Indians and of people in the Orient and in tribal Africa and pre-European Latin America offered many possibilities for choice. If two or three students wanted to investigate the same religious branch, they were permitted to do so. Their written reports were graded for each item, A through O, and their class presentation was done as a panel: they took turns presenting those points on which they had done the best job. They all answered questions on the religion together and were also graded on how well they did in oral presentation and in answering questions. In some instances this revealed student knowledge not exhibited in written work.

Role-playing is a valuable tool for achieving insight into the motivation of others and the dynamics of group interaction. Because of the nature of the meaning of religious practice, however, students should not be asked to role-play religious ceremonies. They may, however, learn a great deal from role-playing under other circumstances, for example: an English, French, or German peasant, a clergyman, a nobleman, a merchant, or a papal representative during the Reformation. They may also be made aware of religious services they can attend and be taken as a class to visit the sanctuaries of many religious denominations.

In the classes under discussion here, the students visited six to eight churches and synagogues during an all-day field trip in the spring of the year. Forty-five minutes were allotted each religious institution visited. The institutions were chosen to give a historical sweep of what

131

was available in the community (Judaism, Roman Catholicism, Greek Orthodoxy, Lutheranism, and several others) and to present sanctuaries equally beautiful in architecture and clergymen equally knowledgeable as academicians of religion. A picnic lunch was taken and eaten on the grounds of one of the churches. All of the participating clergymen were given a copy of the total schedule, were told that we had already studied the historical development of their tradition, and were asked particularly to discuss (1) what they felt to be especially distinctive about their group to which they wished to draw attention and (2) their attitude toward social action as a religious group. Students had time to ask questions, were encouraged to take notes, and spent several days debriefing the field trip in class.

Every available medium was used to aid in teaching: art, film and filmstrip, slides, visiting specialists, lecture, discussion.

Students did not make reports on Judaism and Christianity (unless they wanted to do an extra written report for their own information) but studied them in class under the direction of the teacher. This was done for several reasons. One was to provide all students with the experience of studying a religion different from the overwhelming religious background of our country. This made possible an in-depth experience with thinking nominally outside the Judeo-Christian tradition. It was also felt that there could be so many imponderables of religious prejudice, self-justification, and competition among the students that such a procedure would lighten the emotional load of student-led discussion.

During the last month of the year, a member of the religion faculty of a local university, a scholar in the field of academic religious study, was asked to discuss "Contemporary Currents in Christianity" with each class.

Evaluation

During the year students were led to verbalize certain understandings which could be expected from the study undertaken. Testing included such understandings, and a few are included here as examples of the level of thinking engaged in.

1. Religious reformers appeal to the sanctity of returning to early traditions in the religion. (Concept: reform.)

2. Religious power, when held by political leaders, is used for political purposes. (Concept: power.)
3. All tradition, but especially religious tradition, can maintain the loyalty of its followers for centuries, even when the original purpose of the tradition is obscured by history. (Concepts: tradition, traditionalism.)

Sample test item: Religious reformers, in order to achieve support for their programs, usually place first emphasis in their appeal on: (1) the progressive spirit in a religion, (2) the inadequacy of present practice, or (3) return to the earlier, purer tradition.

At various times during the year students chose to do a report on a conflict in church-state relationships: Christianity and Rome, Russia and the Eastern Orthodox church, the Dreyfus affair, Mao's agricultural reform and ancestor worship, the *Kulturkampf* in Germany. The possibilities are endless.

During the first few days of every year, it was this writer's practice to share with students the basic value system which dictated the classroom organization, content, and teaching methods chosen. The students were advised to evaluate the teacher on the basis of this philosophy: every person's right to his or her own individuality is sacred and protected by the basic political doctrine of our country. Students were not required to subscribe to this position, but they were required to know the thinking supporting it and be willing to identify arguments supporting any competing philosophy which they wished to espouse. Making this value system explicit seemed to make the question of competing value systems irrelevant. Students were reassured by knowing what the teacher believed and by the fact that they were free to hold their own beliefs.[6] Students expected the teacher to answer questions as a proponent of whichever religion was under study at the time; as far as class work was concerned, there was no emotional investment in any one viewpoint. This was very important in building an understanding that every religion responds to the needs of its adherents and fits into its culture, and in creating respect for the validity of differing religious expressions.

The reward of such teaching is immediate: minds and hearts open to show respect for the dignity of humankind. The students take responsibility for orienting newcomers and visitors to the *modus operandi*. Religion achieves a place commensurate with its importance in the curriculum.

BIBLIOGRAPHIC CONCERNS

Identifying an appropriate bibliography poses several difficult problems. There is a wide range of reference sources for teachers, but materials for students have just begun to be published. In both kinds of materials the reader must be wary of a variety of pitfalls: use of terms such as "the Buddhist church" and "Mohammedanism," theology presented as history in early Christianity, great sensitivity displayed in some areas not matched by equal sensitivity in others, the posing of questions which become evaluative of the religion in question, unequal treatment of religions (glossing over contradictions in some faiths while drawing the attention of the students to contradictions in others), and the problem of which tradition is normative and best exemplifies a religion. These are generally more of a problem in the material published for students than in that suggested for teachers.

There are several other problems for the teacher to keep in mind. With the current emphasis on primary source data, there are frequently extended quotations from various scriptures. When taken out of context, the meaning and import of the material quoted are not always evident. Also, students should be exposed to at least three references when researching a single religion, to see firsthand how differently a religion is viewed by different eyes. Finally, the volumes written for high school students which are devoted totally to religion frequently lapse into vocabulary, syntax, and organizational style which are far beyond the capabilities of most of the students.

There has been no attempt to survey all materials available. The references included here are those the writer has found useful. There has been an attempt, however, to report on as many materials published for student use as the writer had access to. Some of the teacher references can be given to gifted students. There are very few audiovisual materials listed, as most of what has been seen did not meet the criterion of sensitivity to the concerns of members of the various religions: judgmental terms were used and the most exotic practices were emphasized. The bibliography has been prepared for both the novice and the experienced teacher about religion. For the beginning teacher in this field, the books asterisked (*) will provide sufficient information of themselves without requiring the reading in scholarly material indicated elsewhere. This in no way impugns the scholarship of the works so indicated: they are just easier to take in large doses by the social studies teacher who is unfamiliar with the language and approach of the field of academic religion.

Two references which are not specifically related to religion studies have been included at the end of the teacher's bibliography because of their general helpfulness in the field.

Teachers References

Breasted, James Henry. *Development of Religion and Thought in Ancient Egypt.* Harper Torchbook. New York: Harper & Row, 1959. Pre-Old Kingdom to the Roman Empire. Includes influence of and on others. Relatively easy reading except for primary quotations. Good material for social studies.

Burtt, Edwin, A. *Man Seeks the Divine: A Study in the History and Comparisons of Religions.* New York: Harper & Row, 1970. Part I: How Religion Outgrows Its Primitive Forms. Part II: The Religions of the East. Part III: The Religions of the West. Scholarly style.

Contenau, George. *Everyday Life in Babylon and Assyria.* Paperback. The Norton Library. New York: Norton, 1966. Divided into four chapters, one of which is "Religious Life." Between adult and scholarly writing style.

Gersh, Harry. *The Sacred Books of the Jews.* New York: Stein & Day, 1968. A not-too-difficult introduction to the Bible; Prophets; wisdom literature; Talmud; Midrash; Commentaries; Responsa; philosophy, mysticism, and liturgy of Judaism. Good appendixes.

Gurney, O. R. *The Hittites.* Baltimore: Penguin Books, 1961. Paperback. Eight chapters, of which one is on religion. Between adult and scholarly writing style.

Hays, H. R. *In the Beginnings; Early Man and His Gods.* New York: Putnam's, 1963. Paleolithic Europe, the Near East, Neolithic to Iron Age, Asia, Africa, the Pacific, the Americas. Preliterates in history and today. Scholarly style.

James, E. O. *The Ancient Gods.* New York: Putnam's, 1960. Deals with the Near East, including: the Mother Goddess, sacral kingship, festivals, cosmology, Cult of the Dead, divination, astrology, prophecy, and the diffusion of these influences beyond the area in which they arose. Scholarly style.

McCants, Billie Lee. *School Prayers as Symbolic Acts of the Civil Religion.* Unpublished Ed.D. dissertation at the University of Tulsa. 170 pp. Very helpful analysis of the role of civil religion in American life and the differing personality needs of those who subscribe to the hegemonic and cultural-pluralism models.

*McNeill, William H. *The Rise of the West: A History of the Human Community.* Chicago: University of Chicago Press, 1970. Available hardback or paperback. Despite the title, includes the Orient, Africa, and Latin America. Not a history but an interpretation of history for the reader already familiar with history. Outstanding attention given to religion as a part of the total civilization.

Mircea, Eliade. *Images and Symbols: Studies in Religious Symbolism.* Translated by Philip Mairet. New York: Sheed & Ward, 1969. Part I: Symbolism of the "Centre."

Part II: Indian Symbolism of Time and Eternity. Part III: The "God Who Binds" and the Symbolism of Knots. Part IV: Observations of the Symbolism of Shells. Part V: Symbolism and History. Scholarly style.

————.*The Sacred and the Profane.* Translated by Willard Trask. New York: Harcourt, 1968. Includes topics such as sacred time, sacred space, sacrality of water. Scholarly style.

*Noss, John B. *Man's Religions.* 5th ed. New York: Macmillan, 1974. Good historical approach; shows where a religion came from and the influence of the religion on history. Part I: Primitive and Bygone Religions. Part II: The Religions of India. Part III: The Religions of the Far East. Part IV: The Religions of the Near East.

Parrinder, Geoffrey. *Religions in Africa.* Paperback. Baltimore: Penguin Books, 1969. Traditional religions, Christianity, Islam, and a short concluding section which deals with other religions and interpretation of the African religious scene. Includes effects of social and political events on religious development. Relatively easy adult reading.

Renou, Louis, *Hinduism.* Paperback. New York: Washington Sq. Press, 1961. Forty pages of an overview of Hinduism, 175 pages of selected textual material. The latter includes selections from the major Sanskrit sources, and from non-Sanskrit sources which bring Hindu religious thought up to modern times.

Schoeps, Hans-Joachim. *The Religions of Mankind: Their Origin and Development.* Paperback. Anchor Book. New York: Doubleday, 1966. Translated from the German. The science of religion, extinct religions outside of Europe, extinct religions within Europe, the great religions of the East, the religions of biblical revelation. Section on holiness, mana, taboo, sacred kingship particularly helpful to social studies teachers. Relatively easy adult reading.

Smith, Homer W. *Man and His Gods.* Boston: Little, Brown, 1956. From Neolithic time through contemporary satanism, evolution, problems within Christianity. Interestingly written.

Smith, Huston. *The Religions of Man.* New York: Harper & Row, 1958. Chapters on eight specific religions. Adult writing but interesting enough to be given to the serious high school student.

Williams, J. Paul. *What Americans Believe and How They Worship.* rev. ed. New York: Harper Bros., 1962. Practical. Shows how beliefs influence the practice and organization of religion. Makes clear the differences among many Christian groups and within Judaism. Easy to read.

Wright, Conrad. *Religion in American Life: Selected Readings.* Paperback. Boston: Houghton, 1972. From the colonial period through "recent tendencies"; synthesizing introductions to primary sources which enable the teacher to pick and choose the material desired.

Zaehner, Robert Charles, ed. *The Concise Encyclopedia of Living Faiths.* New York: Hawthorn Books, 1958. Small print. Philosophical. Interesting introduction and conclusion. Religions treated under two headings: I. Prophecy, II. Wisdom. Scholarly style.

Teaching Methods

Sanders, Norris M. *Classroom Questions: What Kinds.* Paperback. New York: Harper & Row, 1966. Of great help in developing skills in asking questions requiring more than recall.

A Strategy for Teaching Values. "First Things" series. Pleasantville, N. Y.: Guidance Assoc. Two cassettes, three filmstrips. Outstanding discussion guide. Can be used alone or for faculty training. Based on work of Lawrence Kohlberg. Prepared for primary-grade teachers but applicable to secondary.

Student Materials

Bach, Marcus. *Had You Been Born in Another Faith.* Englewood Cliffs, N.J.: Prentice-Hall, 1961. Hindu, Parsee, Buddhist, Confucianist, Shintoist, Jewish, Muslim, Roman Catholic, Protestant. Gives some sense of what is done in the religion as well as what is believed. Suggested for library.

Dicks, Stewart; Mennill, Paul; and Santor, Donald. *The Many Faces of Religion: An Inquiry Approach.* Paperback. Canada: Ginn, 1973. 311 large pages. Attractive format. Pictures, charts, maps. High reading level but short, interesting readings followed by questions at all levels of the taxonomy. Explores major branches and present practices of Hinduism, Buddhism, Judaism, Christianity, Islam. Concluding chapter includes astrology, witchcraft and magic. Baha'i. Material is not included to answer all the questions asked; requires knowledgeable teacher, much student research, or visiting specialists. Prepared for Canadian schools, so a number of examples refer to Canada. Developed to be used as a class set.

Evans, Allan S.; Moynes, Riley E.; and Martinello, Larry. *What Man Believes: A Study of the World's Great Faiths.* Paperback. Toronto: McGraw-Hill Ryerson, 1973. 402 large pages. Attractive format. Pictures, maps, charts, symbols. Includes the nature of religion, origin of religion, religions of the ancient world, Eastern religions, Western religions, contemporary trends in religion. Classical, traditional approach. Tries to put college-level course in senior high terms. Includes very interesting stories as examples of what is presented. Chapters, which are essentially minilectures, followed by questions at all levels of the taxonomy. Prepared for Canadian schools, so includes study of over a dozen Christian sects in Canada (analogous to those in the United States). Developed for use as a class set but can also be used for individual reference.

Gaer, Joseph. *What the Great Religions Believe.* New York: Dodd, 1963. Easy, popular style. Suggested for the library.

Guttmann, Allen. *God and Government: The Uneasy Separation of Church and State.* Paperback. The Amherst Project. Menlo Park, Calif.: Addison-Wesley, 1972. Forty-seven pages. Original sources with conflicting viewpoints on (1) prayer in schools, (2) Catholic attitudes toward the relationship of church and state, (3) tax support of parochial schools. High reading level of last two topics too difficult for most students.

Hayes, Carlton J. H., and Hanscom, James H. *Ancient Civilization: Prehistory to the Fall of Rome.* 1968. Soft cover. 512 pages.

————, and Clark, Frederick F. *Medieval and Early Modern Times: The Age of Justinian to the Eighteenth Century.* 1966. Soft cover. 491 pages.

————, and Faissler, Margaret. *Modern Times: The French Revolution to the Present,* 1965. Soft cover. 522 pages. These three volumes make up the "Mainstreams of Civilization" series, New York: Macmillan. They are of high quality in every area of social studies. They are more sensitive to the need for including religion than many high school history texts, and do so in a scholarly manner. Volume I, in particular, does an outstanding job. Unlike other texts, it gives Judaism and Christianity more than a few sentences. It treats them as it does other religions, as a part of history. Volume III has the least amount of material for religion. Good enough to use as a class set for general introduction.

National Council for the Social Studies. JUDGMENT: *Bible Reading and Prayer in Public Schools.* 1965. Eight-page pamphlet of terminology, background, arguments, decision, and dissents in the *Schempp* case. Four pages of extra material for the teacher. Excellent presentation of opposing viewpoints.

Nigosian, S. A. *World Religions.* Paperback. Evanston, Ill.: McDougal, 1976. 190 small pages. Section on Zoroastrianism has more information than most. Other sections are difficult reading for high school. Suggested for library.

Oliver, Donald W., and Newman, Fred M. *Religious Freedom.* Middletown, Conn.: Xerox, 1967. Forty-seven-page pamphlet. Suggest starting with "Trouble at Camp Lone Pine." Senior high.

Ratcliffe, Robert H., Ed. *Great Cases of the Supreme Court.* "Trailmarks of Liberty" series. Boston: Houghton, 1971. Five cases on "Freedom of Belief" (two of which are the same as in title below). High junior high reading level.

————. *Vital Issues of the Constitution.* Rev. ed. Paperback. "Trailmarks of Liberty" series. Boston: Houghton, 1975. Includes five cases on "Freedom of Belief" which have been important in our history from 1659 to 1970. Background is given for each case and then the case itself, including arguments. Questions at various levels of the taxonomy follow. The class can role-play the Supreme Court. Decisions are given separately in a "Decisions" supplement. Senior high reading level.

Snyder, Louis L. *The Making of Modern Man: From the Renaissance to the Present.* Princeton, N.J.: Van Nostrand, 1967. 742 pages. Outstanding text for social studies. Includes data for handling questions of church-state relationships. Limited mostly to European history. High school reading level.

Sociological Resources for the Social Studies. *Religion in the United States.* "Episodes in Social Inquiry" series. Paperback. Thirty-seven pages. For two weeks of study on (1) the extent of organized religion in the United States and (2) the influence of religion in our society. Extensive teacher's guide. High school.

Spivey, Robert A.; Gaustad, Edwin S.; and Allen, Rodney F. *Religious Issues in American Culture.* "Issues in Religion" series. Paperback. Menlo Park, Calif.: Addison-Wesley, 1972. 165 pages. Quotes heavily from original documents, weaving them into a narrative of critical questions in American religious life from the earliest settlements through contemporary problems of an increasingly vocal and expanding pluralistic religious community. Creative activities. Questions at all

138

levels of the taxonomy, with data provided to answer. Very extensive teacher's guide. Would be a valuable book to use in teacher education.

———. *Religious Issues in Western Civilization.* Second of three volumes in the above series. 256 pages. Investigation of religious values and priorities in Babylonian, Greco-Roman, Jewish, and Christian (seven studies) religious history. Detailed teacher's guide. Level of thought required appropriate for gifted students or college-level work. A real effort has been made in these volumes to go beyond the content available in regular high school social studies texts.

———. *Religious Issues in World Cultures.* Third in the series. 270 pages. Eight studies in world cultures beginning with "What is Religion," leading to studies of Islam, Hinduism, Confucianism and modern China, Buddhism in Burma, Japan's old and new religions, Latin America's social revolution, and Eastern and Western conceptions of nature. Original sources and questions for thought are particularly helpful.

Starr, Isidore. *The Supreme Court and Contemporary Issues.* Paperback. Chicago: Encyc. Brit. Educ., 1969. Forty-three-page unit on "Separation of Church and State." Well written, including reasons for majority and dissenting opinions.

Welty, Paul Thomas. *Man's Cultural Heritage: A World History.* rev. ed. Philadelphia: Lippincott, 1969. 642 pages. Excellent world history treating each part of the world from its ancient history to the present time in one section. Particularly sensitive to and aware of religion in history. Accompanying paperback includes selections from the scriptures of the religions, religious movements, and events studied.

———. *Readings in World Cultures.* Philadelphia: Lippincott, 1970. Paperback. Both text and readings are at the level of the average student but are interesting enough for all.

The World's Great Religions. New York: Time Inc., 1957. Hinduism, Buddhism, China, Islam, Judaism, Christianity. Pictures in color. Adult writing, especially in introduction, but interesting. Covers salient points and includes some philosophy. Suggested for library.

Recording: William O. Douglas, *The Bible and the Schools.* CMS Records, Inc., 14 Warren St., New York, N.Y. 10007.

16mm film: *The Schempp Case: Bible Reading in Public Schools.* B/W or color, 35 min. Chicago: Encyc. Brit. Introduction and conclusion by Robert Maynard Hutchins above most high school students, acting overdone, characterization stereotyped, but valuable nevertheless to give students a feel for the problem.

NOTES

1. The relationship of such taboos to racial differences are obvious. Exploration of the psychological and sociological constructs underlying both sets of attitudes can be undertaken. The teacher should be prepared to handle the questions of whether the eradication of racial differences by intermarriage is a desired good or whether the

blurring of religious differences is a desirable good. Students should know that there is no agreement on answers to these questions. Some people believe that the biological differences of race are culturally irrelevant and that there is no reason to perpetuate racial differences to safeguard the survival of differing cultural traits, while some militant leaders of minority and majority racial groups, for a variety of reasons, believe it necessary to cultural pluralism or to cultural "purity" to continue biological separation of the races. On the other hand, except for those holding the view that all individuals should and can join their own particular religious persuasion, there is widespread belief that differing religious traditions emphasize different insights, all of which are of value to the human experience and which, therefore, should be kept alive.

2. The writer is indebted to a little book by the great conservative, Justice Benjamin Cardozo, for stimulating this line of thought.

3. For gifted students, teachers might ask for some thinking correlating what de Tocqueville had to say about the role of voluntarism in American life in solving problems usually dependent upon government initiative in other cultures with the leadership role of the religious person in the Civil Rights movement.

4. In addition, when field-testing material organized around evaluating religions according to an introductory definition, it was found that the students felt stifled.

5. This was part of an overall departmental restructuring which also offered such a course with emphasis on Africa, Latin America, Asia, Greece and Rome, or Europe.

6. Study of evolution offered no problem. Material was always submitted "according to the paleoanthropologist" or "according to Scripture as the revealed word of God."

Jewish Studies in the Social Studies

Rika Zimmerman

> The laws of Moses as well as the laws of Rome contributed suggestions and impulse to the men and institutions which were to prepare the modern world; but if we could but have the eyes to see the subtle elements of thought which constitute the gross substance of our present habit, both as regards the sphere of private life and as regards the action of the State, we should easily discover how very much besides religion we owe to the Jew.[1]

The history of the Jews is inseparable from that of the West. Logically therefore, the history and thought of the Jewish people who have made contributions to Western civilization should be an integral part of the school's curriculum. Moreover, the majority of our students come from Christian backgrounds. An affiliation with the church, even if tenuous, may introduce the young person at the very least to such terms as Jews and Israel, as well as to a few of the main characters and stories of the Old Testament. For Christians, Judaism is an essential component of their religious heritage.

> Christianity, whether it wants it or not, by its very nature, is bound to take a stand on the question of Judaism . . . because its New Testament implies the existence of an Old Testament, because its founder and all its first disciples were Jews, because it was once a part of Judaism.[2]

Therefore, it appears that some understanding of Jews and of Judaism would be important for our students.

We speak of the Judeo-Christian ethic of our culture, but few are familiar with the Judaic part of the ethic, or indeed with the differences between the two respective components. We still often hear and read the quotation of the ruthless law of "An eye for an eye" as though it were a current Jewish ethical teaching. Very few non-Jews know or teach that this saying was interpreted some two thousand years ago by the Pharisees in a reasonable, compassionate, and thorough manner to mean requirement of an equivalent payment for damages.

Another common misconception has been the portrayal of Judaism as an old, senselessly exacting, law- and obedience-oriented religion devoid of love. Listening to the lyrics of the popular musical, *Jesus Christ: Superstar,* do we not even today hear about "a *new* command, that we should love our fellow man" or that the "Temple should be a house of prayer and [not] a den of thieves"? Both of these ideas expressed by Jesus were a reflection of the Pharisaic revolution going on within Judaism during his lifetime.

The contemporary reference which follows is one of many to be found in scholarly writings exemplifying the misconceptions still existent: "Of the two major roots of Western culture, the Hebraic and the Greek, in the former there was relatively little respect for reason, man's overriding duty being to obey the commands of God."[3]

These misrepresentations demonstrate a persistent ignorance of major developments which shaped Judaism during the Pharisaic period and in later years. For the vast majority of our populace, understanding of Jewish ethics is based on the limited frame of reference of the Bible, that is, Judaism as it is presented in the Old and New Testaments and in later Christian theology. Thus, in the earlier instance, the understanding is derived from a view of Judaic thought at a particular stage of development which does not accurately reflect the major shifts in emphasis in later years. In the second and third instances, the source is secondhand interpretation of Jewish thought for its own purposes rather than an attempt to present Jewish thought within its own context. As a consequence of the general societal misunderstanding of the Judaic heritage, we are deprived of an acquaintance with a rich, ongoing, varied religious tradition which, in its own way, has raised fundamental questions and has offered insight into the human condition.

There are many possible ways to study the rich and abundant material available on Jews and Judaism. The utilizable approaches are multiple since the Jewish people are not a monolithic group professing a single religious doctrine. Rather, they are a diverse people with a complex history and different sets of beliefs who share a sense of a common fate. Thus the avenues for study suggested here are not intended to be regarded as the "correct" ways, the only ways, or even the accepted ways to view Jews and Judaism. Rather, several disciplinary approaches can be employed, as indicated below.

A cross-cultural analysis leads to some interesting insights into human development. One can compare the cultural achievements of biblical societies with their counterparts in the ancient Near East. The Mosaic Law can be compared to Hammurabi's Code, and the story of Noah and the Flood to the Babylonian epic of Gilgamesh. Archaeological and geological findings can be introduced to further substantiate and explain the chronicled events. The Egyptian idea of monotheism introduced during the reign of Pharaoh Akhenaten can be examined in relation to the monotheism of Moses and the Hebrews at the time of the Exodus. The similarities and the differences between the Jewish experience and its Egyptian counterpart can be analyzed. Biblical stories can be treated as windows to the cultures of the time. They can be viewed as a repository of historial experiences and subsequent societal developments. They can also be compared with concepts and beliefs dominant in our contemporary society. Here again the unique, the particular, the different will clearly be seen; but so, too, will the commonality.

This very early period can also be taught as a basis for understanding the ties which have bound the Jewish people to the land of Israel. The Covenant and the special meaning the land assumed in the relationship between God and the people, and the ideas which have thrived in Judaism down through the millennia, find their first expression in the Bible. Further insight into these ties can be found in Jewish literature throughout the centuries. The Talmud, the Midrash, the Jewish prayerbook, and medieval poetry are but a few examples of sources which shed light and reveal the extent of the ties between the people, the culture, and the land. What was the impact of the ancient Covenant on this relationship? How do the sayings of the talmudic sages explain it? How was the loss of Jewish sovereignty and independence in 70 C.E.* explained by the people? What role did the idea of messianic redemption play? Why and how has the trauma of the fall of Masada and of the watershed rebellion of a small people against an overwhelming superpower in the year 135 C.E. echoed through the

---

*C.E.=Common Era. Time frame parallels the Gregorian calendar.

143

consciousness of the people into our very time? What meaning does the Israeli statement of belief and hope, "Again Masada shall not fall," have to the student of Jewish and Israeli realities? What is the relationship between these events and ideas and their resulting cultural developments? How does the collective traumatized memory of a people that has experienced two thousand years of persecution, which reached its infamous zenith in the Holocaust (the persecution under Hitler, which led to the destruction of six million Jews), affect its actions and reactions? One could hardly expect to understand a movement such as political Zionism without taking cognizance of its historical backdrop and the old religiocultural unity it reflects. Certainly politics in the Middle East today could be better understood in light of the composite, intertwined melange of historical events and cultural developments.

The historical approach must be utilized when the Holocaust is studied since it cannot be understood except against the background of the long centuries of anti-Semitism and persecution suffered by the Jews. Even then the Holocaust can be taught and examined in many different ways. The questions stirred by the murder of six million Jews have produced some unique answers that illuminate the meaning of life. Viktor Frankl, a famous psychiatrist and survivor of the death camps, tells us that an individual should "realize that it is not up to him to question—it is he who has to answer, by answering for life";[4] that is, for the quality of the individual's own life even in the concentration camp itself. What were some of the answers given by ordinary persons as well as by the sophisticated in the camps? What can we learn about humanity from the captors and the captives alike? How far does one's responsibility for another go? The questions are indeed endless, and the answers are not easy to come by.

What impact has the Holocaust had on Jews and on Christians? Certainly the reaction of the Jewish community both in Israel and the Diaspora (the Jewish community outside Israel) to nearly all subsequent events concerning Jews is conditioned by this unbelievable trauma. But its effects are felt in Christian thinking and attitudes as well. These emerging thoughts and attitudes, these questions asked, will affect our thinking and can be investigated by students.

There is no parallel to Jewish history in the annals of humankind. Scattered and persecuted for almost two thousand years, the people developed and held onto a culture and to a dream of returning to their homeland. Where did the dream of returning originate? How did it come to hold sway over the people for such a long time? How did the people survive as a people? How is it that their culture survived so long? Each one of these questions can be developed into a separate unit with a number of approaches.

The exemplary unit of study provided here attempts to examine the development of Jewish ethical thought in its seminal period. Father John T. Pawlikowski observed that "all branches of modern Judaism, despite their often profound differences, have their origins in Pharisaism which, practically speaking, was the sole form of Judaism to survive the war with Rome in the first and second centuries A.D."[5] It was in the period of approximately 200 B.C.E.* to 300 C.E. that Judaism experienced an intellectual ferment and Pharisaism gained dominance. Christianity was born of this ferment. It was formed in an intellectual atmosphere which witnessed the encounter between the Hellenic and Judaic traditions and philosophies on the one hand and the surrounding cultures of the time on the other. Both Judaism and Christianity accepted some ideas from the prevailing intellectual climate, and rejected or modified others. The Pharisees, the rabbis who compiled the Halachah, Haggadah, Midrash, Mishnah, and finally the Talmud (which incorporates these materials) were the moving force behind these developments in Judaism. A brief introduction to the Pharisees, their philosophy, and their literature provides a background for the resource unit which follows.

BACKGROUND INFORMATION ON THE PHARISEES

By approximately the second century B.C.E., the foundations of Jewish civilization were consolidated. The written Torah, the Laws of Moses, was accepted as the supreme authority of the people and was studied intensively. However, as early as the third century B.C.E. it became apparent that if, indeed, the Torah were to serve as a definitive guide for Jews, it would need interpretation and an expansion of its scope. The Torah needed to be interpreted, as is our Constitution. It provided the guidelines for the interpreters, who interpreted it in the spirit of the Law. From the Torah new laws were derived, and old ones were adapted to the new needs of the time.

---

* B.C.E.=Before Common Era.

145

Through the device of the Oral Torah, the Pharisees were able to free Israel from the letter of the past and find an open way into new futures, while simultaneously making it their intention to preserve every jot and tittle of that past itself.[6]

The society for which these laws were written and which they reflect was in its early stages of development. Some laws reflect an agricultural society whose concepts could not meet the needs of a developing urban and commercial society. For instance, how much would the more affluent have to give to be considered charitable? How should charity be given? Should donor and recipient be known to each other? What actions would constitute an expression of honor accorded to a mother and a father? To what length would one be obligated to go in order to fulfill this injunction? How should the cancellation of all debts during the Jubilee Year (Lev. 10:43) be handled legally and morally? Practically speaking, why would anyone consider lending money on the forty-ninth year knowing the debt would be canceled? How could one reconcile the injunction not to lend money on interest with the realities of a commercially developed society? Similarly, the Torah did not address all the possible problems encountered by the people of its time, let alone future generations living in changing times. Many *minhagim* (customs) developed, but which ones were to be accepted as congruent with the spirit of the Law?

The Pharisees built on the ethics of Sinai and the prophets which they found lacking in specificity. They expanded the role religion played in people's daily lives. They expounded on the ideas of justice as well as social and personal responsibility. They deepened the meaning of the Torah beyond the framework of its laws and its historical accounts in the direction of loving-kindness *(chesed)*. This idea of loving-kindness in human behavior was brought into daily actions through concrete examples and guidelines. God's loving-kindness was also perceived in history. The rabbis applied thoughtful analysis to historical events and to questions concerning the origin and goal of the world as well as to the most secular, trivial, ordinary daily actions of human beings. This interpretation not only helped organize the community life around a legal system and a world view in accord with a few basic principles, but it also afforded every person the opportunity to know how to apply these same principles in every conceivable facet of life. These precepts and deeds became the essence of a people's culture. No longer were the priests, who still fostered sacrificial practices, the leaders of religious activity. The Pharisees succeeded in democratizing religion. According to the Pharisaic vision, every individual—and hence the people—was to live as a kingdom of priests.

The Pharisees postulated that the Temple should be everywhere. Instead of an altar for atonement and purification, daily life must be purified. Quoting the Torah, the rabbis noted that the injunction, "You shall be unto Me a kingdom of priests and a holy nation" (Exod. 19:6), could be achieved through the way a person treated self and fellow human beings—through the manner in which one conducted one's life. Succinctly stated, this was the mission of the individual and the group. The idea of peoplehood and the responsibility of the individual to the group, through which the idea could be perpetuated and manifested and in which the tradition could live, was the focal point of Pharisaic philosophy and became the pivotal idea in Judaism.

Through their studies the rabbis arrived at, and left as a legacy to the people, broader concepts of God, humanity, life, history, and the universe. They expressed their feelings about God through the new names which they introduced to describe him: Our Father in Heaven; the Compassionate One, the Loving One; Omnipresent. Humans were perceived born free of sin, free and full of opportunities. Within them they were believed to carry a good inclination (*yetzer hatov*) and an evil inclination (*yetzer hara*). Both impulses were acknowledged and accepted as part of the human condition. They were viewed as part of the holy scheme: both impulses are good when regulated. The rabbis preferred a systematic and orderly consideration of the principles by which one must act. For them "the moot issue [was] not how to repress, but how to reshape, the primal energy."[7] This control and shaping process could be achieved through a continuous intellectual analysis which places doubt as its hallmark, but commits itself to making decisions (no matter how hard the choices and how varied the opinions are), lest paralysis set in. To the rabbis, then, the intellect was to be used "not in search, but in the service of God."[8]

When the Temple was destroyed and the revolts against Rome—which the Pharisees opposed—failed, it was the Pharisees, with their expanded world view, who stood ready to help their people and their religion adapt to the new situation. The rabbis and the synagogue replaced the priests and the Temple. Acts of loving-kindness, study, and prayer, which had been developing as the central themes of Judaism, supplanted the old ritualistic aspect of the religion and the culture.

This new form of Judaism, founded by the Pharisees, became a portable culture which could be transplanted from land to land and which continued to unite the people in far-flung parts of the world for some two thousand years. The Torah became the constitution on which Jews built. It could evolve without becoming petrified by dogma. The synagogue became the center of the people's life and activities; in it the study of the written Torah (the Hebrew Bible) and the oral Torah (the Talmud) and the perpetuation of the culture, the tradition, and the people took place. Here were kept alive the individual and collective hopes of redemption, a return to the homeland, a rebuilding of the kingdom of David, the coming of a Messiah and a messianic age. Here the laity, no less than the clergy, strived to become a holy kingdom of God. Here through learning were expounded righteous ways of life according to a specific code of conduct. According to this code, various other institutions of self-government were developed.

THE MISUNDERSTOOD PHARISEES— THEIR VIEW OF LIFE AND HUMANITY

This unit of study introduces students to the historical and cultural milieus in which Judaism was undergoing a process of revolutionary and far-reaching change. The unit examines the period of 200 B.C.E. to 300 C.E., the 500-year time span including the two centuries before the advent of Christianity and the subsequent three centuries. While emphasizing the development of Pharisaic Judaism, the study attempts to provide perspective for the significant development of both Christianity and Judaism during this period.

Through a study of the sayings of the Pharisaic rabbis, the students become acquainted with the ethics and world view of Judaism at the time. This introduction to Judaic thought, coupled with a cursory examination of Greek philosophy, affords the students a better understanding of both Judaism and Christianity's background. Comparison of Pharisaic sources with other contemporary literature of the period, including the New Testament, offers insight into humanity's moral and ethical development. Within the material,

148

values which were accepted and transferred into our American life through the Judeo-Christian influence are noted.

It is hoped that the learning experience fosters the idea of human brotherhood within the framework of individual and group differences. The quotations used introduce many values throughout the unit. Thus this unit can serve not only as a lesson in history and a guide to understanding Judaism and the Jewish people but also as an opportunity for reflection and an investigation of private and social values.

This unit is intended for high school students of average to above-average ability. A period of approximately four weeks is required for its implementation. The unit can be expanded for use over a longer period of time.

Content

GENERALIZATIONS AND SUPPORTING SUBJECT MATTER

I. Every society adapts its own system of beliefs, knowledge, values, traditions, and skills, which make up its culture according to the needs of the times.
    A. Pharisaic democratization of religion; the opportunity to achieve the highest levels of religious expression open to all, not just to the priests
       1. Priestly conduct in daily life for everyone
          a) Acts of loving-kindness
          b) Prayer
          c) Study
       2. Leadership in the community attained through the study of the Torah
    B. Freedom of choice between good and evil in the hands of the individual
    C. The responsibility of the individual to the group
    D. The responsibility of the group to implement and perpetuate its ideals
    E. Eschatology—views concerning a Messiah and hopes for a messianic era
    F. The centrality of the Land of Israel

II. The decisions, policies, and laws that have been made for a given society are reflected in, and are based on, the values, beliefs, and

149

traditions of that society. In the Pharisaic revolution (the Sadducees vs. the Pharisees) these values, etc., revealed themselves as follows:

Pharisees	*Sadducees*
1. Acts of loving-kindness	1. Duties connected with the Temple cult
2. Prayer; repentence	2. Sacrifice
3. Equality of the people	3. Separateness of the priests
4. Study of the Torah, a privilege of all the people	4. The priests as the keepers of the tradition
5. Moral and religious influence exerted by the rabbis and the people	5. Political and religious influence in the hands of the priests

III. Changes in economic developments cause changes in life-styles and customs. A society must continuously evaluate and modify its culture to adjust to changing conditions.
   A. The oral Torah—a response to change
      1. Change from a simple agricultural society to a more complex commercial society
      2. Loss of the Temple as the center for religious activity
      3. The synagogue—the new center for religious activity
         a) House of study
         b) House of prayer
         c) Focal point of community activity
            i)   Meeting place
            ii) Organizational center—charity, social welfare
   B. The loss of independence
      1. Messianic hopes
      2. Yohanan ben Zakkai—the academy of Yabneh
      3. The oral Torah—regulating the life of the people

IV. Each society has empowered a body which makes decisions and establishes social regulations that carry impelling power for the group.
   A. The rabbinate
      1. Ordination of rabbis
      2. The rabbi—judge, spiritual and communal leader
   B. Sanhedrin—Bet Din

V. Contact between various cultures results in cultural diffusion, cultural borrowing, and cultural exchange.
1. Judaic and Hellenistic views during the era under study (Areas of interaction rather than exact parallels)

Judaism	*Hellenism*
a) The concept of God; the Torah—the word of God	*a)* Stoics—the animating cosmic force
b) A controlled life as sanctification of life	*b)* Self-control, as virtue
c) Care of the body as temple of the soul	*c)* The derogation of the body; the body as a prison to the soul
d) Wisdom literature	*d)* Logos
e) Coexistence of the soul and the body (changed from no distinction between body and soul)	*e)* Preexistence of the soul
	f) The hereafter—immortality of the soul only
f) The hereafter—the resurrection of body and soul	

VI. A time of upheaval is a time of change in which new ideas are adopted.
   A. The oppressive Roman occupation
      1. Taxation
      2. Laws restricting Jewish independence
   B. Rebellions
      1. The Zealots
      2. Josephus in the Galilean revolt
      3. The fall of Jerusalem, 70 C.E.; the Western Wall
      4. Rabbi Akiba and the Bar Kokhba rebellion
      5. Masada
VII. The affairs of human societies have historical antecedents and consequnces; events of the past influence those of the present.
   A. Judaism did not consider Jesus the awaited Messiah
      1. Jesus' teaching seen against the backdrop of his time
      2. The Jewish Christians
      3. The Jewish Christians' feud with Paul over Hellenistic Christianity

B. The parting of the ways
   1. The Old and the New Covenant—the role of the Old Testament and its adherents viewed as supplanted
   2. The Crucifixion and its meaning to Jews and Christians
   3. Emperor Constantine—Christianity now the religion of the Roman Empire
   4. Nicaea, 325 C.E.
   5. The ascendency of the Church and its consequences for the Jews
   6. Anti-Semitism—the Holocaust
C. Judeo-Christian and Hellenistic ideas and their influence on our American value system and beliefs
   1. Equality
   2. Legal justice
   3. Social justice—responsibility for members of our society
   4. Responsibility of the individual
   5. The Constitution of the United States as the embodiment of our political beliefs

VIII. Failure to recognize and become familiar with changes and differences can lead to prejudice and social disorganization.
A. The outside perspective of the Jews
   1. The separate nature of the Jewish culture
   2. The beginning of anti-Semitism in the pagan world
   3. The people of the Law; preoccupation with legal minutiae and with strict obedience
   4. The Jews as viewed in the Hebrew Bible without consideration for the temporal setting and without analytical inquiry
   5. The Pharisees as viewed in the New Testament
B. Racial and ethnic problems in our country and in the world

Vocabulary

Tzedakah	Plato
Chesed	Hellenism
Monotheism	Dead Sea Scrolls
Mitzvah	Synagogue
Original sin	Qumran

Logos	Diaspora
Omniscient	Septuagint
Omnipotent	Apocrypha
Torah	Proverbs
Oral Torah	Sirach
Stoicism	Sanhedrin
Midrash	Rabbi
Talmud	Holocaust
Mishnah	Anti-Semitism
Diety	Asceticism
World-to-come	The Western Wall
Essenes	Apocalypse
Zealots	Theology
Pharisees	Construction of the Law
Sadducees	Rabbi Akiba
Hillel	Mysticism
Shammai	Halachah
Josephus	Haggadah
	B.C.E., C.E.

Cognitive Objectives

1. Given a selection of the Talmudic sayings, students will identify and list rabbinic attitudes on:

   a) equality;   e) love;
   b) acts of loving-kindness;   f) study;
   c) charity;   g) life.
   d) justice;

2. Students will explain:

   a) what is meant by the term "the Jewish people;"
   b) why Jews are often referred to as "the Jewish people;"
   c) what actions on the part of individual Jews demonstrate a relationship to a peoplehood;
   d) which of the sayings of rabbis explain the phenomenon of peoplehood in Judaism. (Information gathered in the investigation of Jewish organizations can be used as examples in fulfilling the above objectives.)

3. Students will compare and contrast some of the main differences between the Sadducees and Pharisees.

4. Using examples such as the rabbis' interpretation of the biblical injunction "An eye for an eye" and their conclusions as to its meaning and intent, students will demonstrate how the rabbis adjusted to changing times and mores and strengthened the Torah as a source of guidance and wisdom.

5. Students will analyze factual content to determine how the synagogue became important and the expanded view of religion came to be accepted by the Jewish people by virtue of the loss of the Temple and national independence.

6. Students will explain how the unity forged through the adherence of the Jews to one code of conduct in their daily and social lives as well as how the organization of life around accepted institutions helped preserve them as a separate group, a people.

7. Students will define the term "construction of the Law" and give an example of such an activity in the writings of both the Supreme Court and the rabbis.

8. Students will explain ten sayings from the Talmud and will provide examples to illustrate what was meant.

9. In a brief summary, students will describe some similarities between Hellenistic and rabbinic attitudes.

10. Students will compare and contrast the attitudes toward death and toward body and soul as they appear in the Old Testament, Hellenistic thought, Pharisaic Judaism, and the New Testament.

11. Given a list of some of the main tenets of Pharisaic Judaism, students will compare and contrast them with the main beliefs of their own religion.

12. Arranging the above material into two lists, one of similarities and one of differences, students will note differences and similarities in belief vis-à-vis those in ethical requirements, and write their conclusions of the findings.

13. Based on the readings, students will write a critical essay on the subject: It has been suggested that the Pharisees stressed legalism and not love. Based on your studies, how would you respond to this statement?

14. Reading one or more of the articles listed in the bibliography, students will record a few of the arguments given as possible reasons for the portrayal of the Pharisees as the archenemies of Jesus. (A description of the Pharisees can be found in Matt. 23.)

15. Given the reading assignment, students will explain the historical importance and the interpretation given to the events of the fall of Jerusalem and Masada by Jews and by Christians.
16. Given the four different eschatological views which prevailed during the time under study, students will compare and contrast the different eschatological positions which Christianity and Judaism eventually adopted.
17. Students will identify the main issues of contention between the rabbis, the Jewish Christians, and Paul.
18. Students will explain why the accusation of deicide against the Jews was unjustified.
19. Students will interpret the terms "Old" and "New" Testaments in light of Christian theology. Why do Jews prefer the term "Bible" or "Hebrew Bible" to the term "Old Testament"? What were the historical consequences of this theology?
20. Students will explain both the personal and historical meaning of the Crucifixion to Christians and to Jews.
21. Students will interpret the importance of the conversion of Emperor Constantine and of the Council of Nicaea to both Jews and Christians.
22. "Pull yourself up by your own bootstraps," "rugged individualism," "equality of opportunity," "equality before the law" as well as social security, welfare, and unemployment benefits are expressions of various ideas concerning equality and justice. Students will write an essay identifying the ethical attitudes of Judaism and Christianity in reference to these stances.

Affective Objectives

1. Students will compare their pretest reports covering their feelings and attitudes towards Jews and Judaism with their culminating-activity reports. At their own discretion, students will tell the class about any changes of feelings or attitude.
2. Students will select two or three of the Talmudic sayings studied and describe how the sayings relate to their own views of life.
3. Students will suggest how improving the understanding between Jews and Christians would help overcome prejudicial views and thus benefit both groups.

SAMPLE ACTIVITIES

When conducting interviews with the clergy or with lay people of the Jewish and Christian faiths, it is extremely important to be aware of differences within the groups. It is always beneficial to solicit as many divergent viewpoints as possible, paying major attention to the largest, most representative groups. Within Judaism the three main branches are Reform, Conservative, and Orthodox.

Initiatory Activities for Students

1. Pretest—a multiple-choice or true/false test on Jews and Judaism to establish your attitudes and knowledge base.
2. Write what you know about Jews, Judaism, any expressions or sentiments you have or have heard of.
3. Filmstrip: "Christians and Jews, a Troubled Brotherhood."

Developmental Activites for Students

1. Read assigned books, articles, quotes, and sayings, and answer accompanying questions provided by the teacher.
2. Choose a number of activities from the activity sheet and be responsible for:
   a) a class presentation (subject and form to be contracted with the instructor);
   b) written report(s);
   c) contact(s) or interview(s) in the community.
3. Write a report about Hillel, Josephus, Masada, Rabbi Akiba, or other topics and personalities investigated during this course of study. The topics are to be contracted with the instructor.
4. Invite a rabbi or a qualified person from the local Jewish community to explain the role the Pharisees and the Talmud played in the lives of individual Jews and in Jewish history.
5. Enact a few of the Midrashim.
6. Contact the Jewish Community Center in your area for names, addresses, and materials about Jewish organizations in the community and in the United States. Investigate the origins, traditions, and purposes which were instrumental in establishing these organizations. How do these modern-day expressions of Judaism relate to the Pharisaic teachings?

7. Set up a debate between groups representing Sadducees and Pharisees in which their differing viewpoints on the essence of the Jewish religion are presented.

8. Read one of the articles or chapters stressed in the bibliography and answer the questions provided by the teacher.

9. Invite a rabbi to bring a volume of the Talmud to class. Using one talmudic tractate, ask the rabbi to demonstrate the style, form, and content characteristic of the volume.

10. Filmstrip: "The Gossamer Thread."

11. Make a mural diagram depicting the role of the synagogue in the daily life of the Jewish community as it evolved in the period under study.

12. Investigate the phenomenon of a self-government which lacked physical coercive powers (as, for example, in the Sanhedrin and the rabbinate) and determine the sources of its authority.

13. Leaf through the book of Sirach in the Apocrypha or the book of Ecclesiastes in the Bible and record verses which seem to indicate Jewish and Hellenistic origins.

14. Make a collage to illustrate some of the sayings which you have learned.

15. Check in an encyclopedia for the roles wisdom and self-control played in Stoicism.

16. Interview a number of priests, ministers, and rabbis, and make a chart comparing various Jewish and Christian beliefs and concepts such as God, Messiah, Hereafter, original sin, freedom of choice, etc.

17. Search out statements about life and death in the Torah (The Five Books of Moses). Summarize the attitude toward life and death contained in the Torah. Did you find any references to body, soul, or Hereafter?

18. Leaf through the New Testament. Read statements about the Jews, the Pharisees, or the priests and Levites. Copy some of the verses and tell in your own words what impressions you received about the people described.

19. Invite a rabbi or a qualified person from the local Jewish community to tell how Judaism differs from Christianity and why Jews do not accept Jesus as the Messiah.

20. Based on the sayings and on the reading material, list similarities and differences in Pharisaic Judaism and New Testament

Christianity on such matters as the view of humankind, ethics, the responsibility of the individual, etc.

21. Compare the Sermon on the Mount (Matt. 5–7) with some of Hillel's sayings or with quotations from the Talmud.

22. Compare the English translation of the Kaddish with the Lord's Prayer. What similarities do you find?

23. Interview a member of the Jewish community or perhaps a visiting Israeli Jew (a student in a local university) and ask for the meaning of the statement "Again Masada shall not fall" for that person in particular and for Jews generally.

Culminating Activities for Students

1. Judaism has often been characterized as a legalistic religion. Based on the Pharisaic sayings, write an essay showing how this characterization is accurate or inaccurate. Substantiate your claims with supporting quotations.

2. Report your findings on the concept of peoplehood in Judaism as discovered in your interviews and readings. Write your own thoughts and feelings about this phenomenon.

3. Prepare a newspaper of the time and describe the events leading to the Crucifixion of Jesus.

4. Read the Vatican II statement concerning the question of deicide and explain why the declaration was necessary.

5. Visit a synagogue. What functions does the synagogue serve today?

6. Filmstrip: "Christians and Jews, a Troubled Brotherhood" (shown for the second time). Discuss the film in light of understandings gained in this course. Sample questions:

   a) What were some of the questions which arose as Gentiles began to embrace the Jewish Christian faith, and why did these questions cause friction between the Jews and Paul?

   b) What were the political and religious differences between Jews and Christians during the first and second centuries C.E.? What were the consequences of these differences?

   c) Why do you think so few people are fully aware of the long history of persecution experienced by the Jews?

Valuing Activities for Students

1. The "whys" and "hows" of charity.

   a) Why do people give charity?

b) If you needed financial help, how would you want to receive your help? Would you want to know who the donor was? What kind of help would you want to receive beyond the immediate need at hand?

c) Why did the rabbis maintain that it is better not to give charity at all than to give it in public?

d) What do you suppose is the best kind of charity?

2. Why did Hillel say, "If I am not for myself, who will be for me? And if I am only for myself, what am I?"

a) What kind of help is he referring to? Can we always help ourselves? Why does he find fault with a person who is only for himself or herself? Is there a contradiction between the two parts of his question?

b) How does this saying apply to Pharisaic ideas and to our political system?

c) Do you agree with Hillel? How do your social and political opinions reflect your agreement or disagreement with this statement?

3. The rabbis spoke of an evil inclination and a good inclination, and of the individual's freedom of choice.

a) Write out various choices that you have made or anticipate making, from frequent daily choices to the less frequent choices. How are these decisions made? What roles do personal experience, social pressure, economics, and advice of parents and peers play in the decision-making process?

b) List the class decisions on the chalkboard, grouping them in terms of the frequency with which they were made. Discuss the various groupings. How and to what extent are our choices limited? Can we, under the circumstances of our lives, still claim to be in control of the quality of our lives? What part do the values of our society play in shaping our value systems and our lives?

c) Can you see a correlation between Hillel's saying, "If I am not for myself who will be for me? And if I am only for myself, what am I?" and the rabbis' view of the coexistence of both evil and good inclinations within human beings as an expression of their freedom of choice?

d) What life-style—what actions and behavior—would you have to manifest if you were to believe in either one or both of the discussed viewpoints?

4. What did Hillel mean when he said "Do not unto thy fellowman what is hateful to thee, the rest is commentary"? Could he have really meant that this is the essence of Judaism? Why is commentary needed? What does it comment about? Does our country possess such a body of commentary? Why is it needed? What kind of hateful actions can one person perpetrate against another (physical, economical, psychological, etc.)? What actions or attitudes of others bother you the most? What grievances do various groups in our country voice? Could you and they sum up their grievance by saying "Do not unto thy fellowman" when addressing our society?

5. "A person will have to give account on Judgment Day for every good thing that his eyes saw and he did not sample."
    a) How does this saying compare with "If it feels good, do it"? How does a person determine what is good?
    b) Jews traditionally drink wine on happy occasions—for the Sabbath, festivals, Bar/Bas Mitzvahs, weddings, etc. In the blessing over the wine they thank God for the creation of the fruit of the vine. Does this tradition encourage drinking?
    c) Is there a difference between drinking when one is happy and drinking to become happy? What difference can you see?
    d) Can the enjoyment of wine be evil? When? How?

EVALUATION

1. Each activity and objective will have a predetermined point value. The student will be responsible for completing the activities and objectives as directed or contracted with the instructor. Evaluation will include:
    a) oral presentations;
    b) essays;
    c) the answers to questions handed out with the reading material;
    d) arrangements and contacts with a speaker;
    e) interviews;

f) extra credit work; and

g) some of the culminating activities can be used for evaluative purposes if desired.

2. Each grade level will be assigned a predetermined point count. The total accumulated point value will determine the grade.

3. Tests: essay and objective.

   a) Essay test. Sample questions:

   (1) What is the contribution the Pharisees made to Judaism? Discuss their unique position vis-à-vis the Sadducees and in light of the destruction of the Temple and the loss of Jewish national independence.

   (2) Hillel's saying "Don't do unto thy fellowman" has been viewed to this very day as the essence of Judaism. On the basis of what you have learned, support or refute this statement.

   (3) The Pharisees and the Jews in general did not become Christians. What were some of the reasons? (Note some basic differences between the two religions.)

   b) Objective test. Sample questions:

   (1) Matching: Match the term in the right column with the answer in the left column by marking the letter preceding the term in the space in front of the correct answer.

_____ The developers of the oral Torah.	A. Bar-Kokhba
_____ A famous Jewish historian.	B. Sanhedrin
_____ A leader of a rebellion, called "Son of a Star."	C. Pharisees
	D. Herod
_____ The highest religious authority in Judea.	E. Josephus

   (2) True/False: Mark T or F (true or false) in the space in front of the question.

   _____ Jews believe the Messiah has come.

   _____ The Talmud was written by Hillel.

   _____ The Zealots fought for Jewish independence.

   _____ Judaism advocates asceticism.

4. Extra credit.

   Extra credit assignments will be contracted with the instructor for subject matter, form, and point value.

QUOTATIONS AND SAYINGS

Sayings from the Talmud

The Midrash tells of "a lady who asked what God had been doing since
Creation. Rabbi Jose ben Halafta replied: 'He has been building
ladders for some to ascend and for others to descend.' Man is
endowed with the freedom of will to ascend or descend the ladder of
divinity."[9]

Rabbi Akiba, when asked by a Roman general "Why does your God
who loves the needy not provide for their support Himself?"
answered: "God, the Father of both rich and poor, wants the one to
help the other so as to make the world a household of love."[10]

Actions speak louder than words; God helps those who help themselves; the end does not justify the means.[11]

Better to give no charity at all than to give to the poor in public.[12]

Of everything God created nothing was created in vain, not even the
things you may think unnecessary, such as spiders, frogs, or
snakes.[13]

Sayings of Hillel

Do not separate yourself from the community.[14]

Say not: When I have leisure I will study: perchance you will never
have leisure.[15]

In the hour when the Holy One, blessed be He, created the first man,
He took him and let him pass before all the trees of the garden of
Eden and said to him: "See my works, how fine and excellent they
are! Now all that I have created for you have I created. Think upon
this, and do not corrupt and desolate my world; for if you corrupt it,
there is no one to set it right after you.[16]

The Lord loveth the righteous (Ps. 146:8) because their righteousness
is not a matter of heritage or family.[17]

Thou shalt love thy neighbor as thyself (Lev. 19:18). Rabbi Akiba says:
"This is the greatest principle of the Torah."[18]

Whence do we know that even a Gentile who engages in the Torah is
like a high priest? We learn it from: "Ye shall therefore keep My
statutes, and Mine ordinances, which if a man do, he shall live by
them"(Lev. 18:5). "Priest, Levites, and Israelites" was not said, but
"a man"; thus you may learn that even a Gentile who engages in the
Torah—lo, he is like a high priest.[19]

The world rests upon three things: On justice, on truth, on peace. Yet, those three are one and the same thing. For if there is justice, there is truth, and there is peace.[20]

Quotations

Rabbi Yohanan ben Zakkai: "God can only be served by free moral agents; not by slaves."[21]

Hillel: "If I am not for myself, who will be for me? And if I am only for myself, what am I? And if not now, when?"[22]

Hillel: "Do not unto thy fellowman what is hateful to thee; the rest is commentary." (The essence of Judaism as seen by Hillel.)[23]

In the hour of man's death, neither silver nor gold nor precious stones nor pearls go with him, but only Torah and good works.[24]

A person will have to give account on Judgment Day for every good thing which his eyes saw and he did not sample.[25]

If a person who denies himself only the enjoyment of wine is a sinner, all the more so one who denies himself all the enjoyments of life.[26]

The sword comes into the world for the delay of justice, and for the perversion of justice and for the sin of interpreting the Torah not according to its true sense.[27]

It is not up to you to complete the work, yet you are not free to abstain from it.[28]

A sage taught: "If anyone puts his neighbor to shame in public it is as if he shed blood."[29]

Hillel said: "Judge not your companion until you have been in his place."[30]

Why was man created singly? Why did God create only one man? So that no one can boast, "I am of nobler lineage," our Sages explain. All mankind is descended from the same man. All are equal before God.[31]

Once as Rabban Yohanan ben Zakkai was coming out of Jerusalem, Rabbi Joshua followed after him and saw the temple in ruins. "Woe unto us," Rabbi Joshua cried, "that this place where we atoned for our sins through sacrifices is now laid waste!" "My son," Rabban Yohanan said to him, "be not grieved; we have another atonement as effective as this. And what is it? It is Gemilut Hasadim [acts of loving-kindness] as it is said, 'For I desire mercy and not sacrifice' (Hos. 6:6)."[32]

163

Better the lowest born who is a scholar than a high priest who is an ignoramus.[33]

The Torah declares concerning itself, "It is not up in heaven;" that is to say, once the Torah was given on Mount Sinai, we pay no heed to heavenly voices but, as the Torah ordains further, we follow the opinion of the majority.[34]

Whoever does not dwell in *Eretz Israel* (the Land of Israel) is like one who does not believe in God. This is to tell you that whoever dwells outside the land is likened to one indulging in pagan worship.[35]

Settlement in *Eretz Israel* equals in importance all the *mitzvot* (commandments) of the Torah.[36]

NOTES

1. Woodrow Wilson as quoted in "The Jew and Judaism," from a series of pamphlets based on *A Book of Jewish Thought*. selected by Joseph Herman Hertz (New York: Nat'l Assoc. of Jewish Community Centers, 1966).

2. Jack Riemer, "Teaching about Non-Jews in the Jewish School," *Catholic Mind* (March 1974), p. 44.

3. Glenn Tinder, *Political Thinking: The Perennial Questions* (Boston: Little, Brown, 1970), p. 30.

4. Viktor Frankl, *From Death Camp to Existentialism: A Psychiatrist's Path to a New Therapy* (Boston: Beacon Press, 1959), p. 107.

5. John T. Pawlikowski, "On Renewing the Revolution of the Pharisees: A New Approach to Theology and Politics," *Cross Currents* (Fall 1970), p. 415.

6. Rosemary Radford Reuther, "The Pharisees in First Century Judaism," *The Ecumenist* (November-December, 1972), 2:1.

7. Jacob Neusner, *Invitation to the Talmud* (New York: Harper & Row, 1973), p. 231.

8. Ibid., p. xviii.

9. W. Silverman, "The Jewish Concept of Man" (Washington, D.C.: B'nai B'rith Youth Organ., 1962), p. 24.

10. "The Good Life" in *A Modern Treasury of Jewish Thought*. ed. Sidney Greenberg (New York: Nat'l Jewish Welfare Board, no year given), p. 20.

11. Ben Zion Bokser, "Why I Am a Jew," *Jewish Information* (Summer 1962), 3:24.

12. Azriel Eizenberg, ed., *Tzedakah. a Way of Life* (New York: Behrman House, 1963), p. 32.

13. Albert Vorspan, "The Crisis of Ecology, Judaism and the Environment" (New York: Union of Amer. Hebrew Cong., September 1970), p. 5.

14. Nahum N. Glatzer, *The Judaic Tradition* (Boston: Beacon Press, 1969), p. 194.
15. Ibid.
16. Ibid., p. 206.
17. Ibid., p. 211.
18. Ibid., p. 223.
19. Ibid., p. 229.
20. Ibid., p. 234.
21. Seymour Rossel, Hyman Chanover, and Chaim Stern, *When a Jew Seeks Wisdom: The Sayings of the Fathers* (New York: Behrman House, 1975), p. 97.
22. Ibid., p. 30.
23. Ibid., p. 47.
24. Ibid., p. 53.
25. Ibid., p. 88.
26. Ibid., p. 88.
27. Ibid., p. 243.
28. Ibid., p. 109.
29. Ibid., p. 190.
30. Ibid., p. 159.
31. Ibid., p. 151.
32. Ibid., p. 132.
33. Milton Steinberg, *Basic Judaism* (New York: Harcourt, 1947), p. 68.
34. Ibid., p. 71.
35. Yosef Tirosh, ed., *Religious Zionism. an Anthology* (Jerusalem: Ahva Cooperative Press, 1975), p. 245.
36. Ibid., p. 176.

BIBLIOGRAPHY

When teaching Judaic or related subjects, the teacher is well advised to check with the local synagogues and temples and their school principals, with the Jewish Community Center, and with Jewish Hebrew schools or Jewish day schools. There is an ever-growing pool of books and material available on these topics. Many of the books mentioned in the bibliography might be found in the schools and libraries of the Jewish community. Films, filmstrips, or at least the catalogues listing them can often be located in one or more of these institutions. Other help in the form of clarification of ideas or identification of speakers can also be obtained by contacting these organizations.

For the "beginner," the asterisked (*) resources are recommended as a starting point for establishing a foundation for teaching the suggested resource unit. Other recommendations:

1. Use summarized handouts and questionnaires about the material to be learned based on suggested resources.
2. Use one of the articles about the Pharisees listed in the bibliography as the basis for handouts to students.
3. Use simple comprehension questions.
4. A suggested introduction to the material for the teacher: read two of the articles and three of the suggested student texts.

Reference Works for Teachers and Students

Encyclopedia Judaica. 16 vols. Jerusalem: Keter, 1972.

The Jewish Encyclopedia. 12 vols. New York: Funk & Wagnalls, 1901.

Margolis, Max L., ed. in chief. *Holy Scriptures According to the Masoretic Text.* A New Translation. Philadelphia: Jewish Pub. Soc. of Amer., 1955.

May, Herbert G., and Metzger, Bruce M., eds. *The New Oxford Annotated Bible with the Apocrypha.* (Revised Standard Version. An Ecumenical Study Bible.) New York: Oxford Univ. Press, 1973.

Sandmel, Samuel, gen. ed. *The New English Bible with the Apocrypha: Oxford Study Edition.* New York: Oxford Univ. Press, 1976.

Teacher Sources

Agus, Jacob B. *The Evolution of Jewish Thought.* New York: Arno, 1959.

Baeck, Leo. *The Pharisees.* New York: Schocken Books, 1947.

Baum, Gregory. *The Jews and the Gospel: A Re-examination of the New Testament.* Westminster, Md.: Newman Press, 1961.

Birnbaum, Philip. *Ethics of the Fathers.* New York: Hebrew Pub. Co., 1949.

Cahn, Zvi. *The Philosophy of Judaism.* New York: Macmillan, 1962.

Daube, David. "The New Testament and Rabbinic Judaism." *Jewish People: History, Religion, Literature.* New York: Arno Pub., 1956.

Eizenberg, Azriel; Goodman, Hannah; and Kass, Alvin, eds. *Eyewitness to Jewish History.* New York: Union of Amer. Hebrew Cong., 1973.

Flannery, Edward H. *The Anguish of the Jews.* London: Colliers Macmillan, 1965.

Glatzer, Nahum N., ed. *Hillel the Elder: The Emergence of Classical Judaism.* New York: Schocken Books, 1959.

————. *The Judaic Tradition.* Boston: Beacon Press, 1969.

Herman, Edward, comp. *Jewish Americans and Their Backgrounds: Sources of Information.* Chicago: Amer. Library Assoc., 1975.

Hertz, Joseph H. *Sayings of the Fathers.* New York: Behrman House, 1945.

Heschel, Abraham. *God in Search of Man: A Philosophy of Judaism.* New York: Harper & Row, 1959.

Isaac, Jules, *The Teaching of Contempt: Christian Roots of Antisemitism.* New York: Holt, 1964.

Klausner, Joseph. *Jesus of Nazareth.* Boston: Beacon Press, 1964.

Lehrman, S. M. *The World of the Midrash.* London, New York: Thomas Yoselof, 1962.

Moore, George F. *Judaism in the First Centuries of the Christian Era.* 2 vols. New York: Schocken Books, 1971.

Neusner, Jacob. *Invitation to the Talmud.* New York: Harper & Row, 1974.

*Olson, Bernhard E. "Christian Education and the Image of the Pharisees." *Religious Education,* 4 (November-December, 1960): 410.

Parkes, James W. *Antisemitism.* Chicago: Quadrangle Books, 1969.

————. *The Conflict of the Church and the Synagogue: A Study in the Origins of Antisemitism.* New York: Atheneum, 1969.

————. *The Foundations of Judaism and Christianity.* Chicago: Quadrangle Books, 1960.

*Pawlikowski, John T. *Christian Education and the Jewish People.* New York: Paulist Press, 1973. (See especially chap. 6, "Catechetics and Prejudice.")

*————. "On Renewing the Revolution of the Pharisees: A New Approach to Theology and Politics." *Cross Currents* 20 (Fall 1970).

*Reuther, Rosemary Radford. *Faith and Fratricide: The Negative Myth of the Jews and Its Development in Early Christianity.* New York: Seabury, 1974.

Rivkin, Ellis. *The Shaping of Jewish History.* New York: Scribner, 1971.

Schuerer, Emil. *A History of the Jewish People in the Time of Jesus.* New York: Schocken Books, 1961.

Strober, Gerald S. *Portrait of the Elder Brother: Jews and Judaism in Protestant Teaching Materials.* New York: The Amer. Comm. Nat'l Conf. of Christians and Jews, 1972.

Student Sources

Bokser, Ben Zion. *Judaism and the Christian Predicament.* New York: Knopf, 1967.

Fackenheim, Emil L. *Paths to Jewish Belief.* New York: Behrman House, 1970.

Finkelstein, Louis. *Akiba: Scholar, Saint and Martyr.* New York: Atheneum, 1970.

Freehof, Rabbi Solomon B. *In the House of the Lord.* New York: Union of Amer. Hebrew Cong., 1951.

Miller, Milton G., and Schwartzman, Sylvan D. *Our Religion and Our Neighbors.* New York: Union of Amer. Hebrew Cong., 1971.

"Popular Studies in Judaism." Commission on Interfaith Activities of The Union of Amer. Hebrew Cong., the Central Conf. of Amer. Rabbis, the Jewish Chautauqua Soc., and the B'nai B'rith Youth Organ.

Rossel, Seymour; Chanover, Hyman; and Stern, Chaim. *When a Jew Seeks Wisdom: The Sayings of the Fathers.* New York: Behrman House, 1975.

Samuels, Ruth. *Pathways Through Jewish History.* New York: Ktav Pub., 1967.

Schweitzer, Frederick M. *History of the Jews: Since the First Century A.D.* New York: Macmillan, 1971.

Union of Amer. Hebrew Cong. "Judaism and Christianity: The Parting of the Ways." *Keeping Posted,* 19 (December, 1973).

Easy Reading

Klaperman, Gilbert and Libby. *The Story of the Jewish People.* vol. 2, chaps. 7–14. New York: Behrman House, 1957.

Levin, Meyer. *Beginnings in Jewish Philosophy.* New York: Behrman House, 1971.

———, and Kurzband, Toby K. *The Story of the Synagogue.* Chaps. 16–24. New York: Behrman House, 1957.

Pilchik, Ely E. *Hillel—The Book Against the Sword.* New York: Schuman, 1951.

Films and Filmstrips

"Christians and Jews and Jesus." Filmstrip/record, 65 frs., color guide. 1966. Thomas S. Klise.

The "Gossamer Thread." 28 min., color. Alden Films. The development of the synagogue from its legendary origins in Babylonia to the Spanish period.

"Jews and Christians, A Troubled Brotherhood." Filmstrip/record. 1972. Alba House. A historical survey of the relationship between the two groups.

"Masada." 14 min., color. Alden Films. A tour of the archaeological remains with archaeologist Yigael Yadin.

Sources for Films and Filmstrips

Alba House Communications
Canfield, Ohio, 44406
This company produced the filmstrip/record set titled "Christians and Jews: A Troubled Brotherhood."

Alden Films
7820 20th Ave.
Brooklyn, N.Y. 11214

Anti-Defamation League of B'nai B'rith
315 Lexington Ave.,
New York, N.Y. 10016

Bureau of Jewish Education
Jewish Community Council
590 N. Vermont Ave.
Los Angeles, Cal. 90004

Eternal Light Catalogue
National Academy for Adult Jewish Studies
The United Synagogue of America
155 Fifth Ave.
New York, N.Y. 10010

Jewish Media Service
65 William St.
Wellesley, Mass. 02181

Program-Film Listing
Hadassah National Program-Film Department
65 East 52d St.
New York, N.Y. 10022

The Jewish Audio-Visual Review
American Association of Jewish Education
114 Fifth Ave.
New York, N.Y. 10011

Thomas S. Klise, Co.
P.O. Box 3418
Peoria, Ill. 61414

Part 4

Exemplary Courses and Units of Study

Religion in Human Culture

Lee H. Smith
and
Wesley J. Bodin

Social studies education has long focused on education for effective citizenship. To some this has meant that students acquire an understanding of United States history and how the American political process works. These have been appropriate goals, especially in times when large numbers of immigrants were being integrated into American society. These goals remain an appropriate challenge to social studies education in the United States. However, a broader perspective on what is needed for effective and participatory citizenship suggests that much more than United States history and civics is required. Participants in our culture must have an understanding of the entire cultural complex. This entails a knowledge not only of the political system but also of the social and economic systems. Further, if the total culture is to be understood, the aesthetic, educational, technological, religious, and value systems must also be explored. Social studies and history courses need to explore all aspects of the culture and, especially, its pluralistic dimensions. In an age of change and mobility it is increasingly important that students expand their global perspective, learn to deal with aspects of life which lead to tension and conflict, and broaden their understanding of human interdependence.

Social studies programs which seek to address such goals seem clearly inadequate if they neglect the religious dimensions of human history and contemporary communities. Traditionally, history courses have been followed with specific courses in economics, government, and sociology. Elective courses about religions are fully appropriate in both public and private high schools.

The number of schools in communities across the country instituting courses about religions has been increasing significantly in the past several years. These innovative courses are often the result of community efforts to resolve the problems attending the relationship of the schools to religion in the context of the United States Constitution and the Supreme Court decisions. The community of St. Louis Park, in suburban Minneapolis, began an effective venture when the local school board appointed a citizens' advisory committee to study the role of religion in the schools and to formulate appropriate recommendations. Among its many recommendations, the committee suggested that an elective course about world religions be offered at the senior high school level.

The social studies department of St. Louis Park High School acted upon the committee recommendation and developed a proposal to secure a grant under Title III-IV C of the Elementary-Secondary Education Act. The proposed innovation, supported by the grant, resulted in the establishment of the World Religions Curriculum Development Center and the "development and dissemination of a model course about world religions." The center has addressed itself to the production of materials suitable for teaching high school students about religions. Two additional grants from the Northwest Area Foundation have been awarded to support the center's activities. These funds have aided the development of audiovisual components, teacher training, field-testing, and revision of materials developed by the center.

The center staff has made a serious effort to involve a student advisory committee and a community advisory committee in its decision-making procedures. Professional consultants were employed by the center to help delineate the structure of religions and identify the central concepts of the study of specific religious traditions. These consultants were drawn from the academic fields of religion, history, and the various social sciences, especially anthropology and sociology. Suggestions from field-test teachers and their students over a three-year period of time have been most instrumental in shaping the final revision of the course.

Religion in Human Culture, the course developed by the center, is intended for high schools that choose to teach about religion. It is a social studies course about religion designed to enhance human dignity. Religion in Human Culture utilizes *rational processes* in its learning activities and seeks to maintain the *imprecise, delicate, and very human qualities* religions represent. It is a course which helps

174

students learn about the religious diversity of the world and develop attitudes of understanding and respect for the beliefs and practices of others and the legitimacy of those beliefs and practices in a world of pluralism and mobility. It is consistent with the U.S. Supreme Court decision that schools shall not practice or teach religion, but should teach about religion.

The course objectives for *Religion in Human Culture* lie within the four categories established by the National Council for the Social Studies *Curriculum Guidelines* (1971), as briefly outlined below:

I. Knowledge objectives.
    A. Religious expression.

        Students will demonstrate, by specific examples, illustrations, and explanations, a knowledge of religious expression.

        Students will demonstrate a knowledge of the diversity of religious expression.

        Students will demonstrate a knowledge of the problems of interpreting and attaching meaning to various forms of religious expression.

        Students will demonstrate a knowledge of causes and sources of motivation giving rise to certain specific expressions of religion.

        Students will demonstrate a knowledge that religious expression provides a data base for studying about religion.

    B. Religious Diversity.

        Students will be able to demonstrate, by specific examples, illustrations, and explanations, a knowledge of religious diversity and the diversity of religious expression.

        Students will demonstrate that religious diversity is normal and legitimate.

        Students will demonstrate a knowledge of factors which cause or contribute to religious diversity.

        Students will demonstrate a knowledge of the complexity of religious diversity.

    C. Functions of religion.

        Students will be able to demonstrate, by specific examples, illustrations, and explanations, a knowledge of the functions of religion.

Students will demonstrate a knowledge of certain "universal" functions of religions.

Students will demonstrate a knowledge of certain "unique" functions of specific religions.

D. Continuity and change.

Students will demonstrate, by specific examples, illustrations, and explanations, a knowledge of the concepts of "continuity" and "change" as they relate to religious phenomena.

Students will demonstrate a knowledge of how historical experience shapes religion.

Students will demonstrate a knowledge of how religion shapes historical experience.

Students will demonstrate a knowledge of factors which cause and inhibit change.

E. Stereotypes.

Students will be able to demonstrate, by specific examples, illustrations, and explanations, a knowledge of religious stereotypes and their effects.

F. Conflict and conflict resolution.

Students will demonstrate, by specific examples, illustrations, and explanations, a knowledge of the nature of conflict, its causes and effects, and conflict resolution as they relate to religion.

II. Ability and skill objectives.

A. Awareness and perception abilities.

Students will have demonstrated the ability to perceive religious phenomena by utilizing the skills of observation, and formulating questions, hypotheses, and definitions.

B. Information-gathering abilities.

Students will have demonstrated the ability to gather information by utilizing skills of locating, listening, reading, interviewing, and participant observation.

C. Information-processing abilities.

Students will have demonstrated the ability to process information by utilizing the skills of organization and classification, analysis (checking bias, objectivity, appropriateness), synthesis, and evaluation.

D. Information-utilization and -application abilities.

    Students will have demonstrated the ability to utilize and apply information by employing the skills of generalizing, speaking, writing, presenting, and problem-solving.

E. Effective-participation abilities.

    Students will have demonstrated the ability to participate effectively by utilizing skills of active listening, sharing, cooperation, and leadership.

III. Valuing objectives.

  A. Curiosity.

    Students will have demonstrated an attitude of curiosity toward their own religious ideas, traditions, and practices and those of others by their willingness to ask questions, listen, and learn.

  B. Objectivity.

    Students will have demonstrated a value of objectivity toward religious beliefs, practices, and information by their ability and willingness to ask pertinent questions, suspend judgment, respect the use of reason, and respect the quantity and quality of evidence as a test for accuracy.

  C. Respect.

    Students will have demonstrated an attitude of respect for the religious ideas and practices of others based on the value of human dignity and the value of the right to individual choice.

IV. Social-participation objectives.

    Students will be able to demonstrate an ability to participate effectively in society by dealing with people as individuals rather than as categories, by using their abilities and knowledge in working toward the solution of problems related to religion which affect individuals and groups in society and in the world.

The semester course has been planned to be used on an elective basis. However, when completely developed, there will be more than adequate material to encompass an entire academic year. Many of the course components can be used effectively in courses less than a semester in length, and selected components may be useful in other social studies courses such as area studies, American History, and others.

The components of the course include a teacher's manual which delineates the objectives, student materials, teaching procedures, and teacher background for each lesson. The teacher's manual is the heart of the course; it integrates the materials and activities, serves as an in-service training kit, and at the same time requires the teacher to be a decision-maker about teaching-learning strategies rather than a programmed follower of a set of directions.

In addition to the teacher's manual, each unit has a booklet of student readings containing both primary and secondary source materials. Other essential components in the course include sound-synchronized filmstrips, cassettes, artifacts, and pretests and posttests to measure growth in knowledge and attitudes.

The course emphasizes inquiry strategies and process development as well as substantive content. Students are encouraged to become curious, objective, and capable in learning about religion. Religion in Human Culture is divided into four parts, each made up of several units:

   I. Building a Model for Learning about the Diversity of Religions.
  II. Exploring Selected Religious Traditions—Application of the Model.
 III. Independent Study and Field Work—Application of the Model.
  IV. Religious Issues in Contemporary Society.

The following is a description of some of the units which have been completed and field-tested.

PART I. BUILDING A MODEL FOR LEARNING ABOUT THE DIVERSITY OF RELIGIONS.

The three units comprising Part I of the course represent an attempt to build a World Religions course for high school students without the use of a definition of religion per se. This is done because of the dynamic tension between narrow and broad definitions of religion and the limited agreement on definitions among the scholars and specialists in the academic study of religion.

Educators and school decision-makers must take cognizance of the fact that most students probably carry a definition of religion into the classroom, though it may lack sophisticated formulation and/or articulation. As human beings and members of American society, students have a perfect right to make such definitions; they should in no way be discredited. Rather than proceeding from definitions, Part I suggests an approach which involves the development of an open-inquiry process about religions. Essentially, there are four steps in the process:

1. *Observing* religious behavior or activity as it is expressed in primary and secondary sources, artifacts, literature, music, and other forms of religious expression.
2. *Describing* what has been observed.
3. *Finding meanings* in what has been observed and described.
4. *Developing appreciation for, understanding of, and sensitivity to the range of meanings* people find in religious expression that can be observed and described.

The merits of this process seem multiple: beginning where the student is, without forcing a definition of religion on the individual or the class by consensus; an open framework or model to manage new and additional data; a frame of reference congruent with objectivity and respect for diversity, human dignity, and individual choice; a safeguard against dogmatic "right answerism."

In Part I, Unit A, "Religious Expression in Human Culture," students are asked to explore their own environment for evidences of religious expression. Their ideas are validated with a sound-synchronized filmstrip. Unit B, "The Function of Religious Expression in Human Culture," removes the students from their own environment to consider the question, "What does religion do to and for people?" This is done by focusing on several case studies in which the people and their religious expression are removed from the student by time and place. Part I, Unit C, "Perceiving and Understanding Religious Expression," affords students the opportunity to explore the range of religious expression, with the caution that assigning meaning to what has been observed and described is considerably difficult and risky. In the consideration of expression as a source of data, students learn that human communication and expression, in the forms of rites, symbols, literature, and so forth, are essentially symbolic in nature and are, therefore, subject to interpretation. Students learn that it is possible to misinterpret religious expression, which can lead to inaccuracies, stereotypes, and distortions—all of which can result in ill will and poor relations among people. In studying symbols, rites, and religious literature, art, and music, students come to recognize that it is essential to have an "inside" as well as an "outside," view.

PART II. EXPLORING SELECTED RELIGIOUS TRADITIONS— APPLICATION OF THE MODEL.

Part II of the course gives students the opportunity to practice the skills, ideas, and concepts acquired in Part I as they explore some of the world's religious traditions. Obviously, not all traditions can be taught in one semester, and the teachers and students must make choices. It would seem most appropriate to make choices which reflect increasing attention to religions of the East as well as to the traditions of the West. Consistent with the rhythmic pattern of alternating from far to near in the course, it is suggested that the students begin Part II with an Eastern tradition. Beginning with an Eastern religion also serves to lessen the possibility that the class will deal exclusively with Western religions and give the East no exposure at all. The five traditions cited below are exemplary of emphases which comprise Part II of the course.

Hinduism

Hinduism poses a challenging study for the high school youngster because of its diversity, its antiquity and obscure origins, and its concepts of time and life. To fully know and truly understand Hinduism is to miss the essence of the tradition, for it is probably unknowable. The aim of the unit is to get a feeling for the religion's essence, which is accomplished by exploring student perceptions, gaining insight into Hindu concepts of "the *Divine*," and moving toward an understanding of the relationship of "the Divine" and "the human." The unit focus then shifts to the nature of people and the soul—the "four goods" in life, the "four stages" in life, the "four stations" or "castes," the "four paths" of life—and concludes with a summation of Hinduism which emphasizes the application of the model for studying about religion.

Buddhism

Buddhism, like Hinduism, is a religious system which proves difficult for the Western mind to comprehend. If the students have a background of Hinduism, the concepts and ideas in Buddhism will be easier to grasp. The unit concentrates on the origins of Buddhism, the Buddha, the Path, Nirvana, and variations within Buddhism. The purpose of the unit is to gain insights into the major aspects of Buddhism and then to analyze how people in different parts of the world attempt to reach the goals of Buddhism. The students are asked to use the skills and the model introduced in Part I of the course.

Judaism

In the study of Judaism students confront a complex, long, and rich history. They encounter a people in a dynamic way of life with considerable diversity and immeasurable contribution to the Western and American cultural systems. The unit centers on two themes: "The pursuit of life and meaning," and "What it means to be Jewish." "The pursuit of life and meaning" is essentially historical, philosophical, and theological. The concepts of *God, history, people, Covenant, law, life,* and "What is a Jew?" are dealt with.

"What it means to be Jewish" focuses on some of the practices and observances of Judaism and its concerns today, such as Sabbath, calendar, holidays, Passover, life-cycle rituals, worship, study, persecution, the Holocaust, and Israel. Students work with a variety of primary and secondary source materials.

Christianity

The great complexity and diversity of most religious traditions is established by teachers and students early in the course, and the study of Christianity offers no exception to these considerations. The unit on Christianity begins with a focus on some of the major Christian concepts set forth in the Nicene Creed and the life and teachings of Christ presented in the Gospels. Topics considered include: the creeds, faith, belief, commitment, Trinity, sin, salvation, grace, Incarnation, the church, the Reformation, liturgy, sacraments, denominations, and polity. Major periods in the historical development of Christianity are examined briefly. Contemporary American Christianity is explored through representative case studies.

Islam follows the study of Judaism and Christianity effectively because of the common historical roots of the three religions. Recent political developments appear to have increased interest in the study of Islam. Some Muslims feel that Western knowledge about Islam has distortions and misconceptions; and the unit attempts to deal with that possibility. Lessons concentrate on the topics of misconceptions, basics of Islam, Muhammad, the Koran, the Path, Pillars; do's and don'ts of Islam, Allah, Brotherhood of Islam; and sectarianism. The idea of Islam being a way of life is built upon throughout the unit.

PART III. INDEPENDENT STUDY AND FIELD WORK— APPLICATION OF THE MODEL.

In this part of the course individuals, or small groups of students, select topics or issues for study. They are required to develop a proposal which includes what is to be studied, how it is to be studied, resources to be used, and a method of reporting. Topics have included the study of various sects; the development of religious traditions in music, art, and architecture; death and how it is dealt with in one or more religious traditions; religion in nonliterate societies; and a host of other topics.

PART IV. RELIGIOUS ISSUES IN CONTEMPORARY SOCIETY.

The final part of the course relates to the fact that we live in a world of mobility and dynamic cultural change. There is often tension between tradition and change. A major question to be explored is, "How do individuals and societies identify these changes and tensions and deal with them?" This category of investigation includes topics related to science, technology, and mobility. Another area of change is the increasing awareness of pluralism in American society. The topics of religious minorities, ethnoreligious minorities, women and religion, and intergenerational tensions are appropriate areas for investigation in this part of the course. Contemporary society is plagued with many issues regarding religion and public policy. Among these issues might be listed the Middle East crisis, the situation in Northern Ireland, morality and government, the role of religion in schools and public life, and numerous other areas of values and value conflicts.

Religion in Human Culture and the activities of the World Religions Curriculum Development Center have been monitored by an independent evaluation contractor. An evaluation plan to measure the cognitive and affective growth of students taking the course was developed and refined during the first two rounds of field-test teaching. In the third round of trial teaching there were 37 teachers and over 2,000 students involved. The evaluation results demonstrated that Religion in Human Culture was successful in producing cognitive and affective growth at a statistically significant level.[1]

BIBLIOGRAPHY

The following bibliography is a list of books which the WRCDC project directors have found especially useful. In general, they have served as background material for high school teachers and, to a limited extent, for advanced high school students. The list is very limited, and the authors recognize that many useful sources are excluded. Inclusion of a work in the list does not represent an endorsement but rather an experience of utility. Exclusion from the list does not represent a judgment of the validity of many other sources. Further, the list represents resources which have been useful to the WRCDC project directors in the development of curriculum materials for high school students. The omission of entire religious traditions and certain specific topics in the academic study of religions reflect the fact that, *to date,* the Center has limited or no experience in that area. For example, while a unit on Japanese religion is planned by the Center, no work has been done on it at the time of this writing.

General:

Ahlstrom, Sidney E. *A Religious History of the American People.* New Haven, Conn.: Yale Univ. Press, 1974.

Ballou, Robert O., ed. *The Portable World Bible.* New York: Viking, 1973.

Brandon, S. G. F., ed. *A Dictionary of Comparative Religion.* New York: Scribner, 1970.

Elwood, Robert S., Jr. *Religious and Spiritual Groups in Modern America.* Englewood Cliffs, N.J.: Prentice-Hall, 1973.

---

[1] *Religion in Human Culture* is a forthcoming publication of Argus Communications, a Division of DLM, Inc., Niles, Ill.

Farugi, I. R., and Sopher, D. E. *Historical Atlas of the Religions of the World.* New York: Macmillan, 1974.

Garvin, Philip, and Welch, Julia. *Religious America.* New York: McGraw-Hill, 1974.

Gaustad, Edwin Scott, *Religious Issues in American History.* New York: Harper & Row, 1968

Glock, Charles Y., and Stark, Rodney. *Religion and Society in Tension.* Chicago: Rand McNally, 1965.

Greeley, Andrew M. *The Denominational Society.* Glenview, Ill.: Scott, Foresman, 1972.

Hammond, Phillip E., and Johnson, Benton, eds. *American Mosaic: Social Patterns of Religion in the United States.* New York: Random House, 1970.

Handy, Robert T., ed. *Religion in the American Experience.* New York: Harper & Row, 1972.

Kitagawa, Joseph M. *Religions of the East.* Philadelphia: Westminster, 1974.

Knudten, Richard D. *The Sociology of Religion.* New York: Appleton, Educational Division, Meredity Corp., 1976.

McNamara, Patrick H. *Religion American Style.* New York: Harper & Row, 1974.

Monk, Robert C.; Hofheinz, Walter C.; Lawrence, Kenneth T.; Stamey, Joseph D.; Afflick, Bert; and Yamamori, Tetsunao. *Exploring Religious Meaning.* Englewood Cliffs, N.J.: Prentice-Hall, 1974.

Norbeck, Edward. *Religion in Human Life: Anthropological View.* New York: Holt, 1974.

Rosten, Leo, ed. *Religions of America: Ferment and Faith in an Age of Crisis, A New Guide and Almanac.* New York: Simon & Schuster, 1975.

Schneider, Del Byron. *No God but God: A Look at Hinduism, Buddhism, and Islam.* Minneapolis: Augsburg, 1969.

Smith, Huston, *The Religions of Man.* New York: Harper & Row, 1958.

Streng, Frederick J. *Understanding Religious Man.* Encino, Calif.: Dickenson, 1969.

Stroup, Herbert. *Founders of Living Traditions.* Philadelphia: Westminster, 1974.

Wallace, Anthony F. C. *Religion: An Anthropological View.* New York: Random House, 1966.

Zaretsky, Irving I., and Leone, Mark P., eds. *Religious Movements in Contemporary America.* Princeton, N.J.: Princeton Univ. Press, 1974.

Hinduism

De Bary, William Theodore, ed. *Sources of Indian Tradition.* 2 vols. New York: Columbia Univ. Press, 1958.

Edgerton, Franklin, tr. *The Bhagavad Gita.* Cambridge, Mass.: Harvard Univ. Press, 1975.

Hopkins, Thomas J. *The Hindu Religious Tradition.* Encino, Calif.: Dickenson, 1971.

Kirk, James A. *Stories of the Hindus.* New York: Macmillan, 1972.

Organ, Troy Wilson. *Hinduism: Its Historical Development.* Woodbury, N.Y.: Barron's, 1974.

Prabhavananda, Swami, and Isherwood, S., tr. *The Song of God: Bhagavad-Gita.* New York: New Amer. Library, 1957.

Reymond, Lizelle. *My Life with a Brahmin Family.* Baltimore: Penguin Books, 1972.

Zaehner, R. C. *Hinduism.* New York: Oxford Univ. Press, 1975.

Zimmer, Heinrich. *Myths and Symbols in Indian Art and Civilization.* Harper Torchbook. New York: Harper & Row, 1962.

Buddhism

Beyer, Stephan. *The Buddhist Experience: Sources and Interpretations.* Encino, Calif.: Dickenson, 1974.

Ch'en, Kenneth K. S. *Buddhism: The Light of Asia.* Woodbury, N.Y.: Barron's, 1968.

Conze, Edward, tr. *Buddhist Scriptures.* Baltimore: Penguin Books, 1959.

De Bary, William Theodore. *The Buddhist Tradition: In India, China, and Japan.* New York: Vintage Books, 1972.

Gard, Richard A. *Buddhism.* New York: Washington Sq. Press, 1969.

Kapleau, Philip, ed. *The Three Pillars of Zen.* Boston: Beacon Press, 1967.

Rahula, Walpola. *What the Buddha Taught.* New York: Grove Press, 1974.

Robinson Richard H. *The Buddhist Religion: A Historical Introduction.* Encino, Calif.: Dickenson, 1970.

Ross, Nancy Wilson, ed. *The World of Zen.* New York: Vintage Books, 1960.

Judaism

Donin, Rabbi Hayim. *To Be a Jew.* New York: Basic Books, 1972.

Epstein, Isidore. *Judaism.* Baltimore: Penguin Books, 1970.

Friedlander, Albert H., ed. *Out of the Whirlwind: A Reader of Holocaust Literature.* New York: Union of Amer. Hebrew Cong., 1968.

Garfiel, Evelyn. *The Service of the Heart: A Guide to the Jewish Prayer Book.* North Hollywood: Wilshire Book Co., 1971.

Gersh, Harry. *The Sacred Books of the Jews.* New York: Stein & Day, 1972.

Glazer, Nathan. *American Judaism.* Chicago: Univ. of Chicago Press, 1972.

———. *A Jewish Reader.* New York: Schocken Books, 1969.

Goldin, Judah. *The Living Talmud.* New York: Mentor Books, 1955.

The Holy Scriptures. Philadelphia: Jewish Pub. Soc. of Amer., 1955.

Jacobs, Louis. *What Does Judaism Say About . . . ?* New York: Quadrangle/New York Times, 1973.

Neusner, Jacob. *The Life of Torah: Readings in the Jewish Religious Experience.* Encino, Calif.: Dickenson, 1974.

———. *The Way of Torah: An Introduction to Judaism.* Encino, Calif.: Dickenson, 1974.

Sabbath and Festival Prayer Book. New York: Rabbinical Assembly of Amer. and the United Synagogue of Amer., 1946.

Siegel, Richard; Strassfeld, Michael; and Strassfeld, Sharon, eds. *The Jewish Catalogue.* Philadelphia: Jewish Pub. Soc.

Stadler, Bea. *The Holocaust.* New York: Behrman House, 1974.

Steinberg, Milton. *Basic Judaism.* New York: Harcourt, 1974.

The Torah. Philadelphia: Jewish Pub. Soc. of Amer., 1973.

Wiesel, Elie. *Night.* New York: Avon Books, 1972.

Christianity

Bainton, Roland H., ed. *Christendom: A Short History and Its Impact on Western Civilization.* 2 vols. New York: Harper & Row, 1966.

Bettenson, Henry. *Documents of the Christian Church.* New York: Oxford Univ. Press, 1973.

Common Bible (Revised Standard Version: An Ecumenical Edition with the Apocrypha/Deuterocanonical Books). New York: Collins, 1973.

Cross, Z. L., and Livingstone, E. A. *The Oxford Dictionary of the Christian Church.* New York: Oxford Univ. Press, 1974.

Harvey, Van A. *A Handbook of Theological Terms.* New York: Macmillan, 1964.

The Layman's Parallel Bible. Grand Rapids, Mich.: Zondervan, 1973.

Leith, John H., ed. *Creeds of the Churches.* Richmond, Va.: Knox Press, 1973.

Mead, Frank S. *Handbook of Denominations in the United States.* New 6th ed. Nashville, Tenn.: Abingdon, 1975.

Islam

'Abd-Al'Rahman' Azzam. *The Eternal Message of Muhammad.* New York: New Amer. Library, 1965.

Cragg, Kenneth. *The House of Islam.* Encino, Calif.: Dickenson, 1969.

Farah, Caesar. *Islam: Beliefs and Observances.* Woodbury, N.Y.: Barron's, 1970.

Galwash, Amad A. "Religion of Islam." *Al-Azhar Magazine.* Cairo: 1945.

Hammudah Abd Al-Ati. *Islam: in Focus.* Edmonton, Ont.: Canadian Islamic Centre.

Pickthall, Mohammed Marmaduke, tr. *The Meaning of the Glorious Koran.* New York: New Amer. Library.

Williams, John Alden, ed. *Islam.* New York: Washington Sq. Press, 1969.

Chinese Traditions: Confucianism and Taoism

Bynner, Witter, ed. *The Way of Life According to Lao Tzu.* New York: Capricorn Books, 1962.

Chai, Chu, and Chai, Winberg. *Confucianism.* Woodbury, N.Y.: Barron's, 1973.

De Bary, William, Theodore; Chan, Wing-tsit; and Watson, Burton. *Sources of Chinese Tradition.* 2 vols. New York: Columbia Univ. Press, 1960.

Fung Yu-Lan. *A Short History of Chinese Philosophy.* New York: The Free Press, 1969.

Kaltenmark, Max. *Lao Tzu and Taoism.* Stanford, Calif.: Stanford Univ. Press, 1969.

Lao Tzu; Lau, D.C., tr. *Tao Te Ching.* Baltimore: Penguin Books, 1972.

Legge, James, tr. *The Texts of Taoism.* 2 vols. New York: Dover Pub., 1962.

Mackintosh, Charles, tr. *Tao.* Wheaton, Ill.: Theosophical Pub. House, 1974.

Thompson, Laurence G. *Chinese Religion: An Introduction.* Encino, Calif.: Dickenson, 1975.

Tudisco, A. Jeff. *Confucianism and Taoism.* San Francisco: Field Edu. Pub., 1969.

Van Over, Raymond, ed. *Taoist Tales.* New York: New Amer. Library, 1973.

Ware, James R., tr. *The Sayings of Confucius.* New York: New Amer. Library, 1955.

Welch, Holmes. *Taoism: The Parting of the Way.* Boston: Beacon Press, 1966.

Yang, C. K. *Religion in Chinese Society.* Berkeley: Univ. of Calif. Press, 1970.

An Introduction to Islam

John L. Esposito

Islam is the second largest of the world's religions, incorporating over 550 million people. Islam spawned a civilization which encompassed the various ethnic groups and cultures of the Middle East. Thus Islamic civilization spanned a vast area from North Africa to South Asia, from Morocco to Pakistan. From A.D. 650 to A.D. 1650, Islam was the major alternative to Christendom and at various times was its conqueror, both politically and culturally. Islam views itself as encompassing the sociopolitical sphere and constituting a total way of life.

During the modern period Islam continues to be a strong force. Many of the modern nation states carved out of past Islamic empires gained independence through nationalist movements which relied heavily upon Muslim ideology. Most of these states officially give recognition to their Islamic character in their constitutions. Therefore, an understanding of the sources and riches of Islamic civilization is important for a better understanding not only of past history but of present attitudes and values.

This unit is geared for upper-level high school students in a college preparatory or honors program and as described should take four to six weeks to complete. The unit could be used in a minicourse format or as a component of a variety of social studies courses—world history, world culture, world religion, Middle Eastern area studies, and so forth.

GOALS AND OBJECTIVES

While numerous specific behavioral objectives can be developed by the individual teacher, the unit should encourage the students to:

1. Examine the historical and cultural context for the development of early Islamic belief and practice.
2. Identify those beliefs and practices unique to Islam.
3. Examine the diversity and variety of religious belief and practice within Islam itself.
4. Analyze aspects of Islamic religion in order to understand the practical thrust of Islam and its development of a total way of life as reflected in the Shari'ah.
5. Compare and contrast Islamic belief and practice.
6. Examine the historical and cultural impact of the world's second largest religion.
7. Analyze the role of Islam in shaping the sociopolitical order of Muslim nations, particularly in the recent period.

CONTENT

I. Generalizations
    A. Islam, along with Judaism and Christianity, traces itself back to the patriarch Abraham and his son Isma'il. For this reason, Muslims recognize the previous revelations of God to Jews and Christians and recognize their prophets.
    B. Islam means "submission" to the will of God, i.e., realization of the divine will in history.
    C. The essence of the Islamic religious experience is a radical monotheism. Allah alone is God, one and transcendent.
    D. Islam emphasizes practice more than belief. Thus the primary, earliest, and most developed discipline is the sacred law (*Shari'ah*), which encompasses all of man's duties to God and to his fellowmen.
    E. Islam permeates every aspect of life—religion, culture, society, and politics. The material sources for the Muslim "way" (law and ethics) are the *Qur'an* (the revealed scriptures) and the *Sunnah* (exemplary behavior) of the prophet Muhammad.
    F. The Islamic community *(Ummah)* brought a new sociopolitical order in which religion, rather than tribal affiliation, provided the common bond. Ideologically, there was an organic relationship between religion and the sociopolitical order. Thus, we speak of the Islamic state or empire(s).

G. Islam is a world religion with a universal mission. This mission resulted in its early astounding geographic expansion and can be seen today in the successes of Islam in East and West Africa.

H. From a very early period there were those Muslims who, in addition to following God's will through the performance of their duties, sought direct knowledge or personal religious experience of God. This mystical movement in Islam is called *Sufism.*

I. Although the modern period has seen the disappearance of Islamic empires, the role and influence of Islam can be seen in modern religious reform movements, nationalist movements, and the constitutions and ideologies of many Muslim nations.

II. Subject matter outline and related readings

(For ease in identifying appropriate sources on the content described below, specific references are included in the subject matter outline.)

A. The study of religion and its role in a civilization
   1. Ways of viewing reality and establishing meaning (Streng)
   2. Religion as a "cultural system" (Geertz)
   3. The sacred and profane (Eliade)

Readings

M. Eliade, *The Sacred and Profane* (New York: Harcourt, Brace Jovanovich, 1968).

C. Geertz, "Religion as a Cultural System" in W. Lessa and E. Vogt, *Reader in Comparative Religion: An Anthropological Approach,* 3rd ed. (New York: Harper & Row, 1972), pp. 204–15.

F. J. Streng, *Understanding Religious Man,* 2nd ed. Encino, Cal.: Dickenson, 1975).

B. Pre-Islamic Arabia and the advent of Islam
   1. Political and social order of Central Arabia.
      a) Bedouin tribal society. Tribal affiliation was the basis of identity and social bond.
      b) Majority of bedouin tribes were nomadic, following a pastoral life.
      c) Minority lived in cities which were sedentary oasis settlements involved in agriculture (Medina) or trade centers (Mecca).

d) The status of women and the family was poor. Men enjoyed unfettered rights regarding marriage (polygyny) and divorce.
2. Religious order
   a) Reflected bedouin tribal societal structure.
   b) Allah was the supreme, high God. He was the creator but was remote from man's everyday concerns and thus not the object of cultic worship. Associated with Allah were three female deities: Allat, al'Uzza, and Manat.
   c) Myriad tribal deities (gods and goddesses) who served as protectors of individual tribes and were associated with sacred objects—trees, stones, etc. These active deities were the objects of cultic rites of supplication and propitiation. Sacrifice and soothsayers were part of the religious scene.
   d) Mecca served as a religious center for festival and pilgrimage. The *Ka'ba* in Mecca was a cube-shaped building which contained sacred idols or objects associated with the tribal deities and therefore was the focus for religious pilgrimage.
   e) Justice was rooted in the threat of vengeance. There was little sense of cosmic moral purpose or individual or communal moral responsibility.
   f) Destiny—no belief in the resurrection of the body or afterlife.

Readings

Marshall G. S. Hodgson, *The Venture of Islam* (Chicago: Univ. of Chicago Press, 1975), vol. 1, chap. 1, "The World Before Islam", pp. 103ff.

C. Muhammad: prophet and statesman (570–632). Muhammad differed from the pattern of prophecy as found in the Judeo-Christian traditions, since he was both a messenger *(rasul)* from God and the leader of a religiopolitical community.

1. Early life and career
2. Crisis and conversion (610)
3. Meccan period—persecution and rejection by majority of clansmen
4. Emigration *(hijrah)* to Medina (622)

5. Medinan experience—formation and leadership of community *(Ummah)*
6. Muhammad as exemplar—human *not* divine, no divine attributes or miraculous powers
    a) Exemplary behavior *(Sunnah)* of the Prophet collected, preserved, and transmitted in traditions *(hadith)*
    b) Seal of the prophets, i.e., Muhammad is the last of long line of prophets from Abraham to Moses to Jesus
7. Muhammad and his image in the West

Readings

Kenneth Cragg, *The House of Islam,* 2nd ed. (Encino, Calif.: Dickinson, 1975), pp. 1–29.

Fazlur Rahman, *Islam* (New York: Doubleday-Anchor, 1968), pp. 1–24.

W. Montgomery Watt, *Muhammad: Prophet and Statesman* (New York: Oxford Univ. Press, 1961).

D. The *Qur'an:* God's final revelation to mankind

1. Theory of revelation *(wahy)*
    a) The *Qur'an* is the final and literal revelation sent down from God and revealed to Muhammad through the angel Gabriel.
    b) It is an Arabic *Qur'an* which exists in heaven with God.

2. The *Qur'an* vis-à-vis Judeo-Christian revelations
    a) Muslims acknowledge that the one true God sent his revelation to the Jewish people *(Torah)* and the Christians *(Injil* or Gospel). The original revelation to the Jews was falsified, as witnessed by the ethnocentrism and legalism that crept in.
    b) This distortion led to God's revelation through the prophet Jesus, who declared the universal message and mission and emphasized the spirit over the letter of the Law. Again, the revelation was soon distorted by early Christian teachings that the prophet Jesus was the Son of God and related doctrines such as the Redemption and Atonement.
    c) Therefore, God in his mercy again sent down his true revelation a final time in the *Qur'an.*

3. Major themes
   a) God
      (1) Radical monotheism. Allah is one and transcendent. The doctrine of the oneness of God *(Tawhid)* dominates Islamic thought. There are no associate deities (contrary to the polytheism of pre-Islamic Arabia), no incarnations (contrary to the Christian teaching regarding Jesus).
      (2) Creator, ruler, and judge of the world
      (3) Traditionally God's attributes are encompassed in the 99 Names. Preeminent among these, as witnessed by the *Qur'an,* are justice, mercy, and compassion.

   b) Creation: God is the creator of everything that exists.
      (1) The world is good and has been given to mankind as a divine trust *(amanah).*
      (2) Man and woman are God's viceregents on earth.
      (3) Their vocation is to carry out or realize God's will in history.
      (4) Man and woman were created higher than even the angels. They are the noblest of creatures; they have no original sin. Since all are responsible before God for their own actions, the sin of Adam and Eve is just that—their sin.

   c) Last day and judgment (wrathful day of reckoning)
      (1) Day of wrath, which should motivate faithful to be God-fearing.
      (2) God is omnipotent judge: just and yet merciful.
      (3) Individual responsibility, no vicarious suffering or atonement.
      (4) *Book of Deeds* contains every act of a Muslim, and it is according to scales of strict justice that judgment occurs.

   d) Destiny
      (1) God-fearing will be rewarded with paradise.
      (2) Sinners will be punished with eternal damnation in hell.

Readings

K. Cragg, *The House of Islam,* chap. 3, "The *Qur'an,*" pp. 30–43.

H. A. R. Gibb, *Mohammedanism* (New York: Oxford Univ. Press, 1968), chaps. 3 and 4, "The Koran" and "Doctrine and Ritual in the Koran," pp. 24–41.

F. Rahman, *Islam,* chap. 2, "The *Qur'an,*" pp. 25–41.

E. The Islamic community *(Ummah)*: Its historic, geographic, and cultural development. As Muhammad was a prophet-statesman, so the Islamic community was not simply a spiritual one but a religiopolitical entity, i.e., a state-empire.

1. The Arab expansion

   a) Causes of stunning success, i.e., spread within 100 years from Arabia west across North Africa and east to India

   (1) Religious: Islam provided a common bond to bridge the divisiveness of tribalism and a moral-spiritual force to inspire armies.

   (2) Political and military: Byzantium and the Persian Sasanid empires were weak from the long wars they fought against each other. For their subjects who had born the brunt of long wars, both in lives lost and taxes, it was no more than an exchange of masters. Indeed, their lot was often viewed as better under Muslim rule.

   (3) Economic: The rewards from conquest of richer, more developed areas.

   b) Muslim conquests and the three options offered to a people

   (1) Conversion to Islam and full privileges of citizenship.

   (2) Protection, i.e., the status of a protected people *(dhimmi)* in exchange for the payment of a poll tax *(jizya).*

   (3) If the first two options were refused, then the sword—warfare. (N.B. The Muslim vocation was to strive *(jihad)* to spread the domain of Islam. Warfare was to be the final, *not* the first, resort.)

2. Overview of historical development
   a) Caliphate—"The Rightly Guided Caliphs" (632–661)
      (1) Early expansion and development of Islam under the early caliphs (successors of Muhammad).
      (2) The idealized past which Muslims have always looked back upon for inspiration and guidance.
   b) Umayyad Empire (661–750)
      (1) The expansion continued and government organization was developed.
      (2) The capital was moved to Damascus, and a dynastic empire was established.
   c) 'Abbasid Empire (750–1258) Baghdad
      (1) Flourishing of Islamic culture. After mid-tenth century, power became increasingly decentralized although caliph remained on throne.
      (2) In 1258 Baghdad fell to Mongols.
   d) Medieval Muslim empires (thirteenth to eighteenth centuries)
      (1) Ottoman Empire
      (2) Safavids of Persia
      (3) Mughals of India
   e) Modern period (nineteenth and twentieth centuries)
      (1) Colonialism
      (2) Independence

3. The flourishing of Islamic culture and its influence on the West. The Arab Muslims encountered highly developed cultures in Byzantium and Persia. They learned from their disciplines, translated them into Arabic, and then built upon these foundations. Thus their contribution was twofold: the transmission of the scientific and philosophical knowledge of Greece, Persia, and India to the West and development in many of these disciplines.
   a) Historical development
      (1) Umayyad Empire. Byzantine scholars utilized as court physicians and advisers at Damascus.
      (2) 'Abbasid Empire
         (a) 750–900 Heavy Persian influence at Baghdad. Translation movement: Many works on medicine, science, philosophy translated from

their original languages (Greek, Persian, etc.)
into Arabic.

(b) 900–1100 Muslim scholars assimilated these
materials and developed and extended this
received body of knowledge.

  b) Areas of Islamic influence

  (1) Medicine: For example, Avicenna, "The Canon of
  Medicine," was influential down to the seventeenth
  century.

  (2) Science: alchemy, astrology, astronomy, mathematics (especially algebra and trigonometry), geology, meteorology.

  (3) Philosophy: In addition to transmitting Greek philosophical thought, Muslim philosophers such as
  Avicenna (d.1037) and Averroes (d.1198) made
  their own contributions.

  (4) Literary culture (*adab*): history, geography, poetry,
  literary criticism.

  (5) Arts: architecture, painting, calligraphy, music.

Readings

Cragg, *The House of Islam,* chap. 6, "Ummah," pp. 73–108.
Gibb, *Mohammedanism,* chap. 1, "The Expansion of Islam,"
  pp. 1–15.
Thomas Arnold and Alfred Guillaume, eds., *The Legacy of
  Islam* (New York: Oxford Univ. Press, 1931).
P. K. Hitti, *The History of the Arabs* (New York: St. Martin's,
  1960), chap. 27, "Scientific and Literary Progress," pp. 363–
  407; chap. 27, "Education," pp. 408–15; and chap. 29,
  "The Development of Fine Arts," pp. 416–28.

F. The *Shari'ah:* "The Straight Path." The *Shari'ah* ("path" or
  "way") is the religious law of Islam which constitutes the
  divine pattern ordained by God for Muslim society. It was the
  early Muslims' task to discover the divine will in order that he
  or she might follow it. The sacred law encompasses both law
  and morality; therefore, its violation constitutes both a crime
  and a sin.

  1. Sources of the *Shari'ah*

  a) *Qur'an,* the revealed word of God, and the *Sunnah,* the model behavior of Muhammad, are the primary source materials.

b) These were supplemented by those customary practices not in conflict with the *Qur'an* and by decisions arrived at through the exercise of reasoning, especially reasoning by analogy.

2. Development

a) Throughout the early Islamic centuries, prodigious work was done by the first Muslim scholars *('ulama'*, "learned ones") in determining and elaborating the Islamic way of life.

b) By the tenth century, the scholars in the schools of law concluded that the ideal way of life *(Shari'ah)* had been elaborated in its essentials. Therefore, no longer would individual reasoning *(ijtihad)* be necessary. Rather, succeeding Muslim generations were to imitate or follow *(taqlid)* that which was to be found in the law books.

c) Content: The *Shari'ah* is a comprehensive law which encompasses both the Muslim's duties to God (e.g., Five Pillars, etc.) and to his fellowman (social transactions such as civil, criminal, and family laws—marriage, divorce, inheritance, etc.).

Readings

Gibb, *Mohammedanism,* chap. 6, "The Shari'a," pp. 60–72.

G. Muslim piety: The Five Pillars (fundamental duties) of Islam.

1. Profession of faith *(Shahadah)*. "There is no god but Allah *(the* God) and Muhammad is his prophet."

a) Radical monotheism.

b) Finality of prophethood of Muhammed, i.e., Muhammad is the last ("seal") of the long line of prophets which included Abraham, Moses, and Jesus.

2. Worship *(Salat)*

a) Prayer should be offered five times a day individually or in congregation. The prayers consist of bodily movements (prostrations) and recitation of *Qur'anic* verses. On Friday, the Muslim Sabbath, the noon prayer should preferably be said at a mosque. However, any place where a Muslim prays is acceptable, since a mosque is not a consecrated building but rather a gathering place.

b) Five times a day the *muezzin* gives the call to prayer from atop the minaret (tower) of the local mosque. A Muslim then performs ritual ablutions *(wudu')*. The inside of the mosque is a large, open area with carpets upon which the prostrations and prayers are offered. There is a niche *(mihrab)* which indicates the direction *(qibla)* of Mecca, the spiritual center of Islam. In addition, there is a pulpit *(minbar)* from which an exhortation is delivered by the leader *(imam)* of the prayer. Mosques often have an official *imam.* However, since there are no priesthood and no sacraments in Islam, any Muslim may lead the prayer and officiate at weddings, burials, etc.

3. Alms *(Zakat).* The giving of alms or religious tithing underscores the early Muslim sense of social responsibility.

4. Fasting *(Saum)* in *Ramadan.* During the ninth lunar month, *Ramadan,* Muslims abstain completely from sunrise to sunset from any and all food and drink. This is also a time for increased attention to prayer and charitable actions.

5. Pilgrimage *(Hajj).* Just as five times daily Muslims throughout the world are united as they face Mecca in worship *(salat),* so annually many travel in body to their sacred city where each day they have traveled in mind and spirit. If health and finances permit, every Muslim should make the pilgrimage at least once. Here all are gathered in the common brotherhood of believers regardless of race, color, or social status. This is symbolized by the pilgrims wearing the *ihram,* a white seamless garment.

Readings

Gibb, *Mohammedanism,* pp. 36–45.

Malcolm X (Little), *The Autobiography of Malcolm X* (New York: Grove Press, 1965), chap. 17, "Mecca."

Annemarie Schimmel, "Islam," in C. J. Bleeker, ed., *Historia Religionum,* vol. 2, pp. 148–55.

H. Sufism: Islamic mysticism (the interior path)

While the thrust of the traditional Islamic way of life was expressed in the *Shari'ah,* there developed at an early stage within the Islamic community individuals for whom merely following the will of God was not totally satisfying. These individuals were driven by a desire to return to the purity and austerity of the earliest period and motivated by a deep love of God which culminated in a quest for a direct, personal experience of the presence of God in this life.

1. The interior path *(tariqah)* of Sufism can be contrasted with the exterior path of the *Shari'ah.*

2. Beginnings: sources and development of Sufism
   a) Ascetics
      (1) They emphasized repentance for sins and fear of the last day—judgment.
      (2) Early Muslim ascetic reaction *(faqir, darwish* or dervish, meaning poor or mendicant) against the lavish excesses of Umayyad court life set in.
   b) Mystics
      (1) Through love and devotion, they sought union with God.
      (2) In time, individuals gathered into loosely organized groups.
      (3) By the twelfth century, organized communities— brotherhoods or orders—became popular religious movements through whose missionaries Sufism swept across the Muslim world.

3. Doctrines and practices of the Way *(tariqah)*
   a) *Fana',* annihilation of the lower self, i.e., to die to self in order to abide in God *(Baqa')*; and gain gnosis *(Ma'rifa).* (The goal of the Sufi was a direct knowledge or personal religious experience of God.)
   b) *Shaykh* or *Pir*—master or guide who trained the disciple *(murid)* in the way of purification and thus led him through successive stages *(maqamat).* Along the way, God would reward and encourage the disciple by granting certain experiences or psychological states *(ahwal).*
   c) Practices: In order to attain their goal, the Sufis adopted many practices—some of which were foreign, in the eyes of the religious leaders *('ulama'),* to early Islamic values.

(1) Celibacy

(2) Veneration of Muhammad and of "saints" as intermediaries between God and man

(3) *Dhikr* ("remembrance," "recollection"). Through a rhythmic, repetitive invocation of God's name(s), the devotee establishes the presence of God.

(4) Music, song *(sama',* spiritual concerts of devotional poems), and dance (e.g., whirling dervishes) in order to move to the experience of ecstatic states.

POSSIBLE ACTIVITIES

I. Initiatory activities

A. Show a filmstrip or film introducing students to the Islamic world. (Suggestions are cited below.)

B. Ask the students to write a paragraph on Islam to determine the extent of their knowledge of the second largest of the world's religions.

OR

C. Begin with an in-class discussion based upon the following questions:

1. Why is the Middle East an important and newsworthy area of the world? (Oil crisis, Lebanese war, Arab-Israeli conflict.)

2. When you think of the peoples of the Middle East, how do you identify them? What are the major religions in the Middle East?

3. What do you know about Muslims and their religion?

II. Developmental activities

A. Discussions and student presentations on course-related topics. For example:

(1) What was the religious belief and practice in Arabia in the period preceding the advent of Islam?

(2) Do additional research to determine Islamic understanding of an afterlife.

(3) What are the basic beliefs of the Islamic faith? How do these religious beliefs affect a Muslim's daily life?

(4) Since Islam historically developed after the appearance of Judaism and Christianity, how does Islam regard the teachings of the other two faiths?

B. Field trips to museums and local mosques. Many teachers will be surprised at the Islamic artifacts to be found in their museums and at the presence of mosques in major cities. Of special note is the permanent Islamic art exhibit at the Metropolitan Museum of Art in New York City as well as the Islamic Center (Mosque) in Washington, D.C.

C. There are a variety of filmstrips, films, and slides which may be utilized throughout the unit. (See the resources listed.)

Readings

Seyyed Hossein Nasr, *Ideals and Realities of Islam* (Boston: Beacon Press, 1972), chap. 5, "The Tariqah: The Spiritual Path and Its *Qur'anic* Roots," pp. 121–46.

Gibb, *Mohammedanism,* chap. 8, "Sufism," pp. 86–99.

I. Islam in the modern period (late nineteenth and twentieth centuries).

1. Breakdown of the medieval Islamic social order in the eighteenth and nineteenth centuries.
2. Impact of political and technological challenge of industrialized West.
3. Muslim self-understanding (i.e., notion of history and the universal mission of Islam) vs. loss of political power to Western colonialist powers and the challenge of political and religious pluralism of the modern nation state.
4. Tradition and change.
   a) Religious reformers.
   b) *Shari'ah* reform (law and courts).
   c) Religion in independence movements and constitutions of modern Muslim states.
5. Black Muslim movement in America.
6. Islam is fastest-growing religion in sub-Saharan Africa.

Readings

Cragg, *The House of Islam,* chap. 7, "Questions of Modern Time," pp. 109–25.

Gibb, *Mohammedanism,* chap. 10, "Islam in the Modern World," pp. 113–31.

II. Vocabulary

Allah, Qur'an, Muhammad, Sunnah, Shari'ah, Ramadan, hajj, Sufi, dervish, mosque, minaret, Mecca, Medina

III. Culminating activities

A. An in-class report on certain Islamic religious practices (pilgrimage, holy war, *Ramadan,* etc.).

B. Trace the contributions of Islamic culture to the development of medicine; science, including astrology, astronomy, and mathematics; philosophy; literature, and the arts, including architecture, painting and music. Prepare your report as creatively as possible using examples—pictures, drawings, slides, records, or tapes—where appropriate.

C. An investigation of similarities and differences between Islam and the student's own religious tradition.

D. A study of the image of Islam or Muhammad in Western literature.

E. Interviews with believing Muslims living in the area regarding Islamic beliefs and practices in America.

F. Comparisons and contrasts of the classical Islamic tradition with that of the Black Muslims (followers of Elijah Muhammad).

G. Descriptions of the Crusades from both a Muslim and a Christian point of view.

H. Write to the embassies of several Islamic countries to ask for copies of their constitution. Examine these statements to see if Islamic infiuences are identifiable.

I. Write Middle Eastern embassies for their official statements of position regarding the Middle Eastern conflict with Israel. Are there any "religious" issues apparent in these statements?

J. Obtain as much information on current life in such strongly Islamic-influenced nations as Libya, Egypt, Saudi Arabia, Pakistan, and Indonesia. How does the religion find expression in the cultures of these different countries?

EVALUATION

The quality of students' work during the culminating activities should be an important part of their evaluation. In addition, examinations which involve both identifications to test mastery of key terms and concepts as well as essays which demonstrate an understanding of the traditional Islamic world view can be effective. Below are examples of the types of questions one might use.

Multiple choice

1. Islam places most emphasis on (a) *practice* (b) belief (c) prayer (d) conversion.
2. Which of the following beliefs is most basic to Islam? (a) The world is good. (b) All individuals are responsible. (c) God-fearing people will be rewarded with Paradise. (d) *Allah is one and transcendent.*

True/False

1. Muslim conquerors forced their new subjects to convert. (F)
2. Islamic culture developed without utilizing the other cultural developments already existent. (F)
3. Muhammad is the last of the prophets. (T)
4. The Sufi stress the quest of a direct, personal experience of the presence of God in their lives. (T)

Essay

1. How do the various beliefs and doctrines of Islam affect the Muslim in his daily life?
2. What beliefs does Islam hold which are similar to Judaism and Christianity?
3. What are the Five Pillars of Islam? What effect does the performance of the Five Pillars have on the worldwide Muslim community?
4. Why is the term "Muhammadanism" offensive to Muslims?

INSTRUCTIONAL RESOURCES

Teacher References*

REFERENCE BOOKS.

Brandon, S. G. F., ed. *Dictionary of Comparative Religion.* New York: Scribner, 1970.

Faruqi, Isma'il R. al-. "Islam," in Chan, Wing Tsit; Faruqi, I. R. al, et al.; eds. *The Great Asian Religions,* New York: Macmillan, 1975.

"Islam," in Faruqi, I. R. al-, and Sopher, M. D. E., eds. *Atlas of World Religions,* New York: Macmillan, 1974.

Gibb, H. A. R., and Kramers, J. H., eds. *Shorter Encyclopedia of Islam.* Ithaca, N.Y.: Cornell Univ. Press, 1965.

Savory R. M., ed. *Islamic Civilization.* New York: Cambridge Univ. Press, 1976.

*An excellent annotated bibliography may be found in K. Cragg's *The House of Islam.* The works listed in this unit were selected for this particular project, keeping in mind the limited time available to most teachers.

BOOKS ON ISLAM

There is no satisfactory introductory text. However, H. A. R. Gibb's *Mohammedanism* and K. Cragg's *The House of Islam,* used jointly, provide an excellent resource for the teacher. Readings related to each topic have been listed after each section.

Student References

The following are but three of many introductory volumes on world religions in which a treatment of Islam may be found.

Noss, John B. *Man's Religions.* 5th ed. New York: Macmillan, 1974.

Smart, Ninian. *The Religious Experience of Mankind.* New York: Scribner, 1975.

Smith, Huston. *The Religions of Man.* New York: Harper & Row, 1965.

Audiovisual Aids

The following are especially recommended for classroom use.

Slides: *Hajj: Pilgrimage to Mecca,* by Sheikh Abdul Majeed. Published by Sheikh Publications, 15 Beekman St., New York, N.Y. 10038.

Filmstrips: *Islam*—Parts I and II (40 min. each). Filmstrips with accompanying commentaries on tape cassettes. This is part of an excellent series on world religions from McGraw-Hill, New York, N.Y.

Films: Though produced by different sources, all of the films listed below may be obtained from The Middle East Institute (Film Library, 1761 N Street, N.W., Washington, D.C. 20036) at a nominal fee for elementary and secondary school teachers. N.B. Rental from other agencies is usually significantly higher.

The Gift of Islam. 19 min., 16mm, sound. Emphasizes the cultural aspects of Islam. Although this overlaps with the film listed below, it may be used in conjunction with it.

Islam. 19 min., 16mm, sound. An overview of the historical development of the Islamic community, incorporating religious, political, and cultural perspectives.

The Islamic Center in Washington, D.C. 15 min., 16mm, sound. A look at the interior and exterior of the Center, with a description of its services and a scene of worship (*salat*).

The Sufi Way. 25 min., 16mm, sound. An excellent film made by Huston Smith which looks at the beliefs and practices of Sufism in India, Iran, Turkey, Tunisia, and Morocco.

Periodical

For teachers dealing with Islam and Middle Eastern culture, the Arab American Oil Company publishes a beautifully illustrated bimonthly magazine entitled *Aramco World Magazine* "distributed without charge to a limited number of readers with an interest in Aramco, the oil industry, or the history, culture, geography and economy of the Middle East." For instance, the Nov.-Dec. 1974 issue is on "The Hajj." Requests for addition to the mailing list should be made to: T. O. Phillips, Arab American Oil Company, 1345 Avenue of the Americas, New York, New York 10019.

Two Asian Religions: Hinduism and Buddhism

Paul J. Will

This course is an outgrowth of an earlier full-year course entitled History of Religions which was first offered at Kimball High School, Royal Oak, Michigan, in 1964. That course paralleled one given at Royal Oak's Dondero High School since 1955. Hence there has been a long-standing involvement in religion studies by the school district. Redesigned as two individual semester courses, this specific seventeen-week offering stresses the two major Asian religions, Hinduism and Buddhism, while the other one deals with Western religions.

The class is an elective open to eleventh and twelfth graders through the social studies department and is planned for average and above-average students. A course dealing with non-Western religions is particularly valuable because it fosters understanding of other human beings and other cultures. A study of religion must avoid an ethnocentric bias, and this class emphasizes that there are a variety of responses to ultimate questions and the human situation.

CONTENT

Among the main generalizations stressed in this course are:

1. There are certain characteristics or components that religions tend to have in common, although their specific meaning and function may differ.
2. Religion provides a sense of continuity by incorporating past religious insights and forms.
3. Diversity and variation within a religious tradition are related to historical and cultural developments.
4. Religious expression, e.g., in the arts, is mediated by the cultural milieu.

Students are exposed to a wide variety of new concepts and vocabulary during their study. Some of these are part of the basic terminology associated with the discipline of religion (ultimate reality, eschatology, rites of passage, ethics, theism). A number of terms are specific to the religious traditions being studied (Hinduism: caste, Brahman, bhakti; Buddhism: Nirvana, Sangha, duhkha). Some concepts are related to the social sciences (modernity, social hierarchy, nationalism).

Given the fact that these two Asian religions are too complex to cover in their entirety (with Hinduism's antecedents going back at least to 2000 B.C. and Buddhism adapting to several different cultural settings), a comprehensive study is impractical. An educator should realistically settle for presenting the salient characteristics and the basic religious components of each tradition in a generalized chronological treatment.

Course Outline

I. Introduction
   A. Objectivity and subjectivity
   B. Religion and how to study it
      1. Definitions of religion
      2. Common characteristics of religion
      3. Academic approaches to the study of religion

II. Hinduism
   A. Features of pre-Aryan India and the Indus Valley civilization
   B. Vedic contributions
      1. Aryan deities and sacrifice
      2. Vedic literature—shruti: "that which is heard" (Samhitas, Brahmanas, Aranyakas, Upanishads)
      3. Upanishadic world view—stressing increased metaphysical speculation
         a) Brahman-atman as the ultimate reality
            (1) Universal self—inner self
            (2) Personal and impersonal interpretations
         b) Reincarnation (samsara)
         c) Moral causation (karma and the law of karma)
         d) Liberation (moksha)
      4. Asceticism and yoga marga

5. Jnana marga (path to salvation through wisdom)
6. Karma marga (path to salvation through works)

C. Post-Upanishadic developments
   1. Secondary sacred literature—smriti: "that which is remembered"
   2. Elaboration of the caste system
      a) Varna—class—social ideal
      b) Jati—caste—social reality
      c) Dharma—rules of conduct and functional aspects
   3. *Bhagavad Gita* as a synthesizing and transitional document
   4. Devotionalism and bhakti marga
   5. Sectarian Hinduism
      a) Vaishnavism
      b) Shivism
      c) Shaktism—the female component
   6. Popular folk religion
      a) Relation of many gods to Brahma (Great Tradition-Little Tradition relationship)
      b) Ahimsa and the place of animals

D. Life-styles and ritual elements
   1. Review of ways to salvation
   2. Goals for the individual
   3. Ideal stages of life for the Brahman
   4. Rites of passage and samskara rituals (birth, puberty, marriage, death)
   5. Worship (puja) and pilgrimage

E. Contemporary Hinduism
   1. Gandhi and the independence movement
   2. Modernity and traditional values
      a) Effect of the secular state ideal on religion
      b) Role of caste in present society
   3. Religious response to the West
      a) Brahma and Arya Samaj
      b) Ramakrishna and Vivekananda
      c) Maharishi Mahesh Yogi and Transcendental Meditation
      d) Swami Bhaktivedanta and Society for Krishna Consciousness
   4. Hinduism today (numbers, location)

III. Buddhism
  A. Introduction—problems of research
  B. Life of Gautama Buddha
    1. Youth and legend of the Four Passing Sights
    2. Renunciation and the six-year quest
    3. Attainment of Nirvana and Buddhahood
    4. Establishment of the Sangha
  C. Teachings of Buddha—emphasis on the Buddhist world view
    1. Three marks of existence
      a) Impermanence (anitya)
      b) Non-self (anatman)
      c) Suffering (duhkha)
    2. Rebirth (samsara) and karma
    3. Nirvana—basic description
  D. General development of Buddhism after Gautama's death
    1. Growth of numerous sects
    2. Spread outside of India
  E. Essential characteristics of Theravada Buddhism
    1. Tripitaka and semicanonical religious writings
    2. Meditation and ethics
    3. Arhat and the laity
    4. Role of ritual
  F. Features of Mahayana Buddhism
    1. Vaipulya "extended teaching" literature
    2. Bodhisattva and Buddhas
    3. Cultic activities
    4. Varied sectarian development
      a) Pure Land Buddhism
      b) Chan or Zen Buddhism
  G. Contemporary Buddhism
    1. Effect of modernization
    2. Communism and traditional Buddhist countries
    3. Buddhist outreach to the West
    4. Buddhism today (numbers, location)

GOALS AND OBJECTIVES

In addition to understanding the generalizations and concepts presented in the content material, the students should be able to demonstrate in a variety of ways a knowledge of the following elements in Hinduism and Buddhism:

Social and cultural setting in which the religion developed.
Sacred writings.
World view—concept of the ultimate reality and human predicament.
Cosmology and cosmogony.
Eschatology.
Ethical injunctions.
Rituals and cultic life.
Role of individuals in affecting religious development.
Basic divisions in each religion and their particular emphasis.
Numbers and location of followers.
Contemporary situation and effect of modernity.

In addition to these intellectual objectives, there are some affective goals set for students. Ideally, the course should:

Promote tolerance for other religious traditions.
Develop respect for the religious dimension in human experience.
Create an appreciation of the values of other cultures.
Result in the realization that each religion must be examined objectively if the phenomenon of religion is to be understood accurately.

Finally, students will develop a number of learning skills and be able to:

Participate effectively in group discussions.
Ask analytical questions.
Gather and integrate information from various media.
Analyze primary source material.
Detect bias and determine the accuracy of interpretations.

POSSIBLE ACTIVITIES

There are a number of learning activities that can be used in initiating each section, among them:

Survey stereotypes about the religion; list terms or statements on the chalkboard and then evaluate them with the class.

View a filmstrip or slide presentation to learn about the cultural setting of the religion.

Play recordings of religious music or scriptural readings to create an experiential mood.

Demonstrate the use of religious ceremonial objects (e.g., rosary, gong, incense, mantra).

Use a bulletin board for pictures stressing a unique artistic or cultural aspect that will evoke discussion.

Place scriptural quotations on the chalkboard for analysis.

Study a number of differing translations of the same scriptural passage and discuss why the variations exist.

Write about and discuss open-ended philosophical questions such as "What is death?" or "What are different views about death?" before examining the religion's attitude.

Some of these initiatory activities can be used as developmental strategies with students, along with the following:

Responding to lectures and discussions on the religion.

Reading and discussing selected passages from primary sources.

Giving classroom reports on some aspect of the religion (e.g., role of women, marriage customs, effect in America).

Going on a field trip to a museum or to Asian religious centers.

Seeing a demonstration of meditation or yoga.

Viewing relevant films, followed by discussion.

Participating in group research projects.

Doing a report on a book concerning Asian religion or culture.

Participating in a class discussion of a novel reflecting Asian religious values (e.g., *Siddhartha*).

Writing a research paper on how religion affects the life of a famous Asian personality (e.g., Gandhi, Tagore).

Listening to an outside speaker or to a tape recording by a spokesman from the religion or culture.

As culminating activities, one can have the students:

See a filmstrip or movie that summarizes and reviews the main features of the religion.

Make a chart individually and/or in class listing the main components of each religion.

Fill out a worksheet listing key concepts.

EVALUATION

Many of the forgoing methods provide a basis for formal or informal evaluation of the student's learning. In addition, objective and essay exams are given. Matching and multiple-choice questions can cover definitions of terms and historical development. Essay questions are particularly effective in evaluating broader conceptual understanding. These questions may take several forms.

1. Discuss the Buddhist view regarding rebirth.
2. When Gautama Buddha said: "All the constituent parts of being are transitory, work out your own salvation with diligence," what was he emphasizing?
3. What research problems are encountered by the student of religion when examining the teachings of Gautama Buddha?
4. Compare the scriptures, ideal goal, and role of ritual in Theravada and Mahayana Buddhism.

Affective goals are evaluated through the use of an extensive questionnaire administered at the end of the course. This form not only covers the content area and methodology but asks for student response in regard to any changes in attitudes and understandings.

INSTRUCTIONAL RESOURCES

There are a wide variety of materials available for use by educators. The following compilation represents the items found to be most useful in the course just described.

References for Teachers

HINDUISM

Basham, A. L. "Hinduism." *The Concise Encyclopedia of Living Faiths*. Edited by R. C. Zaehner. Boston: Beacon Press, 1959.

————. *The Wonder That Was India*. New York: Grove Press, 1968. (Especially the chapter on religion.)

Hopkins, Thomas J. *The Hindu Religious Tradition*. Encino, Calif.: Dickenson, 1971.

Ions, Veronica. *Indian Mythology*. New York: Hamlyn, 1967.

Morgan, Kenneth, ed. *The Religion of the Hindus*. New York: Ronald Press, 1953.

Rowland, Benjamin. *The Art and Architecture of India*. Baltimore: Penguin Books, 1971.

Stroup, Herbert. *Like a Great River: An Introduction to Hinduism.* New York: Harper & Row, 1972.

Zaehner, R. C. *Hinduism.* New York: Oxford Univ. Press, 1962.

Zimmer, Heinrich. *Myths and Symbols in Indian Art and Civilization.* Princeton, N. J.: Princeton Univ. Press, 1971.

BUDDHISM

Ch'en, Kenneth. *Buddhism in China: A Historical Survey.* Princeton, N. J.: Princeton Univ. Press, 1972.

———. *Buddhism: The Light of Asia.* Barron's Educational Series. Woodbury, N. Y.: Barron's, 1968.

Dumoulin, Heinrich. *A History of Zen Buddhism.* Boston: Beacon Press, 1969.

Horner, I. B.; Conze, Edward; and Robinson, R. H. Chapters on Buddhism in *The Concise Encyclopedia of Living Faiths.* Edited by R. C. Zaehner. Boston: Beacon Press, 1959.

Humphreys, Christmas. *Buddhism.* 3d ed. Baltimore: Penguin Books, 1962.

Kapleau, Philip. *Three Pillars of Zen.* Boston: Beacon Press, 1965.

Rahula, Walpola. *What the Buddha Taught.* New York: Grove Press, 1974.

Seckel, Dietrich. *The Art of Buddhism.* New York: Crown, 1964.

Student Materials

Ballou, Robert O., ed. *The World Bible.* New York: Viking, 1972.

Birch, Daniel R., and Allen, D. *Gandhi.* Asian Studies Inquiry Program. Menlo Park, Calif.: Addison-Wesley, 1969.

Dicks, Steward; Mennill, Paul; and Santor, Donald. *The Many Faces of Religion: An Inquiry Approach.* Boston: Ginn.

Hesse, Hermann. *Siddhartha.* New York: Bantam Books.

Johnson, Everett B., Jr. *Buddhism.* Asian Studies Inquiry Program. Menlo Park, Calif.: Addison-Wesley, 1969.

Rawding, F. W. *The Buddha.* New York: Cambridge Univ. Press, 1975.

Ross, Floyd H., and Hills, Tynette. *The Great Religions by Which Men Live.* Premier Book. Greenwich, Conn.: Fawcett, 1973.

Audiovisual Materials

HINDUISM

Gandhi. Film. B/W, 26 min. McGraw-Hill. New York: 1964.

Hinduism. Film. B/W, 18 min. McGraw-Hill. New York: 1963.

Hinduism. Two filmstrips and cassettes/records. Time-Life Education. New York.

Hindu Sacrament of Thread Investiture. Film. Color, 14 min. Syracuse Univ.

Hindu Temple Rites: Bathing the Image of God. Film. Color, 13 min. Syracuse Univ.

Hindu World. Film. Color, 11 min. Coronet Instructional. Chicago.

India-Hinduism. 160 slides plus text. Asian Religions Media Resources. Visual Edu. Serv., Yale Divinity School. New Haven, Conn.

Pilgrimage to a Hindu Temple. Film. Color, 14 min. Syracuse Univ.

BUDDHISM

Buddhism. Two filmstrips and cassettes/records. Time-Life Education. New York.

Buddhism. Film. B/W, 16 min. McGraw-Hill. New York: 1963.

Buddhism in Southeast Asia and Ceylon. 220 slides plus text. Asian Religions Media Resources. Visual Edu. Serv., Yale Divinity School, New Haven, Conn.

Buddhism: Man and Nature. Film. Color, 13 min. Hartley Productions, Cos Cob, Conn.

Buddhist World. Film. Color, 11 min. Coronet Instructional. Chicago.

Mood of Zen. Film. Color, 13 min. Hartley Productions. Cos Cob, Conn.

Requiem for a Faith. Film. Color, 28 min. Hartley Productions. Cos Cob, Conn.: 1968.

Additional Resources

Buddhist rosary and other religious items from Buddhist Bookstore, 1710 Octavia St., San Francisco, Calif.

Material on Indian culture from Interculture Associates, Box 277, Thompson, Conn., 06277.

Outside speakers and field trip possibilities are relatively easy to arrange in the Detroit area. These include the Detroit Insititute of Arts, Hare Krishna Temple, Integral Yoga Institute, and Self-Realization Fellowship.

Toward a Public Education Course on Christianity

Catherine L. Albanese
and
David L. Barr

Teaching about Christianity is in many respects a problematic endeavor. At the same time, it is perhaps the most challenging area of religion studies today, eminently ready for changes in its study which may elicit dramatic new approaches in the classroom. What follows is written from the perspective of the university, where even now ground is being broken in reconceptualizing the subject content of the Christian traditions and implementing the results in changed and changing courses. Much that will be suggested here has never been tried completely. Rather, it has been explored piecemeal in smaller segments of various undergraduate religion courses. The course outline which follows the discussion has been developed for a recently introduced course at Wright State University. Hence, it will no doubt profit from the revisions of thoughtful educators in light of their elementary or secondary teaching experience.

From the vantage point of an involvement in university research and teaching, the study of Christianity in elementary and secondary schools seems particularly fraught with difficulties. In the first place, the subject matter may be all too familiar to many of the teachers and students, and for that reason it may fail to generate the enthusiasm which a course in, for example, Buddhism in Southeast Asia might provoke. Secondly and conversely, because Christianity is still in some sense normative in traditional American attitudes and values, it may be a "tender" and "sensitive" area for teachers and their students in the public schools. Christianity may be the faith commitment of the teachers and their students, both of whom may be neither accustomed to nor comfortable with its academic study. Or to the contrary, the personal stance of teachers and students may involve a rejection of the

Christianity they have known—a disposition which perhaps includes strong emotional dimensions. Even should teachers and students take a middle ground between these positions, the unconscious Christianity of so many of the linguistic and behavioral transmitters of our culture makes it impossible to stand, in any complete sense, outside the Christian framework in order to study it. Hence, we may say that those in the public school classroom may find it difficult to approach Christianity with the same sense of discovery with which they approach other world religions. On the other hand, they may find it difficult to integrate the intellectual and emotional qualities they possess as humans so that the learning process emerges as the academic study of religion—a relatively "objective" presentation, not molded exclusively by individual faith commitments yet not necessarily hostile to them, a presentation able to discern and value a meaningful content within the Christian traditions.

The problems of elementary and secondary teachers and their students are compounded by the limitations of the conventional wisdom which, until very recently, has governed the study of Christianity in the university. Generally, Christianity has been addressed from the perspective of either the history of doctrine or the history of the institution which is the church. Both of these approaches are valid and illuminating. In fact, their very choice over other avenues of investigation tells us something very important about the meanings and values of Christianity. Nevertheless, the history of doctrine alone is inadequate because it concentrates on the *intellectual* content of a religious faith as that which is most significant—a proposition which many devout Christians would dispute. Attention to theology and dogma may lead students of Christianity away from the natural questions which rise concerning what people do when they are being religious and what this doing means at a variety of levels, only one of which is tied to reasoning. Similarly, the study of Christianity as the history of the Christian church leads to a concentration on the social and political manifestations of the Christian traditions. It focuses upon the collective action of Christian institutions in the arena of history and tends to neglect the inner life which helps shape these outward manifestations. Thus, while these categories for the study of Christianity reflect some of the major orientations of the religion, they perhaps neglect others. They tell us only *part* of what is religious about the Christian religion.

How then do teachers and students deal with the quandaries which the academic study of Christianity presents? Do they try simultaneously to rouse their enthusiasm and exercise their emotions? Do teachers mention in passing that there were Gothic cathedrals in the Middle Ages, while students volunteer that many Christians read their Bibles at home without regular church attendance? Clearly such a resolution, even if feasible, would offer at best only a patchwork of semisuccessful efforts. But if teachers and students experience some frustration as they try to utilize old categories, the question easily rises concerning the possibility of searching for new ones. The introduction of new ways of understanding the Christian traditions might stimulate both inquiring minds and the development of new materials so that a richer, more complex, and perhaps more accurate comprehension of Christianity results.

Fortunately, the search for new categories need not revert to the intellectual chaos of totally new beginnings. There is already at hand the considerable body of scholarly reflection which has attended the development of the studies of comparative religions and the history of religions in the nineteenth and twentieth centuries.

In particular, the discipline of the history of religions will prove helpful for our dilemma. The use of the categories which rise out of this discipline avoids the twin pitfalls of familiarity and excessive passion. It gives us a different way of looking at Christianity so that what was once familiar becomes new. Moreover, history of religions prevents theology and church from becoming exclusively determinative categories. At the same time, they remain significant categories and are given their due.

While there are perhaps as many descriptions of what the history of religions does as there are describers, in general it is possible to identify three focuses for its work. History of religions is *phenomenological;* that is, it attends to the phenomenon or manifestation of religion as it appears in a given context. It takes that phenomenon seriously and studies it sympathetically. At the same time, history of religions is *comparative;* that is, it compares the forms or appearances of religion in one culture to the religious data of diverse other cultures. Such comparison leads to an interest in those general forms in which religion presents itself which are valid for every culture. Finally, history of religions is *historical* and investigates each religious phenomenon with a view to understanding its particularity and specificity. Above all, in each of these focuses, history of religions seeks to comprehend religion as religious *experience*. Thus, from the perspective of the history of religions, theological and ecclesiastical records are important because they are viewed as expressions and interpretations of religious experience.[1]

Refracted through the prism of the history of religions, Christianity becomes visible as the religious experience and interpretation of numberless peoples distributed through space and time. Perpetuating the memory of its original heritage and inviting continuing generations to renewed attention to some portions of its past, Christianity has also been open to the possibility of new religious experience and interpretation as the plurality of its traditions gives witness. Elements of the Christian traditions, whether doctrine or churchly structure, liturgy or moral injunction, are a kind of shorthand, a code in which Christians may decipher and sometimes recapture or reinterpret the experience which authenticates their identity. From this point of view, dogma, institution, ritual, and ethical code are all symbols which have the power to disclose the religious meaning of Christianity. Factors which have been repeatedly stressed in the study of the Christian traditions—Christian ideas and Christian institutions—hence receive their due in the history of religions. However, they do not unduly obscure the presence of other religious signs which may tell us as much concerning the nature of Christianity.

Thus, the focus of the following suggested course is on religious experience and interpretation, with a deliberate effort to show their distinctive forms in each major Christian tradition. The generalizations attempt to set forth the structures of such interpreted experience and then to show its varieties in Christianity. The subject matter outline takes each major tradition in turn and tries to reveal the dominant forms of religion as they have existed in the historical development of each tradition.

It is hoped that this course will present more than a collection of facts about Christianity, that the student will discover what is *religious* about this religion, and that some comprehensive interpretation of the nature of Christianity will result. These are grand goals, to be sure, but goals worth pursuing. Finally, it must be said again that this is a work-in-progress and not the assured result of critical scholarship. Each teacher is invited to become a participating learner in the attempt to understand the complex phenomena that constitute Christianity.

A SUGGESTED COURSE ON CHRISTIANITY

Course Goals

1. To investigate the Christian tradition within the categories of the history of religions to discover what is *religious* about Christianity.
2. To discover the dominant concerns of the three major Christian traditions.
3. To become familiar with the major events of Christian history.
4. To explore the significance of Christianity in the development of Western civilization.
5. To appreciate the variety of Christian traditions and the variety within each tradition.

N.B. In view of our own perspective, which is that of the university, we have not tried to construct behavioral objectives for this course.

Generalizations

1. Christianity is a form of religious experience and interpretation which includes:
   a) Institutional structures: church, monastery, service organizations.
   b) Mythic patterns: sacred stories, religious thought, theology.
   c) Ritual activities: liturgies, sacraments.
   d) Moral codes/ethical systems: natural law, revelation, tradition.
   e) Community and individual experience: conversion, devotion, mysticism.
2. Christianity exists in three major traditions:
   a) Eastern Orthodoxy.
   b) Roman Catholicism.
   c) Protestantism.
3. Within each tradition one finds orientations toward both this-worldly and otherworldly experience.
4. Thisworldly experience is concerned with achievement in history; examples include the Crusades, the temporal power of the papacy, the social-gospel movement, and missionary enterprise.
5. Otherworldly experience is concerned with attaining inner purity and a relationship to the Divine; examples include the monastic and mystical traditions, millennialism, and liturgical involvement.
6. Relative to the other traditions, each tradition tends to exhibit a dominant orientation.

a) Eastern Orthodoxy tends to exhibit otherworldly concerns.

b) Roman Catholicism tends to exhibit both types of concerns.

c) Protestantism tends to exhibit thisworldly concerns.

Subject Matter Outline

The following outline includes references to important works on the topics covered. In many instances we have referred to specific chapters, but where we have simply listed the book, an examination of its table of contents will indicate the relevant material. When a subpoint is not followed by a reference, either that subpoint is covered in the previous reference to the major point or that subpoint can be easily found in the standard reference works in the bibliography at the end of this article.

I. The structure of religious experience and interpretation in Christianity

    A. Religion as an orientation in community (the people of God) [King, chap. 3; Eliade, *Patterns*]

        1. The religious form of the community in space and time

            a) The internal order of the community: church, sect, denomination [Troeltsch, Mead]

            b) The temporal dynamic of the community

                (1) Thisworldly concerns—involvement in history and an ethic for action [Eliade, *Cosmos and History,* chap. 4]

                (2) Otherworldly concerns—inner involvement with God and the self [Eliade, *Sacred and Profane,* chaps. 3 and 4]

        2. The religious action of the community

            a) Experience and interpretation in language [King, Pt. II]

                (1) The sacred story (Scripture, tradition) [Eliade, *Cosmos and History,* chap. 1]

                (2) Creedal statements (orthodoxy and heterodoxy) [King, chap. 5]

                (3) Theology

                (4) Theological philosophy

             b) Experience and interpretation in ritual

                (1) Sacred space (church buildings, shrines, other places for reaching the divine) [Eliade, *Sacred and Profane,* chaps. 1 and 2]

     (2) Sacred time (separation from profane, transition, incorporation of sacred) [Van Gennep]

     (3) Sacred persons (priests and ministers as conduits for sacred power).

     (4) Sacred objects (sacraments and sacramentals as holy or powerful objects [James]

     (5) Liturgy (the dramatic combination of the ritual elements to express and interpret the sacred story or myth of the community—a solemn and enacted recitation of the myth) [Van Gennep; Turner; Streng, chap. 6]

B. Religion as an individual orientation [Streng, Part II]

    1. General presupposition: community as backdrop

    2. The forms of experience

      a) Conversion

      b) Devotion

         (1) Quest for moral purity

         (2) Relationship to God and to saints

      c) Mysticism

II. The Eastern Orthodox tradition

A. The worship experience in an Orthodox church: the church as sacred space [Ware, chap. 13]

    1. The use of icons [Benz, chap. 1]

    2. The liturgy [Orthodox Eastern Church, *Liturgies of Saints Mark, et al.*]

    3. The taking of the Eucharist

    4. The involvement of all five senses with symbolic transformations to things divine

B. Central ideas of the Orthodox tradition [Benz, chap. 3]

    1. The church as the community in Christ [Ware, chap. 12]

      a) The community as the locus of personal identity

      b) The Spirit in the *whole* church

    2. The centrality of worship: right praise

    3. The interpenetration of matter and spirit: spirit-bearing matter

    4. The continuity of tradition: authority [Ware, chap. 10]

      a) Bible

      b) Councils

      c) The Fathers

        d) The liturgy

        e) Icons

  C. The historical origins of the Orthodox tradition

     1. The nature of the eastern provinces of the Roman Empire at the beginning of the Christian era and their Christianization [Spinka, chap. 1]

     2. Factors differentiating East and West [Ware, chap. 3]

        a) Language

        b) Limited travel

        c) Political instability in the West

        d) Theological differences

           (1) The use of icons in the East

           (2) The development of a celibate clergy and the idea of purgatory in the West

           (3) The issue of organizational unity and primacy

           (4) The addition of *filioque* to the Nicene Creed in the West

     3. The formal schism of 1054 as recognition of the separate forms of religious consciousness in East and West

  D. The Orthodox churches today [Ware, chaps. 7, 8, and 9]

     1. The national bodies

     2. The Orthodox churches in the United States

III. The Roman Catholic tradition

  A. The emergence of the Catholic tradition [Walker, Pts. I and II]

     1. The great doctrinal disputes

     2. The organization of the institutional church

     3. The Roman church and the Roman Empire

  B. Central aspects of the Catholic tradition [McKenzie]

     1. One, holy, catholic, and apostolic church: the organization and the idea

     2. The nature of authority

        a) Scripture

        b) Tradition

     3. Sacramentalism, incarnationalism: ritual, natural theology, social action, humanism

  C. Power in this world: the great medieval popes [Ullman]

     1. Pope Leo I and the primacy of Rome (c. 450)

     2. Pope Leo III and Charlemagne (c. 800)

3. Pope Gregory VII and King Henry IV (c. 1075)
4. Pope Innocent III and the princes of Europe (c. 1200)
D. Pursuit of another world: the spirit of medieval Catholicism
   1. The making of saints [Workman]
   2. The development of monasticism [Workman]
   3. The mystical tradition [Underhill]
   4. The millennial movements [Walker]
   5. The cathedrals [von Simson; Adams]
   6. The Mass [Dix; Thompson]
E. The unity of the two worlds
   1. The great chain of being [Lovejoy]
   2. The papacy as a religious symbol [Ullman]
   3. The scholastic tradition: theology and politics [Gilson]
F. The waning of the Middle Ages
   1. The emergence of nationalism [Ferguson, chaps. 6, 12, and 13]
      a) The rise of French power
      b) The "French popes"
   2. The rise of capitalism and commerce [Ferguson, chap. 5]
   3. The growth of individualism
   4. The division of the church [Chadwick, chap. 11]

G. The continuation of the Catholic tradition
   1. The aftermath of the Protestant schism [Daniel-Rops]
      a) The Council of Trent
      b) The Society of Jesus
      c) The Inquisition
   2. Shifting fortunes in a changing world
      a) The French Revolution
      b) Assertions of authority [Hales]
         (1) The Syllabus of Errors
         (2) Doctrinal developments: doctrine of Mary, papal infallibility
      c) The rise of Catholic liberalism [Hales]
      d) The Second Vatican Council [Abbott]
IV. The Protestant tradition [Dillenberger and Welch; Hillerbrand]
A. The protest of Martin Luther
   1. The cultural context of the Reformation [Ferguson, chaps. 7, 8, and 9]

a) Medieval reform movements [Walker]

b) The conciliar movement [Chadwick, chap. 1]

c) Nominalist philosophy [Walker]

d) Late medieval spirituality: piety and the new humanism

e) Monastic spirituality and Luther's religious quest [Bainton, *Here I Stand*]

f) The worldliness of the church

g) German nationalism and Italian empire

h) The emerging money economy and the new middle class [Weber]

2. The central convictions of the reformers [Dillenberger and Welch, chap. 2; Bainton, *Reformation,* chaps. 2 and 3]

a) Salvation by grace alone

b) Authority of the Bible alone

c) The church as a community of believers/new understandings of ritual [Thompson]

d) The priesthood of all believers

B. The four strands of the Reformation [Dillenberger and Welch]

1. Luther and the Lutherans: the church reformed and faithful [Chadwick, chap. 2]

2. Calvin and the Calvinists: the kingdom of the sovereign God [Wendel; Bainton, *Reformation,* chap. 6]

3. The Anglicans: the way of comprehension [Bainton, *Reformation,* chap. 10; Dickens]

4. The Anabaptists: the gathered church [Bainton, *Reformation,* chap. 5; Williams]

C. The Protestant pursuit of history

1. Puritan England and New England [Simpson; Dillenberger and Welch, chap. 5]

2. The great missionary advance [Glover]

3. Revivalism and/or social reform [Dillenberger and Welch, chaps. 2 and 6; McLoughlin]

4. The ecumenical movement [Von Rohr, chap. 14]

5. Antihistory: Protestant millennial movements

V. The meeting of the traditions in America [Ahlstrom]

A. The Americanization of the traditions

1. The traditions become minorities: denominationalism [Mead]

2. The traditions become "protestantized": democracy and diversity [Ellis; O'Brien; Brauer; Hudson]
3. The traditions stress activism and moralism [Mead, chap. 1; Marty, *Righteous Empire,* chaps. 9 and 19]

B. The distinctively American phenomena
   1. The separation of church and state [Mead]
   2. New denominations: Latter-Day Saints, Churches of Christ, Jehovah's Witnesses, Christian Scientists, Seventh-Day Adventists, Unitarians [Bedell, chap. 4; Ahlstrom; Rosten]
   3. Significant religious developments in America [Ahlstrom]
      a) Fundamentalism [Sandeen; Gatewood, "Introduction," chaps. 1 and 8]
      b) Millennialism
      c) Revivalism and Pentecostalism
      d) Social Gospel [Ahlstrom; Marty, *Righteous Empire,* chap. 19]
      e) Evangelical cooperation
      f) Interfaith dialogue [Bedell, chap. 8]
   4. Christianity in synthesis
      a) The Black churches [Lincoln; Genovese, Book 2, Part I; Barrett]
      b) Civil religion [Richey and Jones, especially chaps. 2, 3, 4, 7, and 10]

Evaluation

We suggest a series of unit exams which test the range of factual knowledge of the student (perhaps with multiple-choice questions) plus an essay which asks the student to analyze the tradition by means of the categories "thisworldly" and "otherworldly," citing evidence for the judgments made. The final examination ought to cover the basic concepts and generalizations of the course about Christian religious experience and interpretation and, thus, should be an essay.

NOTE

1. For a fuller discussion of the usefulness and possibilities of history of religious categories in the context of American and world religion, see Catherine L. Albanese, *Corresponding Motion: Transcendental Religion and the New America* (Philadelphia: Temple Univ. Press, [forthcoming]).

BIBLIOGRAPHY

Reference Works for the Teacher

Bettenson, H. *Documents of the Christian Church*. London & New York: Oxford Univ. Press, 1947.

Brauer, Jerald C., ed. *The Westminster Dictionary of Church History*. Philadelphia: Westminster, 1971.

Catholic University of America. *New Catholic Encyclopedia*. 15 vols. New York: McGraw-Hill, 1967.

Cross, F. L., and Livingstone, E. A., eds. *The Oxford Dictionary of the Christian Church*. 2d ed. New York: Oxford Univ. Press, 1974.

Ferguson, Wallace K. *Europe in Transition: 1300–1520*. Boston: Houghton, 1963.

Gonzalez, Justo L. *A History of Christian Thought*. 3 vols. Nashville, Abingdon, 1975.

Mead, Frank. *Handbook of Denominations in the United States*. 6th ed. Nashville, Tenn.: Abingdon, 1975.

Thompson, Bard, ed. *Liturgies of the Western Church*. N.Y.: Meridian Books, 1962.

Walker, Williston. *A History of the Christian Church*. 3rd ed. N.Y.: Scribner, 1970.

Watts, Allan. *Myth and Ritual in Christianity*. Boston: Beacon Press, 1968.

THE STUDY OF RELIGIONS

Eliade, Mircea. *Cosmos and History: The Myth of the Eternal Return*. Harper Torchbook. New York: Harper & Row, 1959.

———.*Patterns in Comparative Religion*. Cleveland: Collins World, 1958.

———.*The Sacred and the Profane: The Nature of Religion*. Translated by Willard R. Track. New York: Harcourt, Brace, Jovanovich, 1968.

James, E. O. *Sacrifice and Sacraments*. New York: Barnes & Noble, 1962.

King, Winston. *Introduction to Religion: A Phenomenological Approach*. New York: Harper & Row, 1968.

Streng, Fredrick J. *Understanding Religious Life*. 2d ed. Encino, Calif.: Dickenson, 1976.

Turner, Victor. *The Ritual Process: Structure and Anti-Structure*. Chicago: Aldine, 1969.

Van Gennep, Arnold. *The Rites of Passage*. Translated by Monika B. Vizedon and Gabrielle L. Caffee. Chicago: Univ. of Chicago Press, 1960.

EASTERN ORTHODOXY

Benz, Ernst. *The Eastern Orthodox Church*. New York: Doubleday-Anchor, 1963.

French, Reginald M. *The Eastern Orthodox Church*. New York: Hutchinson's Univ. Library, 1964.

Orthodox Eastern Church. *Liturgies of Saints Mark, James, Clement, Chrysostom, Basil.* New York: AMS Press, 1969.

Pelikan, Jaroslav. *The Spirit of Eastern Christendom.* Chicago: University of Chicago Press, 1974.

Schmemann, Alexander. *For the Life of the World: Sacraments and Orthodoxy.* Crestwood, N.Y.: St. Vladimir's Sem. Press, 1973.

Spinka, Matthew. *A History of Christianity in the Balkans: A Study in the Spread of Byzantine Culture Among the Slavs.* Hamden, Conn.: Archon Books, 1968.

Ware, Timothy. *The Orthodox Church.* Baltimore: Penguin Books, 1963.

ROMAN CATHOLICISM

Abbott, Walter M., ed. *The Documents of Vatican II.* Translated by Joseph Gallagher. New York: Association Press, 1966.

Adams, Henry. *Mont-Saint-Michel and Chartres.* Anchor Books. New York: Doubleday, 1959.

Daniel-Rops, Henry. *The Catholic Reformation.* 2 vols. Translated by John Warrington. New York: Dutton, 1962.

Dix, Dom Gregory. *The Shape of the Liturgy.* 2d ed. London: Dacre Press, 1945.

Gilson, Etienne. *Reason and Revelation in the Middle Ages.* New York: Scribner, 1938.

Hales, E. E. Y. *The Catholic Church in the Modern World.* New York: Doubleday, 1960.

Leff, Gordon. *Medieval Thought: St. Augustine to Ockham.* Baltimore: Penguin Books, 1958.

Lovejoy, Arthur. *The Great Chain of Being.* New York: Harper & Row, 1960.

McKenzie, John. *The Roman Catholic Church.* New York: Doubleday, 1971.

Simson, Otto von. *The Gothic Cathedral: Origins of Gothic Architecture and the Medieval Concept of Order.* New York: Harper & Row, 1962.

Ullmann, Walter. *A Short History of the Papacy in the Middle Ages.* London: Methuen, 1972.

Underhill, Evelyn. *Mysticism.* New York: World Pub., 1955.

Workman, Herbert. *The Evolution of the Monastic Ideal.* Gloucester, Mass.: Peter Smith, 1976.

PROTESTANTISM

Bainton, Roland H. *Here I Stand: A Life of Martin Luther.* Nashville, Tenn.: Abingdon, 1951.

———. *The Reformation of the Sixteenth Century.* Boston: Beacon Press, 1956.

Chadwick, Owen. *The Reformation.* Baltimore: Penguin Books, 1964.

Dickens, A. G. *The English Reformation.* New York: Schocken Books, 1964.

Dillenberger, John, and Welch, Claude. *Protestant Christianity.* N.Y.: Scribner, 1954.

Glover, R. H. *The Progress of World-Wide Missions*. Revised by J. H. Kane. New York: Harper & Row, 1960.

Hillerbrand, Hans J., ed. *The Reformation: A Narrative History*. New York: Harper & Row, 1964.

Rohr, John Von. *Profile of Protestantism: An Introduction to Its Faith and Life*. Encino, Calif.: Dickenson, 1969.

Simpson, Alan. *Puritanism in Old and New England*. Chicago: University of Chicago Press, 1955.

Stoeffler, F. Ernest. *The Rise of Evangelical Pietism*. Supplements to *Numen, 9*. Leiden, Nether.: Brill, 1965.

Troeltsch, Ernst. *The Social Teaching of the Christian Churches*. 2 vols. Translated by Olive Wyon. New York: Harper & Row.

Weber, Max. *The Protestant Ethic and the Spirit of Capitalism*. N.Y.: Scribner, 1958.

Wendel, Francois. *Calvin: Origins and Development of His Religious Thought*. New York: Harper & Row, 1950.

Williams, George H. *The Radical Reformation*. Philadelphia: Westminster, 1962.

AMERICAN RELIGION

Ahlstrom, Sydney. *A Religious History of the American People*. New Haven, Conn.: Yale Univ. Press, 1972.

Barrett, Leonard. *Soul-Force: African Heritage in Afro-American Religion*. New York, N.Y.: Doubleday-Anchor Books, 1974.

Bedell, George, et al. *Religion in America*. New York: Macmillan, 1975.

Brauer, Jerald C. *Protestantism in America: A Narrative History*. rev. ed. Philadelphia: Westminster, 1966.

Clark, Elmer T. *The Small Sects in America*. Nashville, Tenn.: Abingdon, 1949.

Ellis, John Tracy. *American Catholicism*. 2d ed., rev. Chicago: University of Chicago Press, 1969.

Gatewood, Willard B., Jr., ed. *Controversy in the Twenties: Fundamentalism, Modernism, and Evolution*. Nashville, Tenn.: Vanderbilt Univ. Press, 1969.

Genovese, Eugene D. *Roll Jordan Roll: The World the Slaves Made*. New York: Pantheon, 1974.

Hudson, Winthrop S. *Religion in America*. 2d ed. New York: Scribner, 1973.

Lincoln, C. Eric, ed. *The Black Experience in Religion*. N.Y.: Doubleday-Anchor, 1974.

McLoughlin, William G., Jr. *Modern Revivalism: Charles Grandison Finney to Billy Graham*. New York: Ronald Press, 1959.

Marty, Martin E. *A Nation of Believers*. Chicago: Univ. of Chicago Press, 1976.

——. *Righteous Empire: The Protestant Experience in America*. N.Y.: Dial, 1970.

Mead, Sidney E. *The Lively Experiment: The Shaping of Christianity in America*. New York: Harper & Row, 1963.

Niebuhr, H. Richard. *The Social Sources of Denominationalism.* Meridian Books. Cleveland: World, 1976.

O'Brien, David. *The Renewal of American Catholicism.* New York: Oxford Univ. Press, 1972.

Richey, Russell E., and Jones, Donald G., eds. *American Civil Religion.* New York: Harper & Row, 1974.

Rosten, Leo, ed. *Religions in America.* New York: Simon & Schuster, 1963.

Sandeen, Ernest H. *The Origins of Fundamentalism: Toward a Historical Interpretation.* Philadelphia: Fortress Press, 1968.

Weisberger, B. A. *They Gathered at the River.* Chicago: Quadrangle Books, 1966.

Zaretsky, Irving I., and Leone, Mark P. *Religious Movements in Contemporary America.* Princeton, N. J.: Princeton Univ. Press, 1974.

References for the Student

Bainton, Roland. *Christendom: A Short History of Christianity and Its Impact on Western Civilization.* 2 vols. New York: Harper & Row, 1976.

Marty, Martin. *A Short History of Christianity.* New York: Meridian Books, 1959.

Audiovisual Resources

The Crusades: Saints and Sinners. Color, 26 min. Learning Corporation of America, Rental Library, 711 Fifth Avenue, New York, N.Y. 10022. 1970.

The Divine Liturgy. (Eastern Orthodox). Color, 30 min. Mottas Films, 1318 Ohio Avenue, N.E., Canton, Ohio 44705.

Eye of the Heart: American Indians and the Church. Color, 30 min. National Council of Churches, TV Film Library, Room 860, 475 Riverside Drive, New York, N.Y. 10027.

Galileo: The Challenge of Reason. Color, 26 min. Learning Corporation of America, Rental Library, 711 Fifth Avenue, New York, N.Y. 10022. 1970.

In the Good Old Fashioned Way. Color, 30 min. Appalshop, Inc., Box 743, Whitesburg, Ky. 41858. (Old Regular Baptist Church; Appalachia.)

Martin Luther and the Protestant Reformation. B/W, 30 min. Time/Life Films, 43 W. 16th St., New York, N.Y. 10011. 1969.

A Matter of Conscience: Henry VIII and Thomas More. Color, 30 min. Learning Corporation of America, Rental Library, 711 Fifth Avenue, New York, 10022. 1972.

Medieval Life: The Monastery. Color, 15 min. Modern Film Rentals, 2323 New Hyde Park Road, New Hyde Park, N.Y. 11040.

Medieval Times: Role of the Church. Color, 13½ min. Modern Film Rentals, 2323 New Hyde Park Road, New Hyde Park, N.Y. 11040.

Religious America Series. 12 videotapes. Color, 30 min. Public Broadcasting System. Contact local station. (Religious services and personal testimonies from a broad spectrum of Americans.)

The Revival Heard Round the World. Videotape. 30 min. Auburn Theological Seminary, 3041 Broadway, New York, N.Y. 10027. (Charles G. Finney; reconstructed revival service, nineteenth century.)

The Vatican. Color, 52 min. Time/Life Films, 43 W. 16th Street, New York, N.Y. 10011. 1976.

The Meeting of Science and Religion: Narratives about Origins

Barbara Ann Swyhart
and
Mark R. Lester

In the summer of 1975, Dr. Roy Harris, Social Studies Specialist in the San Diego Unified School District, invited us to participate in the preparation of a curriculum unit on cosmic and human origins for use in senior high school anthropology courses. Dr. Harris described the project as follows:

> I would suggest that such a document include not merely "both sides of the issue" (i.e., evolution vs. creation), but rather a wide range of explanations that different cultures have put forth to explain the origins of man. The following perspectives are examples of what I had in mind.
> 1. The Judeo-Christian perspective including the range of views from fundamental biblical to liberal Christian;
> 2. Asian-Oriental;
> 3. Mythical including classical Greek and primitive;
> 4. Scientific.[1]

The project was prompted by the long-standing controversy in California centering on the manner in which the theory of evolution is presented in textbooks adopted for classroom use. The Creation-Science Institute of San Diego, most vocal in the argument, requested that the evolutionary position be taught as a hypothesis rather than as a demonstrable theory, along with the Creation narrative in the Bible as the literal account of the origin of the universe and human beings. The suggestion of a curriculum which would include a variety of different interpretations of the origin of humanity and the universe was accepted by the Institute. Members were invited to write a piece exemplifying their own position which would be included in a larger work. They did this most willingly.

The curriculum which was subsequently developed is entitled "Narratives About Cosmic and Human Origins," and contains selections from the world's major religions and from such distinct geographical areas as the Near East, Africa, and Australia.[2] The work also focuses on a historical presentation of key Western commentaries on cosmic and human origins as well as interpretations contained in the Book of Genesis. This essay presents one component of "Narratives"—Western views on the origin of the cosmos and life. The selections reflect philosophical, religious, and scientific viewpoints. Sometimes scientists speak of religion and at other times theologians speak of science.[3]

As planned, the total syllabus could cover a full semester; however, selected readings are ideal for a six-week unit within an anthropology course. The unit we present below runs approximately two weeks. The readings are diverse enough so that a student may choose selections at his or her reading level. The selections are not intended to present every point of view. Rather, they illustrate the wide variety of differing viewpoints on the origin of the universe and life. (The student may fulfill the cognitive competency requirements by becoming acquainted with three or four selections.)

The Western unit contains a preponderance of "scientific" narratives. Care should be taken not to present these narratives and the preceding large selection of "religious" narratives as mutually antagonistic and contradictory positions. Students should be able to see that there is no necessary dichotomy between scientific and religious understandings of cosmic origins. Instead there are multiple interpretations stressing differing perspectives. Thus we have included philosophical elaborations of a scriptural position (e.g., the Talmud), humanistic interpretations of science (e.g., Bronowski), and religious interpretations of evolution (e.g., Pierre Teilhard de Chardin and Asa Gray).

The impression given in most Genesis vs. evolution debates is that there are only two types of narratives and they articulate this question in the mutually exclusive terms: Creation *or* evolution. Not so! This collection demonstrates that many thoughtful people have produced a great variety of answers to this question. Even those who are placed in one school of thought may often be placed in several other different schools. Reducing a person's views on so complex an issue to a single argument often denies the complexity, richness, and sophistication of the narrator's position.

GOALS AND OBJECTIVES

The resource unit covers the beginning of modern thinking about origins and culminates in the modern scientific conceptualization of the late Jacob Bronowski. In presenting these ideas, we have placed the long-range goals primarily within the cognitive-ethical domains. The student is informed about theoretical positions, both religious and scientific; the student is shown the relationship between thought and behavior on both individual and social levels, for example, the relationship between evolution and Social Darwinism, and the influence of Social Darwinism on the development of Marxism.

In the discussion which follows the reading, the student is expected to develop a capacity for critical reflection by responding to such questions as:

1. What is religion?
2. What is science?
3. What is the domain of religion?
4. What is the domain of science?
5. Do they overlap at any points? If so, when? If not, why not?
6. What are the relationships between thinking and believing, believing and knowing, believing and behavior?

CONTENTS

The subject matter of this unit is best presented diagrammatically.[4]

Readings	Concepts	Vocabulary
Charles Darwin, *Descent of Man* (excerpts)	Evolution vs. Genesis Science as providing a different mode of explanation from that of religion Social Darwinism Possible confrontations of science and religion	evolution natural selection

Readings	Concepts	Vocabulary
Asa Gray, *Darwiniana* (excerpts)	The amelioration of science and religion: evolution as evidencing Providential design Evolution as hypothesis rather than proof	teleology hypothesis design
A. G. Hays, "The Scopes Trial," in *Evolution and Religion* by Gail Kennedy	Societal attempts to control the outcome of the meeting of science and religion	fundamentalism
Bertrand Russell, "Evolution," from *Religion and Science*	Historical approach to what is perceived as an essential antagonism between science and religion	agnosticism skepticism
Pierre Teilhard de Chardin, *The Phenomenon of Man* (excerpts)	The religious application of evolution: spiritual evolution	biosphere hominization noosphere convergence Omega point
Langdon Gilkey, *Maker of Heaven and Earth* (excerpts)	Reconstruction of a myth in the light of a separation of science and religion Modes of discourse: levels of meaning	neoorthodoxy existential myth
Robert E. Kofahl, "Creation and Science" and "Biblical Creation"	Fundamentalist attempts to verify Creation by science A religious repudiation of evolution which still desires to be scientifically oriented	radiometry
Fred Hoyle, *The Nature of the Universe* (excerpts)	A scientific narrative which avoids conflict with religion by separating the questions of "how" and "why" things come to be	continuous creation steady state theory

Readings	Concepts	Vocabulary
Jacob Bronowski, *Ascent of Man* (excerpts)	A recognition of the contribution of all perspectives on origins to the understanding of the mystery of the universe	

EVALUATION

Since the *Schempp* decision allows the teaching about religion in the public schools but disallows the fostering of religious commitment, evaluation must be restricted to measuring cognitive development and the acquisition of a knowledge of the religio-ethical options each perspective affords. Thus essay examinations, class projects, debates, and student responses to guest lectures would be the most appropriate means of evaluation.

This does not mean that attitudes of tolerance will not be developed and so listed as a realistic goal. On the contrary, we believe that the right to believe can only be safeguarded when tolerance for others' beliefs and practices is encouraged. Therefore, while it is not our intention to change a person's belief, it is our intention to create an atmosphere of gentle tolerance and critical reflection in religion studies, just as one would create such an atmosphere in any academic discipline. Religion studies is distinct in that it touches the private rights of the individual but does so in an academic setting and with an appropriate method conducive to the preservation of the right to believe. It is in this domain that teacher evaluation is most important. Class conferences should be held intermittently throughout the course. Parents should be informed of the intent and content of the syllabus. If possible, parents should be invited to a sample class or to a group meeting to ask questions.

NOTES

1. Dr. Roy Harris, in a memorandum to Mr. Bennett, San Diego Unified School District, June 12, 1975.
2. "Narratives About Cosmic and Human Origins," San Diego Unified School District, 1976. (A modified version of "Narratives" will be published by Paulist Press.)
3. Ibid.

4. This list represents the selections in "Narratives" as published by the San Diego Unified School District. The version to be published by Paulist Press will contain additions such as Galileo, Theodosius Dobzhansky, and James Watson.

BIBLIOGRAPHY

Basic Works for a Study of the Meeting of Science and Religion: Historical, Thematic, and Methodological Perspectives

Abbott, Lyman. *The Evolution of Christianity.* New York: Johnson Reprint Corp., 1969.

———. *The Theology of an Evolutionist.* Boston: Houghton, 1897.

Barbour, Ian. *Issues in Science and Religion.* New York: Harper & Row, 1971.

———. *Myths, Models and Paradigms.* New York: Harper & Row, 1974.

———. *Science and Religion.* New York: Harper & Row, 1968.

———. *Science and Secularity.* New York: Harper & Row, 1970.

Birch, L. Charles. *Nature and God.* Philadelphia: Westminster, 1966.

Booth, Edwin P. *Religion Ponders Science.* New York: Appleton, 1964.

Brecht, Bertolt. *Galileo.* New York: Grove Press, 1966.

Bronowski, Jacob. *The Ascent of Man.* Boston: Little, Brown, 1973.

Bullough, V. L., ed. *The Scientific Revolution.* Gloucester, Mass.: Peter Smith, 1970.

Burhoe, Ralph Wendell, ed. *Science and Human Values in the 21st Century.* Philadelphia: Westminster, 1971.

Butterfield, Herbert. *The Origins of Modern Science.* rev. ed. New York: Free Press, 1965.

Collingwood, R. G. *The Idea of Nature.* Oxford: Oxford Univ. Press, 1945.

Dampier, W. C. *A History of Science.* New York: Cambridge Univ. Press, 1961.

Darwin, Charles. *The Origin of Species.* Philadelphia: Univ. of Pennsylvania Press, 1959.

De Santillana, Giorgio. *The Crime of Galileo.* Phoenix Book. Chicago: Univ. of Chicago Press, 1955.

Dillenberger, John. *Protestant Thought and Natural Science.* Nashville, Tenn.: Abingdon, 1960.

Dobzhansky, Theodosius. *Evolution, Genetics, and Man.* New York: Wiley, 1955.

Draper, J. W. *History of the Conflict Between Religion and Science.* New York: Appleton, 1897.

Eddington, Arthur. *The Nature of the Physical World.* Ann Arbor, Mich.: Univ. of Michigan Press, 1958.

Educational Research Council of America, Social Science Staff. *Technology: Promises and Problems.* new ed. Boston: Allyn & Bacon, 1972.

Eiseley, Loren. *Darwin's Century: Evolution and the Men Who Discovered It*. New York: Doubleday, 1958.

———. *Francis Bacon and the Modern Dilemma*. Lincoln: Univ. of Nebraska Press, 1962.

———. *The Immense Journey*. Vintage Book. New York: Random House, 1957.

———. *The Unexplained Universe*. New York: Harcourt, 1969.

Francoeur, Robert. *Perspectives in Evolution*. Baltimore: Helicon, 1965.

Fuller, Watson, ed. *The Biological Revolution: Social Good or Social Evil?* Anchor Book. New York: Doubleday, 1971.

Gamow, George. *The Creation of the Universe*. rev. ed. Mentor Book. New York: Viking, 1961.

Gilkey, Langdon. *Maker of Heaven and Earth*. Anchor Book. New York: Doubleday, 1965.

———. *Religion and the Scientific Future*. New York: Harper & Row, 1970.

Gillispie, Charles Culston. *Genesis and Geology: The Decades before Darwin*. Harper Torchbook. New York: Harper & Row, 1959.

Glass, Bentley, et al. *Forerunners of Darwin (1745-1859)*. Baltimore: Johns Hopkins Press, 1959.

Gorney, Roderic. *The Human Agenda*. New York: Simon & Schuster, 1972.

Gray, Asa. *Darwiniana: Essays and Reviews Pertaining to Darwinism*. Edited by A. Hunter Dupree. Cambridge, Mass.: Belknap Press of Harvard Univ. Press, 1963.

Greene, John C. *Darwin and the Modern World View*. Baton Rouge: Louisiana State Univ. Press, 1961.

Habgood, John. *Truths in Tension: New Perspectives in Religion and Science*. New York: Holt, 1964.

Hall, A. R. *The Scientific Revolution, 1500-1800*. Boston: Beacon Press, 1966.

Hesse, Mary B. *Science and Human Imagination*. New York: Philosophical Library, 1955.

Hodge, Charles. *What Is Darwinism?* New York: Scribner, 1874.

Hoffding, Harold. *A History of Modern Philosophy II*. New York: Dover Pub., 1955.

Huxley, Julian. *Religion Without Revelation*. New and rev. ed. New York: Harper & Row, 1961.

Huxley, Thomas Henry. *Science and Christian Tradition*. New York: Appleton, 1968.

Johnson, Roger A.; Wallwork, Ernest; Green, Clifford; Sentmire, H. Paul; Vanderpool, Harold Y. *Critical Issues in Modern Religion*. Englewood Cliffs, N. J.: Prentice-Hall, 1973.

Jung, Carl G., et al. *Man and His Symbols*. New York: Dell, 196 4.

———. *Modern Man in Search of a Soul*. New York: Harcourt, 1933.

———. *Psyche and Symbol*. Anchor Book. New York: Doubleday, 1958.

———. *Psychology and Religion*. New Haven, Conn., and London: Yale University Press, 1971.

Koestler, Arthur. *The Sleepwalkers.* New York: Macmillan, 1968.

Kuhn, Thomas S. "History of Science." *Encyclopedia of Social Sciences* 14 (1968): 74–83.

Maslow, Abraham, ed. *New Knowledge in Human Values.* New York: Harper & Row, 1959.

Meland, Bernard Eugene. *The Realities of Faith: The Revelation in Cultural Forms.* New York: Oxford Univ. Press, 1962.

Overman, Richard H. *Evolution and the Christian Doctrine of Creation: A Whiteheadian Interpretation.* Philadelphia: Westminster, 1967.

Polanyi, Michael. *Personal Knowledge: Toward a Post-Critical Philosophy.* Harper Torchbook. New York: Harper & Row, 1964.

———. *Science, Faith and Society.* Chicago: Univ. of Chicago Press, 1964.

———. *The Tacit Dimension.* Anchor Book. New York: Doubleday, 1967.

Popper, Karl. *The Logic of Scientific Discovery.* New York: Basic Books, 1959 (1935).

Ramsey, Ian T. *Religion and Science: Conflict and Synthesis.* Naperville, Ill.: Allenson Press, 1964.

Russell, Bertrand. *The ABC of Relativity.* rev. ed. New York: New American Library, 1970.

———. *Religion and Science.* New York: Oxford Univ. Press, 1961.

Rust, Eric C. *Science and Faith.* New York: Oxford Univ. Press, 1967.

Schilling, Harold K. *Science and Religion: An Interpretation of the Communities.* New York: Scribner, 1962.

Simpson, George Gaylord. *The Meaning of Evolution: A Study of the History of Life and of Its Significance for Man.* New Haven, Conn.: Yale Univ. Press, 1967.

Teilhard de Chardin, Pierre. *The Phenomenon of Man.* Harper Torchbook. New York: Harper & Row, 1961.

Toulmin, Stephen. "Conceptual Revolutions in Science." *Boston Studies in the Philosophy of Science* 3:331–40. Edited by R. S. Cohen and M. W. Wartofsky. New York: Humanities Press, 1968.

———. *Foresight and Understanding.* New York: Harper & Row, 1961.

———. *Human Understanding: The Collective Use and Evolution of Concepts.* Princeton, N. J.: Princeton Univ. Press, 1972.

Westfall, Richard S. *Science and Religion in 17th Century England.* Ann Arbor, Mich: Univ. of Michigan Press, 1973.

White, Andrew Dickson. *A History of the Warfare of Science with Theology in Christendom.* New York: Appleton, 1896.

White, Edward A. *Science and Religion in American Thought.* N.Y.: AMS Press, 1952.

Whitehead, Alfred North. *Adventures of Ideas.* New York: Macmillan, 1933.

———. *Religion in the Making.* New York: Meridian Books, 1954.

———. *Science and the Modern World.* New York: Macmillan, 1953.

Zygon, Vol. 1 to present. Chicago: Univ. of Chicago Press, 1960.

Audiovisual Materials

The Ascent of Man. Narrated by Jacob Bronowski. Time-Life.

The Emergence of Man. Time-Life series.

Galileo. KPBS.

An Inquiry into the Origin of Man: Science and Religion. Slide presentation. Produced by Biological Sciences Curriculum Study and Science and Mankind, Inc., of The Center For the Humanities, Inc.

Part 5

Religion Studies in Programs with
 Values Clarification and Moral
 Education

Supplying the Missing Dimension

Rodney F. Allen, Sr.

One difficult responsibility of the public schools is to help each of its students come to a knowledge of values. As an institution in a pluralistic, democratic society, the schools have a commitment, as far as their resources permit, to help students become citizens who possess attributes associated with rational, self-fulfilled, moral persons. The schools are obligated to provide self-fulfilling, self-actualizing experiences which promote reflection and inquiry on the one hand, but also promote attitudes and motives conducive to democratic life-styles on the other. By necessity, this striving to help mold the democratic person entails the confrontation of student and societal values in the classroom.

Social education, which includes public issues, values clarification, or moral dilemmas, inevitably involves the study of religious as well as secular values. The lives of persons are governed by the values they hold. Values are human instruments derived from the meaning people have found in the physical and spiritual universe, and in their conception of their place in that universe. Values "are like the stars," as Carl Schurz observed, "you choose them as your guides and follow them until you reach your destiny." Value commitments are involved as persons wrestle with questions involving *should, ought, right, good,* and *desirable.* But for many people, including many of those in our classrooms, the fundamental ingredients that give those specific values coherence and meaning are a religious significance and a religious feeling, which serve as a sacred canopy for them.

While dealing with public issues, clarifying personal values, and making decisions with case studies presenting moral dilemmas, teachers and their students will confront religious and philosophical commitments at their deepest levels. Too often, classroom discussions of public issues are handled as if they only involved secular values or political values. Classroom practices employing values clarification tend to pose serious questions of personal definition, behavior, and policy without fortifying or preparing students for serious reflection and study on the significance and consequences of what they have clarified. Simple moral-dilemma cases which elicit verbal judgments and answers to "Why?" too often ignore the reasons behind those answers. They ignore the religious-philosophical commitments which warrant and give significance to our judgments and reasons.

If we are to deal with public issues, values clarification, and moral dilemmas in the classroom, we are going to have to raise questions for reflection and provide materials for study which get to the ultimate commitments and life goals that lie behind (or above) specific decisions, actions, value choices, and moral principles. For some of us, those ultimate concerns will be called "religious." For others, they will be thought of in "secular" terms. For example, in a classroom discussion of Watergate, one student might approach the issue of truth-telling in terms of political "savvy" and realism wherein the ultimate objective is to survive and maintain power. Another student might speculate on value principles involved in truth-telling grounded in a sense of Christian obligation and love. Similarly, in a classroom discussion of government policies on abortion, one student might argue from a naive existentialist position, another might argue from a utilitarian position, another from personal feelings, and a fourth from a right-to-life position which may be deeply embedded in the student's total world view as a Roman Catholic.

To summarize the discussion to this point, there are three central assertions:

1. Social education dealing with values inevitably involves religious values.
2. Social education using public issues, values clarification, or moral dilemmas confronts religious-philosophical commitments at the deepest level—"Who do I think I am? What am I trying to do? Why?"
3. Social education using public issues, values clarification, or moral dilemmas ought to *deepen* the classroom approach sensitively to raise matters of students' commitments (as well as their decisions and reasons) and to *broaden* the classroom approach sensitively to

provide for studying the decisions, reasons, and commitments of others coming from diverse religious-philosophical traditions.

COURT PROHIBITIONS ON TEACHING RELIGIOUS VALUES

We will return to the third assertion. But first, we need to set forth two limitations. The Supreme Court's prohibitions against teaching for religious commitment has curtailed the practice of religion in classrooms and the teaching of those values which are restricted to a particular religious tradition—commitment to a specific sacred book, person, community, or ceremony or a commitment to a value defined in the context of a particular theological understanding. The public schools may teach *about,* but not *for,* such specific discernment and religious commitment. However, without reducing all religious traditions to a quasi-civic faith, educators may teach about religions and teach for commitment to basic human valuations such as *justice, equity, altruism, sensitivity, dignity of persons,* and *self-realization.* These values are not the exclusive province of any one religious-philosophical tradition and are defined, warranted, and (perhaps) actualized in different ways. The values are deeply embedded in the American politcal tradition as well as a variety of religious traditions. One educator clearly stated the case for teaching for commitment to *justice* in this way:

> The school is no more commited to value neutrality than is the government or the law. The school, like the government, is an insititution with a basic function of maintaining and transmitting some, but not all, of the consensual values of society. The most fundamental values of a society are termed moral values, and the major moral values, at least in our society, are the values of justice. . . . The problems as to the legitimacy of moral education in the public schools disappear, then, if the proper content of moral education is recognized to be the values of justice which themselves prohibit the imposition of beliefs of one group upon another.[1]

The fact that social education involves values and that they may be perceived as religious values is no limitation on the content of instruction, for the Supreme Court proscribed the practice of religion, not the study of religion and religious values. Indeed, the Court encouraged the study of religions.

The fact that social education may not promote the practice of religion or student commitment to specific religious values does not mean that the teacher and the curriculum must be "value free." The teacher might properly value knowledge over ignorance, truth over untruth, justice over injustice. The teacher may engage students in the study of value questions and in the development of value concepts through classroom inquiry, reflection, and reasoning.

Students engaged in a study of capital punishment might well develop their understanding of the value concept *justice* and develop their principles of justice by attending to the arguments of religious and secular community leaders, gathered through personal interviews. They might explore the commitments and reasoning of ancient writers, medieval Christian thinkers, recent *Commentary* authors, and radical activists. They might share their own positions, the reasons for their positions, and the meaning of existence which ultimately gives sense and feeling to their reasons.

VALUES AS SIMPLY NOUN-NAMES

A second limitation involves the process of instruction. Programs which have relied upon textbooks and materials teaching specific values by persistent exhortation and prescriptions have not been successful. Inculcating moral values as noun-names for values and as fixed conventional traits taught students the expected verbal responses, but their verbal responses most often did not reveal commitment or predict moral behavior when removed from the threat of "authorities."

There is no evidence which indicates that being able to recall the noun-names for values in response to teacher questions is translated into appropriate behavior. *Honesty, fairness, integrity, freedom,* and *equity* are noun-names for values. If knowledge about right produced a tendency to do right, moral education would be a simple task. But presenting unquestioned and unreasoned moral precepts, idealized beyond what students know as reality, too often produces student role-playing for authorities and eventual apathy or cynicism.

Rollo May recognized the deficiency in simply teaching ethical codes and values as "facts," without the motive feelings and reasoning abilities which promote moral discernment and behavior:

The triumph of barbarism in such movements as Hitlerism did not occur because people "forgot" the ethical traditions of our society as one might misplace a code. The humanistic values of liberty and the greatest good for the greatest number, the Hebrew-Christian values of community and love for the stranger, were still in the text books, and were still taught in Sunday School, and no archeological expedition was needed to unearth them.[2]

People become intelligent about values as they become intelligent about the conditions upon which they depend and about the consequences to which they lead. In the abstract, persons may subscribe to the noun-names for values, verbalize them, and celebrate them. But it is in specific decision-making situations, when values conflict and alternatives with various consequences are present, that values achieve personal reality.

Rather than learning definitions of values or memorizing the precepts in ethical codes, students need to reason together on real or hypothetical dilemmas in their own experience. As the Educational Policies Commission wrote in 1960:

> Ethical character depends upon the ability to reason sensitively and responsibly with respect to those values in specific situations. Character is misunderstood if thought of as mere conformity to standards imposed by external authority. In a free society, ethics, morality, and character have meaning to the extent that they represent affirmative, thoughtful choices by individuals. The ability to make these choices depends upon awareness of values and their role in life.[3]

THE THIRD ASSERTION

Now we may return to our third assertion:

> Social education using public issues, values clarification, or moral dilemmas ought to *deepen* the classroom approach sensitively to raise matters of students' commitments (as well as their decisions and reasons) and to *broaden* the classroom approach sensitively to provide for studying the decisions, reasons, and commitments of others coming from diverse religious-philosophical traditions.

Disregarding those who would have us teach for commitment to religious values (unconstitutional) and those who would teach inert value noun-names or precepts in codes (uneducational), we can discern some practices which enhance the use of public issues, values clarification, and moral dilemmas and, at the same time, properly recognize the place of religious-philosophical commitments, including our students' values.

First, when using values-clarification techniques, we can deepen the "Choosing, Prizing, Acting" model outlined by Raths, Harmin, and Simon.[4] Students may not only become aware of their choices and priorities, but through sensitive teacher questioning may become aware of and share the reasons for their choices and define the life-style consequences. We can add some of the following questions to the "Choosing, Prizing, Acting" model to deepen the understanding that decisions on personal- and interpersonal-welfare matters involve more than the feelings of the moment or the immediate consequences:

"Who am I? Who are we?"

"What are my motives and intentions as I decide or act here?"

"How do I see what is going on here? How are my perceptions affected by my motives and interests?"

"What do I stand for in life? What principles and character traits are at stake?"

"What am I trying to do in life? What do I live for?"

Second, when using public-policy approaches to values education, we can broaden the consideration beyond power and political values. Advocates of specific public policies base their conceptions of problems and policies upon their own world view and religious-philosophical considerations. Students not only need experience with advocates from a range of religious-philosophical traditions, but they also need the opportunity to share the religious-philosophical basis of their own positions.

Third, when using moral dilemmas in the style suggested by Lawrence Kohlberg,[5] we can be sensitive to the fact that students are responding not only from their "developmental stage" but also from their understanding of their religious-philosophical tradition. To deepen student understanding, we can pose the questions suggested above to complement values-clarification techniques. We can broaden student understanding by class sharing of reasons and by studying the ultimate concerns and reasoning of others from diverse traditions. But the dictates of *justice* and our sense as *educators* should constantly remind us that students are responding out of their persons—reflecting in many cases their deepest sense of religious commitment—and must be treated with respect and empathy by teachers and fellow students.

Fourth, when using any educational approach, the teacher may stand for those middle-range values which are hallmarks of a free, open society: the dignity of each person and the right of persons to be treated equally (fairly, equitably).

Working with teachers of social studies and science on curricula which raised value considerations, we discovered that teachers could and did confront students' religious commitments with sensitivity and understanding. These teachers discovered with us that we could not teach about population problems, environmental issues, or political affairs without eliciting students' religious-philosophical commitments. They found, with us, that this was not to be feared or repressed but was an important development for classroom instruction and for student development.

The following examples of instructional units are drawn from our curriculum-development endeavors to encourage religion study in public elementary and secondary schools. We have tried, and we think successfully, to implement the principles outlined above.

Example I

Third-grade pupils using the Religion-Social Studies Curriculum Project's unit on "Religion and Ethnicity in Urban North America" study about others' values while developing their own. The unit begins with opportunities to learn about the central knowledge concepts of *ethnicity* and *community*. Children first explore ethnicity and religious diversity in their own community by interviewing parents and adult leaders, using the telephone book as a data source, and establishing their own learning center with their books and artifacts gathered in the community. Using the Project's materials, youngsters turn to the San Francisco Bay Area to learn about children in five ethnic-religious groups (Reform Judaism, Roman Catholic, United Methodist, Confucian, and Baptist). As their study progresses, the pupils see the connection between religious and ethnic traditions, values, and behavior. They see how ethnic groups in the Bay Area interact. As they read about others' stories and ways, the third-grade youngsters have an opportunity to share aspects of their own stories and ways.

In the final section of the unit, children return to reflect upon their own community and the interaction among religious and ethnic traditions. Once more the children are involved in interviewing family members and community leaders, discovering the religious-ethnic diversity in their environment, and discerning the problems and opportunities which exist. This study involves the boys and girls in decision-making and reasoning about situations involving *fairness* and *religious pluralism* as the central value concepts in the unit. For example, in the following lesson, youngsters have studied a story about the life-style of Phil of Chinatown and are asked to discern connections between Phil's religious tradition (its value principles) and his actions. In another lesson, children who have explored the value concepts of *fairness* and *pluralism* are asked to assess the fairness of interpersonal relationships in one setting.

CONFUCIAN TRADITION

> *"Pay back kindness with kindness.*
> *Then people will want to do good."*

This is the proverb Phil learned in the story of "Phil of Chinatown." At the Chinese language school, Phil learned about the teachings of Confucius.

Confucius, an ancient Chinese wise man, told the Chinese people that human beings were good. He said that people will do the right thing *if* they try hard, *if* they are treated well, and *if* they are expected to do the right thing. Doing the right thing meant showing respect for others and being concerned about others' happiness and well-being. Confucius told people to think about what they do before they do it.

1. How did Phil show respect and concern for others?
2. On what occasions did Phil think before he did something?
3. Would you say that Phil followed the teachings of Confucius? Why or why not?

FAIRNESS

A young Pakistani man got on a bus. He wanted to go to Toronto. There was only one seat left. He started to sit down, but the lady in the next seat quickly put her bags on the seat. "I am not going to let *you* sit by me!" she said.

The young Pakistani politely asked the lady to move her bags. She refused.

The Pakistani quietly went to get the bus driver. When the bus driver came back to the lady, he started to talk to her and the Pakistani.

1. If you were the bus driver, what would you do? Why?
2. What reason would the Pakistani give for wanting to sit next to the lady?
3. Was the Pakistani right in insisting upon that seat?
4. What reason would the lady give for refusing to move her bags and let the young man sit down?
5. What does this situation tell us about *fairness?*[26]

Example II

Teachers using the fourth-grade materials produced by the Religion-Social Studies Curriculum Project explore various religious traditions' views of the man-nature relationship. The unit opens with a set of activities to help pupils explain why persons have different perceptions of the natural world and to engage them in reflection upon the ways in which they see and act in the natural world. These activities ask boys and girls to read Native North American poetry, songs, and Creation stories as well as the Creation stories and songs from Christian and Jewish traditions. Youngsters discern the values and world views of these diverse traditions, raising three focusing questions: "What do they believe?" "How do they see the world?" "How do they act in the world?" Ample opportunities exist for teachers to elicit pupils' answers to these questions from their own religious or secular traditions.

The class then turns to religion and culture in Japan to see how two religious traditions have influenced a people's sense of place. Using Creation stories, art, poetry, and folk stories from Shinto and Zen, the boys and girls see the development of values and beliefs, perceptions and patterns of behavior. A slide series on contemporary urban-industrial Japan shows some of the problems which have arisen as the Japanese seek to cope with population increases and with a rising material standard of living. Again, youngsters are engaged in reflecting upon their evaluations and explanations of similar phenomena in their own "place"—North America.

The final portion of the unit directs attention to the impact of religion upon the beliefs, values, and behavior of individuals. A

"People Book," with ten biographies of outstanding environmentalists (such as Albert Schweitzer, Rachel Carson, Thoreau, Muir, and Black Elk), shows the class the connections between what a person values and believes and the positions that a person takes on public issues and in personal behavior. Accompanying each biography are alternative activities (thinkers, talkers, doers, helpers) which boys and girls may choose to perform in or outside of classrooms. Each of the biographies includes brief case studies, relevant to the youngsters' community and life space, which will engage them in ethical reasoning based upon and fostering the development of their own values and views of nature.

Two samples from the student materials are reprinted below. The first illustrates the Zen view of sudden enlightenment through observing nature. The second illustrates a similar view held by Albert Schweitzer and is used to help students comprehend Schweitzer's "Reverence for Life" concept.

A BUDDHIST STORY

Buddhists in Japan have many stories telling about people learning good ways to live. These stories are told and retold to children by their parents. If you were a young Buddhist, what would you learn from this story?

A boy wanted to become a famous Buddhist monk, so he went to school. In school he studied hard for years and years. He studied day and night. For years he learned well, but suddenly he became confused. He did not learn as well. His friends and teachers tried to help him without success.

The boy decided he was not smart enough to learn. He said good-bye to his teachers and friends, and he sadly left school.

Leaving the school, he walked with his eyes on the ground. He walked many miles in sadness, thinking about his failure. He was not going to be a famous monk. He was miserable.

Soon it began to drizzle rain. He walked on with his eyes on the stone street. When the sun came out, the little raindrops sparkled in the sun. He noticed the drops falling off the buildings. Along the sides of the buildings and on the stones in the street, he saw little holes as far as his eyes could follow them.

Suddenly, he realized that over hundreds of years these little raindrops had worn little holes in the street stones!

With this Truth, he stood up straight. He smiled. He turned around and went back to school.

If it took a tiny raindrop hundreds of years to make a little hole in the stone street, he too could study hard, no matter how long it took to be a monk.

Many years later he became a famous monk. But he never forgot the lesson taught by tiny raindrops!

LEARNING FROM NATURE

Albert Schweitzer discovered that people can learn about themselves and how they might act by watching nature—its plants and animals. He told two stories, one about geese and one about sparrows, which taught him something important. What do they teach you?

Geese

A flock of wild geese had settled to rest on a pond. One of the flock had been captured by a gardener, who had clipped its wings before releasing it. When the geese started to resume their flight, this one tried to lift itself into the air. The others, observing his struggles, flew about to encourage him; but it was no use. Thereupon, the entire flock settled back on the pond and waited, even though the urge to go on was strong within them. For several days they waited until the damaged feathers had grown strong enough to permit the goose to fly. Meanwhile, the gardener, having learned something from the good geese, gladly watched them as they finally rose together, and all resumed their long flight.

Sparrows

A friend owned a small cafe. He would daily throw out crumbs for the sparrows in the neighborhood. He noticed that one sparrow was injured, so that it had difficulty getting about. But he discovered that the other sparrows would leave the crumbs which lay nearest to their crippled comrade, so that he could get his share, undisturbed.

Example III

For junior high school students, the Religion-Social Studies Project is developing a set of biographical materials. The biographies focus upon persons famous for their roles in religion and American culture. Each of the thirteen biographies is designed so that students are exploring a Personal Concern (e.g., *trust, belongingness, integrity, power, meaning*), a Central Knowledge Concept (e.g., *cause and effect, social status, power, anomie, political system*), and a Central Value Concept (e.g., *equity, truth-telling, fairness, honesty, justice*). The materials focus upon a set of conflicts and issues which the subject of the biography faced in his or her time, and the students have the opportunity to examine and think about similar conflicts and manifestations of the issues in their own experience.

In the biographical study of Frederick Douglass, the Personal Concern is that of "power over one's life"—*efficacy*. The Central Knowledge Concept is *personhood*—"What does it mean to be a person?" The Central Value Concept is that of *equality*—"What does it mean to be equal?" The introductory-discussion springboard elicits students' feelings and perceptions on a person's need to control his or her life and the consequences of not having control. Students are given portions of Douglass's autobiography in which he offers stories of his youth as a slave and the impact of his inability to gain control over his life. Students are asked to search for similarities and dissimilarities with their own views on efficacy from the introductory discussion. Later, portions of the *Autobiography* describe how Douglass was able to gain control over his life, and students are asked to evaluate the appropriateness of his means. Next, with their understanding of Douglass's background and with their analytical skills, students turn to Douglass's condemnation of "slave-owning Christianity." They analyze his argument to discern his conception of Christianity, his conception of "slave-owning Christianity," and his views on what it means to be a person. Quotations from the world of de Tocqueville and Francis Wayland are used to elaborate on the concepts of *personhood* and *equality of treatment*. In these sections, students are asked to discuss their own conceptions of *personhood* and *equality*, comparing and contrasting their views with those of others studied in the unit.

In the final section of the biographical study, students turn from Douglass's time to their own. They analyze an argument regarding the obligations of the affluent (as persons and as a society) to the less fortunate in their communities, their nation, and their world community. A series of ethical problems describing contemporary conflicts engage students in decision making and argumentation, using their concepts of *personhood* and *equality*. The focus is upon how they should act to (1) maintain their own sense of personhood and (2) respect others' needs and interest. Teachers are urged to have interested students interview various religious and secular leaders in their community in order that the students may broaden their study of these concepts.

Example IV

The *Religious Issues in Social Studies* series, developed by the Religion-Social Studies Curriculum Project and published by Addison-Wesley Publishing Company, also involves students in an examination of others' values and religious traditions as well as engaging students in reflection upon their own value commitments. One of the thirty units entitled "The Reformation in Western Civilization," deals with the right to rebel and the rightful means of rebellion. Students open their study by responding to ten unlabeled quotations presenting a spectrum of views on the right to rebel when facing an unjust authority. They are asked to rank-order the quotations according to the quotations' concurrence with their personal views. Following an extended discussion of the students' entry beliefs and attitudes on the issue, the class moves to an analysis of six arguments by Protestant religious leaders in the sixteenth century on the right to rebel and the rightful means of rebellion (e.g., Martin Luther, John Knox, Calvin, Anabaptists, etc.). Several logical schema are provided for student use. The discussion of this analysis focuses upon the diversity within Christianity on the issue and the way that each advocate grounded his position within the religious tradition. Students then turn to the advocacy of rebellion in their own time and world community. They are given time and minimal directions to select a contemporary advocacy person or group (e.g., Henry Kissinger, Eldridge Cleaver, South African Blacks, Liberation Theologists, or others that may be currently of note) and to search out their arguments in the library. Students may elect simply to report their findings, or they may pose counter-arguments from their personal perspectives.

Each of the thirty units in this series follows a similar pattern: (1) initial springboard to elicit student concerns and entry dispositions, (2) study of a religious issue relevant to the students' time and experience, stressing knowledge and skill development, and (3) study

257

of the contemporary manifestations of the issue, stressing the application of knowledge and skills and the development of student value commitments.

CONCLUSION

In our work we have discovered that teachers cannot omit study of religions from the curriculum and still provide young people with an adequate social education. Religious-philosophical beliefs and practices are an integral part of our culture and social institutions. Religious-philosophical beliefs and practices are an integral part of individual behavior. The corollary of this point is that teachers cannot simply deal with values, public issues, and moral education without confronting religious-philosophical beliefs and practices. Reality for many students is a religious reality. Values and actions make sense to them only as they are integrated and justified within a world view which, for them, comes from their religious tradition.

As educators, we are learning the truth of this corollary in ethnic and multicultural education. Now our task is to learn the corollary in the context of the social and moral education of all children in our classrooms.

NOTES

1. See Lawrence Kohlberg, "Moral and Religious Education and the Public Schools: A Developmental Point of View," in T. Sizer, ed., *Religion and Public Education* (Boston: Houghton Mifflin, 1967), pp. 164–83.
2. Rollo May, *Man's Search for Himself* (New York: W. W. Norton, 1952), p. 216.
3. *The Central Purpose of American Education* (Washington, D.C.: National Education Association and the American Association of School Administrators, 1960).
4. Louis E. Raths, Merrill Harmin, and Sidney B. Simon, *Values and Teaching* (Columbus, Ohio: Charles E. Merrill, 1966).
5. Kohlberg, "Moral and Religious Education."
6. Joan G. Dye and Rodney F. Allen, *Exploring Many Traditions* (Niles, Ill.: Argus Communications, 1976). Activity Book for Level 3 of *Learning About Religion/Social Studies*.
7. Robert A. Spivey, Joan G. Dye, and Rodney F. Allen, *Learning About Religion/Social Studies* (Level 4, field test materials).

For bibliography, see pp. 116–118.